OCCASIONAL SERIES NO 2

EMBRACING LIFE AND GATHERING WISDOM

Theological, Pastoral and Clinical Insights into Human Flourishing at the End of Life

Stephen Smith, Edwina Blair
and Catherine Kleemann (Editors)

SCD Press
2020

Embracing Life and Gathering Wisdom
Theological, Pastoral and Clinical Insights into
Human Flourishing at the End of Life
(Occasional Series No 2)
Edited by Stephen Smith, Edwina Blair and Catherine Kleemann

© SCD Press and Contributors 2020

SCD Press
PO Box 1882
Macquarie Park NSW 2113
scdpress@scd.edu.au

ISBN-13: 978-1-925730-19-7 (Paperback)
ISBN-13: 978-1-925730-20-3 (E-book)

Internal layout and design: Lankshear Design
Cover Design: Ben Taylor Creative Enterprises

OCCASIONAL SERIES NO 2

EMBRACING LIFE AND GATHERING WISDOM

Theological, Pastoral and Clinical Insights into Human Flourishing at the End of Life

Stephen Smith, Edwina Blair
and Catherine Kleemann (Editors)

SCD Press
2020

Occasional Series:

1. Peter G. Bolt & James R. Harrison (eds.), *Romans and the Legacy of St Paul. Historical, Theological, and Social Perspectives* (Macquarie Park, NSW: SCD Press, 2019).

2. Stephen Smith, Edwina Blair & Catherine Kleemann (eds.), *Embracing Life and Gathering Wisdom. Theological, Pastoral and Clinical Insights into Human Flourishing at the End of Life* (Macquarie Park, NSW: SCD Press, 2020).

AUTHOR PROFILES

Kirsty Beilharz is the Director of Integrative Studies at Excelsia College. Her particular areas of research and interest include applied theology in aged care, palliative care, ethics, phenomenology of music, Trinitarian theology, and Christian Higher Education amongst culturally diverse students. She is the author of *Music Remembers Me: Connection and Wellbeing in Dementia* and chapters in various books on Wellbeing and Palliative Care.

kirsty.beilharz@exclesia.edu.au

Edwina Blair is a doctoral candidate in the Old Testament at the Sydney College of Divinity and holds a Bachelor of Applied Science (Nuclear Medicine), a Bachelor of Theology, and a Master of Theology. Her current areas of research include anthropomorphism and the senses as represented in the Hebrew Bible. She is the Graduate School Project Manager and Academic Coordinator (Bible) at the Australian College of Ministries and has had extensive experience in pastoral care through local church ministry for over 20 years.

eblair@acom.edu.au

Peter Carblis is the Senior Chaplain (Quality and Standards) in Fresh Hope Engage in the Churches of Christ NSW. He is also a member of the Executive Committee of the Civil Chaplaincies Advisory Committee of NSW. His particular areas of research interest are in ensuring the validity of professional development and standards of practice in ministry. His latest research is titled *Educating for Virtue: The New Covenant as a Framework for the Development of Character*.

Peter.Carblis@freshhope.org.au

Doru Costache is Senior Lecturer in Patristic Studies at St Cyril's Coptic Orthodox Theological College. His particular area of research is the intersection of Christianity and culture, focusing upon early Christian representations of reality. He is the co-author of *Dreams, Virtue and Divine Knowledge in Early Christian Egypt* (Cambridge University Press, 2019). He also authored *The Orthodox Spring: A Diary* and *Reading Scripture in the Orthodox Church: The Festal Cycle* (AIOCS Press, 2020, 2019).

dcostache@stcyrils.edu.au

Matthew Del Nevo is the Associate Professor of Philosophy at the Catholic Institute of Sydney and writes in the area of spirituality and psychology. He is the author of several books on soulfulness published by Routledge. His most recent book is *Finding Harmony* (Wipf & Stock, 2018).

mdelnevo@cis.catholic.edu.au

Michelle Eastwood is a Research Assistant with the Centre for Human Ageing, based at the Catholic Theological College, Melbourne. Her particular areas of research are the Hebrew Bible, worship and liturgy, and building community. She is currently completing her doctorate titled *The Shame of the Old Woman: A Feminist Reading of Psalm 71*.

michelle.eastwood@ctc.edu.au

Carol Flanagan is a practising solicitor in Sydney. She has an ongoing interest in the care of older generations through her legal practice and life-changing personal experiences. Carol has co-authored several books with Jack Flanagan including *Happily Ever After: A Guide to the Best Aged Care for the People You Love*.

carol@therockspractice.com

Jack Flanagan is a semi-retired accounting academic with ongoing research interests in the ethics of financial reporting and the care of our ageing population. Jack has co-authored several books with Carol Flanagan including *Happily Ever After: A Guide to the Best Aged Care for the People You Love*.

jack@therockspractice.com

Daniel J. Fleming leads ethics and formation for St Vincent's Health Australia. He is also an Honorary Research Associate with the Sydney College of Divinity. His research focuses on theological ethics and its application to moral development as well as health and aged care. Dan is the author of *Attentiveness to Vulnerability: A Dialogue Between Emmanuel Levinas, Jean Porter and the Virtue of Solidarity* (Eugene: Pickwick Publications, 2019).

daniel.fleming@svha.org.au

James R. Harrison is Professor, FAHA, and Research Director at the Sydney College of Divinity. His recent monographs include *Paul and the Imperial Authorities at Thessalonica and Rome* (Mohr Siebeck, 2011), *Paul and the Ancient Celebrity Circuit* (Mohr Siebeck, 2019), and *Reading Romans with Roman Eyes* (Lexington/Fortress, 2020). He is also the chief editor of *New Documents Illustrating the History of Early Christianity Vols. 11-15* (forthcoming), co-editor with L. L. Welborn of *The First Urban Churches Vols. 1-6* (SBL, 2015-2020; Vols. 7-9 forthcoming 2021-2023), and is the editor of the Cascade collection of E. A. Judge, *The Conflict of Cultures: The Legacy of Paul's Thought Today* (Cascade, 2019).

jimh@scd.edu.au

David James Hooker is a PhD student at the Melbourne School of Theology. His particular areas of interest are hermeneutics, systematic theology, and the intersection of theology with science.

dahoowork@gmail.com

Catherine Kleemann is Dean of the Graduate School of Leadership at the Australian College of Ministries and a doctoral candidate in Pastoral Practice at the Sydney College of Divinity. Catherine has extensive experience as a local church pastor and church planter and CEO/Director of a not-for-profit that ministers to the marginalised in society, including work with domestic violence, homelessness, children at risk, and the aged. She is the author of 'New Every Morning: Spiritual Care in the Context of Memory Loss,' in *Justice, Mercy and Social Well-being: Interdisciplinary Perspectives* (2020).

ckleemann@acom.edu.au

Mavis Salt is Adult's Ministries Consultant for The Salvation Army, Australia. Her particular area of research and interest is spiritual care. This incorporates understanding spiritual needs and self-care for all ages but in particular the provision of holistic care in our multi-cultural ageing society.

Mavis.Salt@salvationarmy.org.au

Stephen Smith holds doctorates in community health (SYD) and management (SCU). He is Managing Partner of The Colloquium Group and an Associate Professor in Pastoral Theology at the Sydney College of Divinity. Stephen has over 30 years of hands-on ministry experience, has published widely on issues of well-being and human flourishing, and serves on the board of several community-based non-profits serving the disadvantaged in society.

steve@colloquiumgroup.com

Bruce A. Stevens was the Wicking Chair of Ageing and Practical Theology at CSU (2015–2019) and is now an adjunct professor. He is a clinical and forensic psychologist in part-time private practice and an associate minister at Wesley Uniting Church Canberra. His book *The Storied Self: A Narrative Approach to the Spiritual Care of the Aged* (Lanham, Maryland: Fortress Academic, 2018) won the Australasian Journal of Ageing book award in 2019. His latest book is *Before Belief: Discovering First Spiritual Awareness* (Lanham, Maryland: Lexington Books, 2020). He is interested in early spirituality (see www.earlyspirituality.com)

bstevens@csu.edu.au

Chris Swann is the Director of Training for the church planting agency, City to City Australia, as well as an adjunct lecturer in ministry and practice at Ridley College in Melbourne. His doctoral work focused on discipleship in Karl Barth's theology of sanctification. His ongoing research interests include theological ethics, ecclesiology, and the doctrine of the Christian life, particularly as these intersect with soteriology, theological anthropology, and the theology of the body.

chris@citytocityaustralia.org.au

CONTENTS

	INTRODUCTION	1
PART 1	The Practice of Caring for the Ageing	7
Chapter 1	Daniel J. Fleming, *Beyond the Medicalisation of Ageing*	9
Chapter 2	Peter Carblis, *Standards and Continuing Professional Development for Chaplains: Learning Pathways for Aged Care Chaplains.*	37
Chapter 3	Carol Flanagan & Jack Flanagan, *In Providing Aged Care with Compassion and Respect, What Role can Spiritualty Play?*	69
PART 2	The Theology of Ageing	89
Chapter 4	David James Hooker, *Human Biological Ageing: Creation or Curse? Exploring Two Foundational Models.*	91
Chapter 5	Michelle Eastwood, *Theologies of Ageing: A Review of the Literature*	127
Chapter 6	Chris Swann, *Karl Barth on the Dignity and Crown of Suffering: Reimagining the Fourth Age for Discipleship*	145

PART 3	**Holistic & Spiritual Care for the Ageing** 171
Chapter 7	Bruce Stevens, *The Hidden Story: What Might be Missing in a Life Review?* 173
Chapter 8	Kirsty Beilharz, *Theological, Pastoral and Clinical Insights into Human Flourishing at the End of Life: Music and Meaning in Dementia and De-Medicalising Palliative Care* 187
Chapter 9	Mavis Salt, *Spiritual Care Needs in Illness, Dying and End-of-Life Choices* 219

PART 4	**Ageing in Literature** 245
Chapter 10	James R. Harrison, *Two Approaches to Ageing in Antiquity: Comparing Cicero's De Senectute and Paul's Intergenerational Relationships in Philemon and 1 Timothy* 247
Chapter 11	Doru Costache, *Elders and Disciples in Egypt's Early Monastic Literature.* 275
Chapter 12	Matthew Del Nevo, *Old Age* 301

EPILOGUE 314

INTRODUCTION

Simple demographics tell us that each year (for at least the next two decades) more of us than ever before will be over 70 years of age. Ageing invites loss: the potential for the fading of mental and physical abilities, the passing of youthful desires, the diminishment of independence, the unravelling of false pride, and the undoing of identity. So much can be taken away from people during this stage of life including the loss of loved ones, betrayal by family members, and consequences of financial impoverishment. For some the fear of ageing is palpable, ensuring a thriving anti-ageing market that seeks to deny the reality of our human state.

In growing old we each share in the inevitable future of our humanity. Yet ageing is not to be feared. It is a physical decay, yet a theological aspiration—the journey of the created meeting their Creator. In this lies the real difference in the anthropology of the Christian. An assumed purpose and personhood that results from being created in the image of God to be in an intimate relationship with Him. In life, then in the afterlife.

In this way, the Christian approach to ageing is distinct when compared to a purely secular perspective. Christians live with the conviction that people are 'soul beings' first and physical beings second. Our soul integrates the interplay of physical, psychological, spiritual, and social health, and is an inseparable companion to every breath we take. When we experience ageing, the search for meaning that emanates from our soul is radically sharpened. This is God's calling to us, an inevitable search for the sacred.

This book seeks to share a Christian response to the challenges of ageing and arose from the 2018 academic conference, 'Embracing Life and Gathering Wisdom: Theological, Pastoral, and Clinical Insights into Human Flourishing at the End of Life', convened by Professor Jim Harrison, Professor Bruce Stevens, and Associate Professor Stephen Smith and hosted by The Sydney College of Divinity.

In the following 12 chapters, the authors focus on the four themes of practical application, theological understanding, spiritual care, and historical insight.

Part 1: The Practice of Caring for the Ageing: Daniel J. Fleming in Beyond the Medicalisation of Ageing writes about an approach to the care of the aged that is shaped by the Aristotelian and Thomistic traditions of ethics, synthesised in current natural law theory, and informed by the theological anthropology of the Catholic tradition. Through his work, he critiques the reductive approaches to the human person that undermine dignity, which he believes are evident in the current trend towards the medicalisation of ageing.

Concerned about the training standards for chaplains, Peter Carblis writes about the increased need for the professionalism of aged care chaplaincies in an environment subject to government scrutiny and regulation. This move towards recognition as allied health professionals requires the adoption of formal standards of practice, as demonstrated in the framework outlined here in Standards and Continuing Professional Development for Chaplains: Learning Pathways for Aged Care Chaplains. This framework will enable the critical evaluation, specification, and continual improvement of the attributes of assistant, practising, accomplished, and lead practitioners, leading to the consideration of faith-based distinctives, specifications of regulatory bodies, professional associations and peak bodies, research on spiritual care in aged care, and research on inter-cultural and inter-faith practices.

Carol and Jack Flanagan share their insights into the practical considerations surrounding care for our ageing loved ones in In Providing Aged Care with Compassion and Respect, What Role can Spirituality Play? With an emphasis on the importance of spirituality in aged care, this chapter explores the reality that we will all be carers or cared for one day.

Part 2: The Theology of Ageing: In Human Biological Ageing: Creation or Curse? Exploring Two Foundational Models, David Hooker explores the claim that human biological ageing is 'good' in the Biblical creation sense by comparing the doctrine of the Cosmic Fall with what he titles Cosmic Disintegration. Finding support for the alternative Disintegration Model, he stresses the fundamental and persistent goodness of God's creation, with biological ageing as an organically original and theologically good component of it. He concludes that to recognise human ageing as 'good' is to provide a strong foundation for the perspective in the practical theology of 'embracing life' in our older years.

Michelle Eastwood identifies a lack of scholarship on the theology of ageing through this thorough review of the current literature and a critical review of key texts within the areas of biblical theologies, including experiential and theological treatises. In Theologies of Ageing: A Review of the Literature, she identifies gaps in the literature and suggests areas for future research, specifically that future theologies of ageing should focus on ageing as a distinct life stage with specific challenges and opportunities, while also developing a deep theology of ageing that considers the intersectional impacts of race, gender, culture, wealth, nutrition, and particular life experiences.

In Karl Barth on the Dignity and Crown of Suffering: Reimagining the Fourth Age for Discipleship, Chris Swann explores some of the more unpleasant realities of ageing, dwelling in particular on the ways the so-called fourth age is imagined as a period of dramatically diminished agency or even non-agency—and the effects of this on the way the preceding third age of active retirement is imagined. In this context, the chapter undertakes a retrieval of a distinction Karl Barth draws between the dignity and crown of suffering in the context of his late doctrine of sanctification and then proposes some important coordinates for its constructive appropriation of the dignity-crown distinction in reimagining the fourth age in terms of discipleship.

Part 3: Holistic & Spiritual Care for the Ageing: Bruce Stevens explores the concept of the life review, an influential approach for finding personal meaning, in his chapter The Hidden Story: What Might be Missing in a Life Review? He explores the possible beginning of a life review in the concept of a hidden story. Various theories with a learning component such as implicit learning, tacit knowledge, the cognitive unconscious, Bourdieu's habitus, and attachment theory are approached to reach beyond the barrier to explore our first story—the hidden story. It is suggested that this can then be incorporated into a more comprehensive life review and, on this basis, we can effectively re-author ourselves into a new life story.

In Theological, Pastoral and Clinical Insights into Human Flourishing at the End of Life: Music and Meaning in Dementia and De-Medicalising Palliative Care, Kirsty Beilharz shares her insights into the way that society has lost touch with the physical, psychosocial, and spiritual experience of dying well. Palliative care has commonly been relinquished to professionals and institutions, which disconnects an individual from the opportunity for prayer, reflection, reconciliation of relationships, pastoral support and intercession, seeking forgiveness, and sometimes causes resistance to a conscious and comfortable passing. This chapter considers the stages of death, facilitation of interaction with friends and relatives, communion with God, and acknowledgement of the individual as a community responsibility.

Mavis Salt explores the way in which there is now more choice about how and when to end one's life when faced with illness or suffering in Spiritual Care Needs in Illness, Dying and End-of-Life Choices. Prompted by recent studies, this chapter highlights that the shared universal experience is, in fact, a spiritual one, with spiritual tasks to be worked through towards the end of life. This chapter does not endeavour to outline an ethical response to assisted dying; rather, it aims to stimulate thinking around suffering and autonomy and the importance of spiritual care.

Part 4: Ageing in Literature: In Two Approaches to Ageing in Antiquity: Comparing Cicero's De Senectute and Paul's Intergenerational Relationships in Philemon and 1 Timothy, James Harrison compares the ideological backdrop established by the only treatise devoted exclusively to ageing in antiquity, Cicero's De Senectute ('On Old Age'), with the Apostle Paul's intergenerational construct of relationships in the Body of Christ (1 Timothy 5). This comparison leads to the exploration of the contribution each approach has made to the Western intellectual tradition and praxis regarding ageing.

Doru Costache examines the written records of the fourth- and fifth-century monastic wisdom produced in and about the ascetic milieus of Egypt in Elders and Disciples in Egypt's Early Monastic Literature. Through the chapter, he explores two aspects of ageing, first, the perception of Christian discipleship as ongoing growth, which culminates in the wisdom of the 'beautiful elder' and second, the understanding of Christian discipleship in terms of novices attending to the needs of elders, leading to the conclusion that, discipleship, in desert literature, means learning wisdom from and taking care of elders.

In Old Age, Matthew Del Nevo explores views about old age that have principally arisen from Simone de Beauvoir's book Old Age, considered by some to be the greatest study of old age of the last one hundred years. This chapter presents some general considerations regarding the subject of old age and broaches once more the subject of a 'late style'—that is, to live to a ripe old age; not only artists, but each one of us, need somehow to develop our own late style or manner.

This book hopes to capture a balance of perspective (theological, pastoral, and clinical), all dealing with the same question: how do we age well? The secular view would see humans as a physiological machine that houses sentient awareness; however, the Christian view sees the human body as a carrier of an eternal spiritual being. While the physical shell is in decline, the soul is maturing and enduring.

Thus, our spirituality is an integral part of human health and not merely an influence on it.[1] Spirituality pervades every part of who we are. It is bonded to our well-being in ways that seem incomprehensible.

---

1   Sean Fleming and David S. Evans, 'The Concept of Spirituality: Its Role within Health Promotion Practice in the Republic of Ireland', *Spirituality and Health International* 9, no. 11 (June 2008), 79-89.

It is central to how we cope and thrive when our life journey reaches its final stages.

We hope that this book provokes discussion and promotes scholarship into Christian theological, pastoral, and clinical insights that shape human flourishing at the end of life.

Editors:
Stephen Smith
Edwina Blair
Catherine Kleemann

A Note on Spelling

It should be noted that there are two acceptable spellings of the word 'ageing' and this book has followed the convention accepted in the United Kingdom.[2] While this has been adopted consistently by our authors throughout this book, any occurrence of the alternative spelling (aging) that occurs in quotes or bibliographic information of other authors has been retained in its original format.

---

2 *Webster's Third New International Dictionary*, Unabridged, s.v. 'aging,' accessed April 28, 2020, http://unabridged.merriam-webster.com.

PART 1

The Practice of Caring for the Ageing

CHAPTER 1

Beyond the medicalisation of ageing

Daniel J. Fleming

Abstract

This chapter reflects on excellence in the care of those who are ageing. Its approach is informed by the Aristotelian and Thomistic traditions of ethics, which are synthesised in current natural law theory and, in this iteration, are informed by the theological anthropology of the Catholic tradition. This approach to ethics holds that any adequate response to the human person must be informed by their human dignity and a robust anthropology which, when held together, provide moral content which can influence, guide and direct both individual responses to moral questions and also broader social projects such as aged care. Using this framework also enables a critique of the reductive approaches to the human person which undermine dignity. This chapter suggests such approaches are present in our current trend towards the medicalisation of ageing.

Introduction

This chapter considers what excellence looks like in the care of those who are ageing. Its approach is informed by the Aristotelian and Thomistic traditions of ethics, which are synthesised in current natural law theory and, in this iteration, are informed by the theological anthropology of the Catholic tradition. This approach to ethics holds that any adequate response to the human person must be informed by their human dignity and a robust anthropology which, when held together, provide moral content which can influence, guide and direct both individual responses to moral questions and also broader social projects, such as aged care. Using this framework also enables a critique of the reductive approaches to the human person which undermine dignity. This chapter suggests such approaches are present in our current trend towards the medicalisation of ageing. The chapter is framed by two case studies, which are referred to throughout to illustrate aspects of the ethical framework so developed. Following the case studies, the chapter develops an understanding of dignity and theological anthropology, which are used to inform what an ethical (and therefore excellent) response to the scenarios would look like. The chapter then reflects on what the actual, first response to these scenarios was and, drawing on the work of Slavoj Žižek, suggests this reflects an ideological construct of the interaction between ageing and medicine in our context. This analysis is advanced further through discussion with Martha Nussbaum and Jeffrey P. Bishop, both of whom provide important critiques of our current trend towards the medicalisation of ageing. The chapter concludes with a critique of the medicalisation of ageing, held up through a deliberate process enacted by those responding to each of the scenarios. Finally, it proposes a vision informed by a more robust ethical framework which better responds to human dignity and, thus, provides a better foundation for excellence in the care of those who are ageing.

Two Case Studies

Each of these case studies is based on personal and professional experiences, and they have been adapted and anonymised to protect the identity of any individuals involved.

Case Study One: An Apartment Block in Sydney

In mid-2018, friends of mine relayed to me a difficult situation they encountered in their apartment block late one weekday evening after a warm day in autumn. At the time, they lived in a block which had a small common area made up of stairs connecting three apartment levels, with each level providing access to two apartments. The apartment block was located in an old area of Sydney and a number of residents had lived there since it was first built in the early 1970s.

One resident, who will be referred to as John hereafter, lived on the top floor of the block. He was 90 years old, a very private person, and committed to his independence. The apartment block did not have an elevator and, therefore, to reach his home, John would need to walk up three flights of stairs. My friends noted this could often take him 20 minutes or more (and longer if he had groceries), and that he would politely refuse assistance if it was ever offered. Sometimes they would hear John struggling down the stairs in the middle of the night when it was garbage collection the following day, carrying his bin down to the roadside. In total, this exercise could take John up to an hour, but he was committed to doing it himself.

One night, my friends arrived home late from an interstate trip to find John was locked out of the common area: 'It's good that you're here', he said to them; 'I've locked myself out'. My friends let him into the common area and asked if he needed a locksmith to get into his apartment. 'No', John said, 'I've left that door unlocked—it was just this one that I needed opened'. Thinking nothing more of it, my friends went into their apartment, unpacked their bags, put a load of washing on, and got ready for bed.

A couple of hours later, as they were about to go to bed, my friends decided they should check to see that John made it into his apartment. They walked up to the top level and found he had not: John was lying down outside his apartment, using newspapers as blankets and a roll of paper towelling as a pillow. They offered for John to come into their own apartment or to call a locksmith for him, but he refused both offers. He preferred to wait out the night and call his sister in the morning, who had a key to his place.

How were they to respond in this case with John?

Case Study Two: An Aged Care Facility in Regional Australia

Colleagues of mine working in aged care relayed to me a case regarding a resident in one of the services they manage. They explained such cases were fairly regular, but this case in particular had caused significant concern.

The case involved Mary, an 87-year-old resident, who was experiencing a condition which led to deterioration in her oesophagus. For Mary, swallowing became increasingly difficult and her care team noted she had recently shown signs of choking risk. At a care-team meeting, it was determined Mary should be put on a liquid diet to mitigate further risks to her health. This decision was to remain in place until Mary recovered or, if she did not, it would remain indefinitely. The care team determined this would be the most prudent way forward in the management of her care.

When they sought to advise Mary of their decision, they encountered great resistance. Upon hearing the news, Mary was extremely distressed and her family subsequently became involved, challenging the caregivers' decision. Her family's position was that Mary should continue to receive solid foods as that is her wish—they were aware of the risk and were willing to accept it. Care staff were distressed at this development: what if they provided Mary a meal which caused her to choke when this was both foreseeable and avoidable?

How were they to respond in this case with Mary?

Human Dignity, Human Flourishing, Excellence and Ethics

The approach I chart out in response to each of these cases derives from the Catholic tradition of theological ethics. Every aspect of this tradition begins with an affirmation of the insatiable dignity of each and every human person, founded in their being created in the image and likeness of God (Gen. 1:27).[1] Furthermore, it affirms that dignity bestows on the person a value which calls for a particular kind

---

1 This foundation is widely articulated in Catholic theological ethics. In authoritative teaching, it is most clearly expressed in John Paul II, *Evangelium Vitae*, no. 34.

of response and for the establishment of social systems and structures which are reflective of a commitment to human dignity.[2] It also generates a commitment to supporting and ensuring a human life is lived in its fullness (John 10:10), which is expressed in Aristotelian and Thomistic language as eudemonia and translated variously as flourishing, happiness, or excellence.[3] The ultimate goal of this life is theological (i.e., union with God), but this goal also integrates all of those aspects of an earthly life well-lived, which themselves are given meaning through their eternal significance.[4]

Towards this view, ethics is the art of considering what dispositions and acts respond to the dignity of each and every human person and support human flourishing. It has interpersonal and social elements since, towards this view, there is a commitment to the common good: 'we are all really responsible for all'.[5] However, these robust foundations for an ethical framework do not provide adequate ethical content. Specifically, a commitment to human dignity might lead to any number of responses to John or Mary, and some of them quite at odds with one another. This means the ethical vision needs to be expanded and, within the Catholic ethical tradition, this happens through the development of a theological anthropology. This is an attempt to provide a response to the question, what does it mean to be human?[6] Only in addressing this question can we properly consider if an adequate response to human dignity is possible. As Charles Curran noted, the way in which one understands the human person coexists with one's understanding of what is due to persons on the basis of their dignity.[7] Accordingly, we turn now to a consideration of the theological anthropology of the Catholic tradition.[8]

---

2   See Pontifical Council for Justice and Peace, *Compendium of the Social Doctrine of the Church*, nos 164–167.
3   John Paul II, *Evangelium Vitae*, no. 38.
4   John Paul II, *Sollicitudo Rei Socialis*, no. 38.
5   John Paul II, *Sollicitudo Rei Socialis*, no. 38.
6   West, 'Prophetic Religion and the Future of Capitalist Civilization', 94–95.
7   See Rudman's *Concepts of Person*, which is a systematic exploration of different understandings of the human person and the ethical implications that follow from these. See also Curran, *Catholic Social Teaching*, 127.
8   The content in the following section is analysed more fully in Fleming, *Attentiveness to Vulnerability*, 137–175.

The Human Person Integrally and Adequately Considered

The theological anthropology I draw from the Catholic tradition is captured in the school of thought known as the human person integrally and adequately considered, which is closely aligned with the work of Louis Janssens and those who followed his lead at the University of Leuven. Janssens' work is founded on the anthropological vision of the Second Vatican Council document *Gaudium et Spes: The Pastoral Constitution of the Church in the Modern World*.[9] In essence, as Roger Burggraeve notes, that document holds that 'it is only when we approach the human person integrally or holistically that he or she is given their due'.[10]

Janssens' work in this area begins with one of the first drafts of *Gaudium et Spes* Part II, in which it is argued sexual ethics needs to be understood according to 'objective criteria based upon the dignity of the human person'.[11] In the promulgated version of *Gaudium et Spes*, the wording is as follows: 'the moral aspect of any procedure [...] must be determined by objective standards which are based upon the nature of the human person and his acts'.[12] Janssens provides the following analysis of this part of the document:

> In the official commentary it is explained: 1, that in this expression a general principle is formulated, one which is applicable not only to marriage and sexuality but also to the entire domain of human activity (*agitur de principio generali*), and 2, that it is affirmed through the choice of this expression that 'human activity must be judged insofar as it refers to the human person integrally and adequately considered' (*actus diiudicandos esse... quatenus illi ad personam humanam integre et adequate considerandam pertinent*). In other words, in order to determine whether or not an act is worthy of man or morally good, one must apply the criterion of 'the human

---

9   Vatican II Council, *Gaudium et Spes*.
10 Burggraeve, 'Holistic Personalism', 31.
11 Janssens, 'Artificial Insemination', 4.
12 Vatican II Council, *Gaudium et Spes*, 51. Cf. Janssens, 'Artificial Insemination', 4.

person adequately considered', i.e., in all his essential aspects or constitutive elements.[13]

Janssens then analyses Gaudium et Spes—and other aspects of Catholic theological ethics—with a view to establishing what these essential aspects or constitutive elements are. In other words, he seeks a comprehensive theological anthropology which can inform ethical judgements regarding what adequate responses to human dignity look like. In doing so, he establishes eight dimensions of the 'human person integrally and adequately considered'. I explore each in turn and, where relevant, provide remarks on how they relate to one or other of our scenarios.

The Human Person is a Subject

The first dimension in Janssens' framework is that the human person is a subject.[14] As Richard Gula explains:

> To speak of the human person as a subject is to say that the person is in charge of his or her own life. That is, the person is a moral agent with a certain degree of autonomy and self-determination empowered to act according to his or her conscience, in freedom, and with knowledge.[15]

This means if one acknowledges human dignity, one must also acknowledge 'that no one may ever use a human person as an object or as a means to an end the way we do other things of the world'.[16] From this, it follows that a truly good response to human dignity happens in support of subjectivity and not at its expense.[17] It must therefore empower the person as a person, providing the opportunity for an appropriate exercise of autonomy, and err away from any form of response which

---

13 Janssens, 'Artificial Insemination', 4; Kelly, *New Directions in Moral Theology*, 29-30.
14 Janssens, 'Artificial Insemination', 5.
15 Gula, *Reason Informed by Faith*, 68.
16 Gula, *Reason Informed by Faith*, 68. Cf. Janssens, 'Artificial Insemination', 5; Kelly, *New Directions in Moral Theology*, 31. See also Vatican II Council, *Gaudium et Spes*, no. 27.
17 Gula, *Reason Informed by Faith*, 69.

'imposes' decisions and forces responses without due reference to the subjectivity of the person in question. This is the realm of shared decision-making in health and aged care, whereby the recipient of care is as active as possible in dialogue with their caregivers in determining what will look like an appropriate response for them. In the context of end-of-life care, for example, this recognition of subjectivity upholds a patient's right to withdraw or withhold life-saving treatments that are overly burdensome from their perspective as subject, rather than from some abstract set of criteria that fails to account for them as an individual.[18]

In the context of John and Mary's cases, attentiveness to their subjectivity would see them as partners in any response to concerns regarding their health and well-being. They are not objects on whom a response can be forced; rather, they are subjects who have a vested interest in the kind of response chosen with them.

The Human Person is a Body

The second dimension that Janssens proposes is that human persons are embodied creatures. Curtailing any dualism between body and spirit, Janssens draws on *Gaudium et Spes* and other elements in the tradition in noting these aspects of our personhood are constitutive of one being—specifically, what 'concerns the human body [...] also affects the person himself'.[19] Kevin Kelly notes this perspective challenges the 'anti-corporeal dualism' that has found its way at times into Christian discourse, including in some cases to the detriment of our understanding of human freedom:

> We have tended to look for some hidden aspect of ourselves where we are completely undetermined and to locate human freedom at that point. In reality, our freedom is embodied freedom. In other words, it is precisely through our bodies that we are able to be free. What we sometimes refer to as our

---

18 Catholic Health Australia, *Code of Ethical Standards*, Section 5.
19 Janssens, 'Artificial Insemination', 6.

"limitations" are in fact simply the current boundaries of our present abilities. They are the package of gifts we have to live our lives with.[20]

Based on this observation of how essential our body is to our humanness, it follows that adequate care of bodily needs is essential for human flourishing. This gives rise to significant basic 'dues' that relate to human dignity as they pertain to bodily flourishing (e.g., adequate food, fluids and shelter). This area is also the remit of healthcare as it pertains to the care of our bodies. I return to this particular point in some detail later in the chapter given that the care of the body absent of other considerations is part of the medicalisation of the ageing ideology I prefaced earlier.

Here, it is sufficient to note that in both John and Mary's cases care of body is a concern (i.e., safety, warmth, adequate food and fluids in John's case; and attention to the risk of choking and other methods for the provision of food in Mary's case). It is the normal work of health and aged care, as well as some social support services, to respond to these needs.

The Human Person is Always in Relationship with the Material World

In the next dimension of the human person, Janssens explains it is through our bodiliness that human persons engage with the material world and, following Heidegger, also explains the person is a 'being-in-the-world'.[21] Accordingly, human persons need the things of this world and, to acquire them, transform the world through labour.[22] Given what we know in the midst of our current ecological crisis, this dimension of our personhood is an ambivalent one. A capacity to transform

---

20 Kelly, *New Directions in Moral Theology*, 33.
21 Christie notes that Janssens himself denied direct parallels between his and Heidegger's work, but that their thought is at least philosophically congruent. See Christie, *Adequately Considered*, 18.
22 Janssens, 'Artificial Insemination', 6. Regarding labour, cf. *Gaudium et Spes*, 33–39. Regarding culture, cf. *Gaudium et Spes*, 53–62.

the world is not a guarantee that this will be done in ways that 'sustain human dignity and the common good'.[23] This observation of our interconnectedness with the material world also invites considerations of how it is we understand ourselves in terms of place (e.g., through concepts of home or land), as well as considerations of the way in which we use the material world—either responsibly or irresponsibly.

In John's case, it became apparent to my friends when they spoke to him that the question of 'home' was a particularly important one, and, indeed, his subjective conception of bodily well-being (drawing on the two features noted above) was integrally bound with his conception of home. John felt the safest just outside his own home, regardless of whether or not he was able to get in the door. Furthermore, given what my friends were able to determine through conversation with John (and from their observations regarding his behaviour outside this incident), it became clear the fear of losing home was driving his ongoing quest for independence, including in this scenario.

The Human Person is Always in Relationship with Others

The fourth dimension of the human person adequately considered refers to relationality. The central observation here is that humans are essentially relational creatures that we come to being through relationship, and that every dimension of our personhood is bound up with our relationships with others.[24] According to this view, human flourishing is inherently related to flourishing in the context of relationship.[25] This points to the importance of relationship quality, the many ways in which relationship is expressed and strengthened, and the way in which relationship influences our worldviews, values, and preferences.

In the context of Mary's case, when my colleagues engaged in further discussion with Mary and her family, they discovered that the ritual of eating (seen on first glance as an act of nourishing the

---

23 Gula, *Reason Informed by Faith*, 70.
24 Janssens, 'Artificial Insemination', 8. Cf. Christie, *Adequately Considered*, 43.
25 *Gaudium et Spes*, no. 12 (Parenthesis added).

body) was in fact a deeply relational act for Mary. They began to see that, coming from a family in which relationship was predominantly expressed and nourished in the context of meals, a decision for Mary which would take away her capacity to eat was seen as detrimental to relationality—an aspect of her humanness that she valued even over bodily well-being.

The Human Person is Always in Relationship with Social Groups and Institutions

The fifth dimension of the human person considered here acknowledges that human relationships are never simply a one-to-one matter; rather, our relationality is expressed in terms of a broader sociality. Specifically, our relationship dimensions are structured in the context of social groups and institutions. When these are orientated towards the common good, they help to support flourishing; when they are not, they can undermine it.[26] This dimension of the human person acknowledges that the way in which our social groups and institutions are structured has an influence on our moral decision-making as well as on the self-understanding of people within them.

In John's case, his previous association with groups such as the Boy Scouts had given him a certain kind of human subjectivity, one which sought after (rather than avoided) certain kinds of adventure (including, in this case, sleeping out). In Mary's case, the very social structure of the aged care facility gave her and her family a sense of disempowerment in the face of decision-making by caregivers. In both cases, attention to the way in which these social groups and institutions functioned gave those responding to John and Mary a better understanding of how to respond.

---

26 Janssens, 'Artificial Insemination', 9. Cf. Kelly, *New Directions in Moral Theology*, 37. See *Gaudium et Spes*, nos. 23–32.

The Human Person is Orientated towards Relationship with God

The sixth dimension of the human person adequately considered points towards the spiritual aspect of each and every person. Within the Christian tradition, this is framed as our response to the invitation to enter into relationship with God.[27] What this dimension of the person acknowledges is that, in a similar way to our relational and social dimensions, relationship with God can have a defining impact on our subjectivity and, through that, every other dimension of our personhood. As an example, it is not difficult to think of individuals throughout history whose Christian faith gave them a sense of subjectivity that led them to a clear sacrifice of bodily or relational well-being in pursuit of their commitments to God. On the other hand, the Catholic health and aged care services I engage with through my current work are set up to support the flourishing of individuals—with a special focus on the body—equally out of a faith commitment.

The cases of John and Mary did not have any clear application of this dimension of their personhood. However, it is not difficult to imagine similar cases in which one's religious views would have an impact on how one engages with questions surrounding care.

The Human Person is a Developmental and Historical Being

The seventh dimension of the human person adequately considered represents both the developmental and historical aspects of the person. The first observation here (espoused by developmental psychology) builds on the fact that each and every one of us has a unique developmental history.[28] In other words, we all have a story, and the structure and flow of that story contributes to the person we are. Additionally, the stage at which we are in our story may influence the kind of person we are at a particular point in time. For example, we recognise with

---

27 Janssens, 9. See *Gaudium et Spes*, 12, 34 & 34, 36, 48, respectively. Cf. Gula, *Reason Informed by Faith*, 68.
28 Janssens, 'Artificial Insemination', 10.

ease that what can be expected from a child differs from what can be expected from an adult.[29] This recognition also highlights an important aspect of shared decision-making, of the kind we encounter in the cases of John and Mary. Specifically, in both cases, it is clear the decisions of others in relation to John and Mary have a significant impact on them in view of their developmental history: what happens at this point in time will become part of their story, and once it is committed to history, an irretrievable aspect of that history. This places a saliency on the kind of response we choose to make, especially at significant moments in a person's developmental history. Simultaneously, both John and Mary—and the rest of us—exist at a particular moment in shared history, which itself adds important features to our response to their situations.[30] In Mary's case, for example, it would not have been possible to provide her with a nourishing liquid diet even 150 years ago and, therefore, that places importance on such an aspect in our decision-making process.

I have already noted aspects of John and Mary's developmental history that link into the quality of response to their cases (i.e., John's history with the Boy Scouts and Mary's history of expressing relationship through meals). What became especially important in both cases for those who responded to John and Mary was a consideration of how that response could contribute to their ongoing developmental history. For example, if an intervention was made with John (such as contacting a healthcare service or one of his family members), would it have had an impact on his capacity to continue living at home, something which he has expressed a clear preference for?

---

29 Janssens' own example is that it is 'essentially important to begin with the meaning of youth to morally judge behaviour within that stage of life'. Janssens, 'Artificial Insemination', 10. Cf. Gula, *Reason Informed by Faith*, 70.
30 Janssens, 'Artificial Insemination', 10. See *Gaudium et Spes*, no. 49.

Each Individual Human Person is Fundamentally Equal to All Other Human Persons While at the Same Time Uniquely Original

The eighth, and final, dimension of the human person adequately considered holds together two central aspects of what we have explored thus far. They are that our dignity makes us fundamentally equal to each and every other person, and yet our own subjectivity; bodies; relationships with the world, others, and social groups; religiosity, developmental journey and moment in history make us totally unique.[31] Our commonalities make possible general responses to each and every person (e.g., medicine would not be possible if each person's body was totally unique), and yet our uniqueness calls forth a response that is attentive to each and every individual. This points to what I have referred to in another work as attentiveness to the vulnerability of each person as a unique person, and invites an application of response to human dignity which honours this attentiveness.[32]

An 'Unknown-Known': Why We Did Not at First See Mary or John Integrally or Adequately

Returning now to a focus on the cases of Mary and John more fully, I note the first response of everyone involved (including my friends, colleagues, and myself when I came into contact with the cases) did not reflect the paradigm of the human person developed above. In fact, it was not even close, and this from individuals steeped in 'person-centred care' and aspects of the paradigm introduced above. What is striking about this is how all involved stepped into a manner of thinking through the issues at hand in an automatic way in which unacknowledged assumptions regarding what was important in response brought themselves to bear on our decision-making. These unacknowledged assumptions reflected a reductive understanding of the human person,

---

31 Janssens, 'Artificial Insemination', 12. Cf. Kelly, *New Directions in Moral Theology*, 53. See *Gaudium et Spes*, no. 29.
32 Fleming, *Attentiveness to Vulnerability*.

which emphasised particular perceptions of their humanness at the expense of an integral and adequate response to them.

This kind of response has some resemblance to what the Slovenian philosopher, Slavoj Žižek, refers to as an 'unknown-known', an ideological framework that underpins a way of thinking, but that remains unacknowledged and so exerts itself in a way that appears as neutral or natural. Žižek's explains this concept with reference to the oft-quoted (and oft-mocked) response of the then US Secretary of Defence, Donald Rumsfeld, to a question on evidence linking the Iraqi Government to weapons of mass destruction in 2002. Rumsfeld's response was as follows:

> As we know, there are known knowns; there are things we know we know. We also know there are known unknowns; that is to say, we know there are some things we do not know. But there are also unknown unknowns—the ones we don't know we don't know.[33]

Žižek observes that, contrary to the mocking that this statement received in popular media, Rumsfeld produces a fairly sophisticated epistemology in these three sentences. What is missing, however, is a fourth sentence: 'there are also unknown knowns—things we don't know that we know'.[34] Reflecting on the phenomenology of Edmund Husserl, the French philosopher Emmanuel Levinas holds out a similar observation:

> Notions held under the direct gaze of the thought that defines them are nevertheless, unbeknown to this naïve thought, revealed to be implanted in horizons unsuspected by this thought; these horizons endow them with a meaning.[35]

The work of these unknown-knowns can be revealed by pointing to aspects of thought that automatically bring themselves to bear on situations and scenarios through the discipline of ideological criticism.

33 Cited in U.S. Department of Defense News Transcript *(February 12, 2002)*.
34 Žižek, *Living in the End Times*, 429.
35 Levinas, *Totality and Infinity*, 28.

The first step in this discipline is to notice them when they appear, and then to provide a compelling vision that shows up their inadequacies. In the cases at hand, what occurred automatically for all those who sought to respond revealed what I will refer to as the ideology of the 'medicalisation of ageing', in contrast to an approach that reflected the framework introduced above.

The medical aspect of this approach emphasises concern for bodily well-being—and interventions that respond to the human body—in a way that relativises or completely removes considerations of other aspects of the person. In the case of Mary, it became present in the way in which the care team first decided for Mary the risk to her health of eating solid foods was too great, and this was used as an unquestioned foundation for a decision Mary had no part in. In the case of John, my friends' first reaction was to do something for John to protect his bodily well-being. His appearance as a frail, elderly gentleman led them to believe the appropriate response was for them to intervene, with a list of possible responses including calling an ambulance, contacting his relatives, ignoring his comment about not wanting a locksmith and contacting one anyway, and so on. With the framework of the human person adequately considered in mind, it is clear to see how these first considerations were deficient in reference to their response to Mary and John's dignity.

In the main, this is because they fail to respond to Mary and John as unique subjects, with due reference to all of those aspects of their personhood which shape their subjectivity, and instead treat them as objects: passive materials on which concern can be exercised, but without adequate involvement of the subject themselves. As a nurse-colleague once said to me, this is 'caring at' rather than 'caring for'. This is common in healthcare contexts across the board. However, my argument here is that Mary and John's status in our socio-cultural context as ageing played a significant role here. Were they younger individuals, the response would have been vastly different (i.e., a 21-year-old John would have been offered a glass of water and a laugh, perhaps, and a 30-year-old Mary would have been more fully involved in decision-making surrounding her eating).

This point has an ethical saliency that is not at first obvious, hence my suggestion that it functions as an ideological 'unknown-known'. To develop this analysis, I draw on the work of Martha Nussbaum, which reflects on the status of the ageing body. Her work on this topic appears in a 2017 book she wrote collaboratively with Saul Levmore, Aging Thoughtfully: Conversations about Retirement, Romance, Wrinkles, & Regret.[36] Within this text, I focus on an essay by Nussbaum entitled Our Bodies, Ourselves: Aging, Stigma and Disgust.[37] Here, Nussbaum advances an argument that the ageing body has become an object of stigma and disgust in our collective unconscious.[38] Like other bodies that have and, in some cases, continue to be objects of stigma and disgust (black bodies, Asian bodies, disabled bodies, women's bodies, homosexual bodies, and so on), that the ageing body elicits stigma and disgust as an unconscious response also inevitably leads us to particular kinds of ways of responding to it.[39]

These responses include the creation of a 'sub-group' within society, who are treated differently from others not necessarily on the basis of genuine differences in need, but on the basis of unfounded bias. Nussbaum draws on contemporary psychological and social research that demonstrates the unconscious level at which this bias rests, illustrating that prompts such as 'old' and 'ageing' 'elicit negative reactions even when the subject is not aware of having any such bias'.[40] Nussbaum goes on to say such 'implicit bias toward the aging is likely to be based on childhood learning, deeply internalized', meaning that 'it will, therefore, be difficult to eradicate'.[41]

Furthermore, categories of bias are used to justify certain forms of treatment, and here Nussbaum suggests we see features in the approach to the ageing that we see in response to other bodies that have been the object of stigma and disgust: fear, an 'othering' of the sub-group, a segregation of the sub-group, a devaluing of the sub-group's capacities, and an over-emphasis on the animalistic characteristics of the

---

36 Nussbaum and Levmore, *Aging Thoughtfully*.
37 Nussbaum and Levmore, *Aging Thoughtfully*, 108–123.
38 Nussbaum and Levmore, *Aging Thoughtfully*, 109.
39 Nussbaum and Levmore, *Aging Thoughtfully*, 110–111.
40 Nussbaum and Levmore, *Aging Thoughtfully*, 115.
41 Nussbaum and Levmore, *Aging Thoughtfully*, 115.

sub-group.[42] More specifically, this includes seeing and responding to the group as strange and alien, using communication strategies that mirror communication to pets or small children (at best) and other animals (at worst), and, at its more extreme end, assigning characteristics of smell, decay, and death, which Nussbaum argues points to the impression that whichever particular body is being considered in this way is at its heart 'just a pile of faeces'.[43]

In terms of more specific beliefs regarding the ageing body among other bodies that are viewed with shame and disgust, Nussbaum points to the following:

> One is that the aging have declining cognitive capacity and memory. Thus, the very same mistakes and instances of forgetfulness are ascribed to normal human frailty when a younger person makes them, but to age when an aging person makes them. Similarly, the same physical problems that are ascribed to treatable disease in younger people are ascribed to the inevitable effects of aging when the patient is older.[44]

She then goes on to observe that, 'since such stereotypes of inevitability have reigned for so long, we actually don't know very much about what the baseline of health is for people at various ages, in a variety of performance areas'.[45]

At the beginning of Nussbaum's essay rests a significant observation about this particular ideological framework. She stands it in contrast to the Our Bodies, Ourselves movement, which women in the Baby-Boomer generation spearheaded in the 1970s. In her words:

> Inspired by the generation-defining tome Our Bodies, Ourselves, we trained for childbirth without anaesthesia, we looked at our cervixes using a speculum, and in general cultivated in ourselves the thought that our bodies were not sticky, disgusting, and shameful, but dynamic, marvellous—and,

---

42 Nussbaum and Levmore, *Aging Thoughtfully*, 110–111.
43 Nussbaum and Levmore, *Aging Thoughtfully*, 115.
44 Nussbaum and Levmore, *Aging Thoughtfully*, 115.
45 Nussbaum and Levmore, *Aging Thoughtfully*, 115.

more importantly, just us ourselves. Today, as we boomers age, male and female, what has happened to that love and excitement? I fear that my generation is letting disgust and shame sweep over us again, as a new set of bodily challenges beckons.[46]

On these points we should observe what typically happens to people who are in groups that are the objects of shame and disgust: in the worst cases, violence is perpetuated against them, and in other cases they are segregated, their subjectivity is undermined, their spirituality undervalued, they are institutionalised, and they are no longer able to flourish according to any reasonable definition of this term. If these are our 'unknown knowns' when it comes to ageing, then they have the capacity to undermine an integral and adequate response to the human person along the lines of what is outlined above. In various forms and at various levels of extremity, we treat people as objects and not subjects, with a de-valuing of every aspect of their humanity that makes their subjectivity so profound. And it is this unknown-known I believe was present in my own, my friends' and my colleagues' first reactions to both Mary and John's cases.

The Entry of Medicine

The presence of medicine produces an additional layer of complexity in this context. When it comes to groups who are the 'objects of shame and disgust', at times medicine has been seen as a solution to the 'problems' such groups are identified with. Sadly, one does not need to list the ways in which medicine has been used as a legitimising force for all range of issues responding to groups considered objects of disgust and shame—the experiments on Jewish and other prisoners of the Nazis immediately come to mind.

Today, this underside is less readily noticed and, in an apparently more benign way and in any raft of issues that humanity faces, medicine

---

46 Nussbaum and Levmore, *Aging Thoughtfully*, 108.

is seen as the transcendental discipline that has insights which will chart a socially responsible course. Anyone who has had experience in politics will know this well: whenever an important social issue arises, the voices considered to have the most authority for response in our society are typically medical professionals. We outsource our decision-making and look to medicine for appropriate responses. This may not be a problem, but only if it can be shown the discipline of medicine itself can provide the most appropriate response. In some cases, it can, but when it is in the middle of its own ideology, this status is debatable.

On this point I turn to the philosopher and medical doctor Jeffrey Bishop, who shares the following story in his article The Sacrifice of Sagging Flesh.[47] This partially autobiographical intervention by Bishop picks up on much of what we have explored with Nussbaum, but then looks further into the question of the ideology that rests at the heart of the discipline of medicine today, which leads to a more in-depth critique of that discipline. I cite Bishop's article at length, for reasons which will become obvious throughout:

> My great-grandmother's flesh was soft under my 5-year-old fingers. Standing beside her as she spent time playing cards or dominoes with her grandchildren—my father and his brothers—or her children—my great aunts and uncles—I would hold onto to her arm, laying my head on her shoulder, touching the loose, sagging flesh of her arm. What today is considered grotesque—wrinkled and sagging flesh—felt good under my young fingers.
>
> I remember this scene fondly, because it was played out on numerous weekend evenings playing cards or dominoes into the wee hours. The laughter and banter around the card table was joyful, as she unleashed her dry wit in an attempt to outwit my father and uncles in cards or dominoes.
>
> She had been a teacher in rural Texas, where my family has been since Texas was a Mexican state. She was born in 1893,

---

47 Bishop, *The Sacrifice of Sagging Flesh*.

and she had been a teacher from age 20. She walked 12 miles each way to teach at one of the rural schools that peppered the southeast Texas landscape in the early Twentieth Century. Her body was marked by the work she had done, and the work done on her by the harsh Texas soil of the farm she ran for nearly 30 years after her husband's death in 1960. Her fingers and toes were gnarled, bending in odd ways; her knees were arthritic and knobby from the wear and tear of the years. They bore traces of her life.

If time is the endurance of things in relationship to themselves and to events around them from moment to moment, then aging is a different kind of time. It is the endurance of a body from moment to moment, but also in relation to change. To some extent, we understand aging as something intrinsic to the body, a kind of decay endured from within. Yet mostly, it seems that we imagine aging as primarily a price exacted on the flesh from the pressures of living, the endurance of the flesh undergoing change in relation to the miles walked or the hours worked against the resistance of soil. Aging is the wear and tear on the body, the endurance by the flesh of the onslaught of insult and injury.[48]

Bishop's article continues by noting that, in cultivating a form of medicine that presents as our constant fight against the ageing body (even by interventions that would remove wrinkles—in this case, the very signs of his grandmother's life story, for example), we reveal a deep-seated ideology that separates the body from all other aspects of the human person integrally and adequately considered. A body from which the signs of ageing are medically removed is a body that medicine separates from its developmental history and, thereby, its subjectivity.

This kind of analysis is consistent with a deeper critique of the ideology of medicine itself, which Bishop has explored in his remarkable book The Anticipatory Corpse: Medicine, Power and the Care of the

---

48   Bishop, *The Sacrifice of Sagging Flesh*.

Dying.[49] Whilst I cannot do justice to the entire book here, one central insight is relevant to this exploration. That insight is captured in one fairly simple observation Bishop makes regarding the training of medical doctors. It begins with a question: when a person first begins medical school, what kind of human body do they first encounter in their medical training?

The answer is a dead body: a body removed from its subjectivity, history, spirituality, relationality, and so on.[50] There are obvious reasons for this—there is no better way of studying human anatomy than by studying a human body, and there are important ethical and logistical barriers to doing this with living bodies. Bishop sees the problem with this not as the practice, but with the normativity arising out of it. He argues the corpse (the dead body) is the normative body for medicine, which leads to a form of practice that sees the human person as effectively a machine (i.e., an object upon which medicine can practice its art). Thus, the patient becomes 'an object of disciplinary power'.[51] On this foundation, Bishop launches into a stunning critique of the bio-social-spiritual medicine characterising our current times as an expression of power over the human subject, imagined as a corpse rather than a person and, thereby, not as an authentic, healing response to the human person. Or, to use the language of this chapter, not as excellence in response to the human person integrally and adequately considered, but rather as a response that sees the person as an object and a body, not an embodied subject.

Bishop explains this as a 'dis-enchantment' of the human subject in a more recent article, Enchanting Medicine: Science, Religion and the Care of the Patient.[52] That article synthesises the abovementioned points. The excerpt I include below focuses on Becca, a patient of Bishop's who removed her own oxygen mask and died under his care, and who he frequently reflects on for what she taught him about the limitations and ideology of his medical profession:

---

49 Bishop, *The Anticipatory Corpse*.
50 Bishop, *The Anticipatory Corpse*, 14.
51 Bishop, *The Anticipatory Corpse*, 7.
52 Bishop, *Enchanting Medicine*.

> Medical science with its technocratic reason distorts the images of bodies, psyches and spirits into manageable mechanisms. We study the body, the psyche and the spirit in order to control them.
>
> The physiologists taught me that the body and the brain are just complicated mechanisms. The psychologists and psychiatrists taught me that the psyche, the mind, is the sum total of all the inputs that result in the outputs of behaviour. The new scientifically-minded chaplains taught me that the spirit just needs to be elucidated by spiritual assessments so that we can prescribe certain spiritual interventions to help the patient better cope with their disease. Together, the biopsychosociospiritual medicine disenchanted Becca, permitting us to offer total care to her—a means to manage every dimension of her illness, her body, her dying.
>
> Yet, in her appearing, Becca taught me that these scientific procedural attempts to describe and control human reality—body, psyche and spirit—are the idolatries to which scientific rationality is given. Becca revealed this to me, in her death.[53]

Bishop compellingly names the risk that medical ideology has for those under the care of medical professionals: they are disenchanted and separated from their subjectivity. In the most egregious cases, physical violence is done to them by applying techniques of care without due reference to the subjects to whom they are directed (as may have been the case for Mary—see more below). Even in more benign cases, we run the risk of other kinds of violence, such as the removal of subjectivity from an individual, their disempowerment, ignorance of their subjectivity, and so on (as may have been the case even outside a medical context with John—see more below). As we have seen above, the temptation to the enactment of an ideology like this is especially salient for those who work in the helping professions and, if not checked, can lead to poor outcomes that do not reflect the dignity or comprehensive humanity of the people who are being served. This is a

---

53 Bishop, *Enchanting Medicine*.

risk as much for those with good will as those with ill—the problem of an unknown-known is that we do not see it unless we take time to critique it. I turn now to the conclusion of the article, in which I propose a method for doing exactly this, in dialogue with the cases of Mary and John.

A Pause and a Conclusion: What Happened with Mary and John?

In the cases of both Mary and John, those involved in responding took a simple action enabling them to critique their initial response: they paused. And then they asked a simple question, one which follows the pattern introduced by Jesus of Nazareth when he asked Blind Bartimaeus 'what can I do for you?' (Mark 10:51). This simple question shifts the power dynamic from the carer to the one cared-for and provides a moment in which the unique subjectivity of the other person can become known. It thereby has the effect of disrupting the automaticity of any ideological approach that has an influence on decision-making, especially when this is unknown to those in the midst of a situation.

In the case of John, this approach opened up a conversation that led my friends to an understanding that he was seeing this night as an adventure. He felt safe (and, objectively speaking, he was—the common area outside his home was warm, quiet, and private), he had eaten dinner, had access to clean water (provided by my friends) and knew he could ask to use their bathroom if needed. They also loaned him a sleeping bag and pillow. John awoke the next morning, contacted his sister, and was able to get back into his apartment. He was home, and later delivered a box of chocolates to my friends as a thank you.

In the case of Mary, the care team was able to coordinate a discussion with her and her family to better understand the significance of meals for Mary, and what it meant to her when she discovered they were considering taking away her option of solid foods. This led to a much richer discussion surrounding Mary's goals for care and an adaptation of her diet that enabled her to enjoy eating and mitigate some, but not all, risk of choking. The care team came to understand some things were worse from Mary's point of view than the risk of choking, and came to an acceptance of this position, even though it was difficult for them.

Both cases led to responses which, I would argue, represented excellence. However, they only did this because those involved took the time to pause and ask the power-inverting question, which had the effect of disrupting their unknown-knowns. Had they not, the responses would have been less than adequate.

This is the crux and conclusion of the argument in this chapter. The ageing body has a particular status in our current context and it is one that intertwined with ideological frameworks that see those who fall into the category of 'ageing' more as objects than subjects. In the context of medicine, this leads to unfortunate decision-making processes, which are also reflected in other care contexts (even the common area of an apartment block). Without critique, this approach will become the dominant one in care and response to those who are ageing, and this would be a tragedy. Medical ideology inflicts itself on people under its care, and does more harm than good. Instead, an approach informed by the full dignity of each and every person, regardless of age and stage, and responsive to their humanness and adequately considered, can lead to excellence in the care of the ageing.

Bibliography

Bishop, J. P.	*Enchanting Medicine: Science, Religion and the Care of the Patient* (2017) <https://www.abc.net.au/religion/enchanting-medicine-science-religion-and-the-care-of-the-patient/10095164> [accessed 25 May 2019].
Bishop, J. P.	*The Anticipatory Corpse: Medicine, Power and the Care of the Dying* (Notre Dame: University of Notre Dame Press, 2011).
Bishop, J. P.	*The Sacrifice of Sagging Flesh* (2018). <https://churchlifejournal.nd.edu/articles/the-sacrifice-of-sagging-flesh/> [accessed 25 May 2019].

Burggraeve, R. 'The Holistic Personalism of Professor Magister Louis Janssens', *Louvain Studies* 27 (2002), 29–38.

Christie, D. L. *Adequately Considered: An American Perspective on Louis Janssens' Personalist Morals* (Louvain: Peeters, 1990).

Catholic Health Australia. *Code of Ethical Standards for Catholic Health and Aged Care Services in Australia* (Deakin West: Catholic Health Australia, 2001).

Curran, C. *Catholic Social Teaching 1891–Present: A Historical, Theological, and Ethical Analysis* (Washington: Georgetown University Press, 2002).

Fleming, D. J. *Attentiveness to Vulnerability: A Dialogue Between Emmanuel Levinas, Jean Porter, and the Virtue of Solidarity* (Eugene: Pickwick Publications, 2019).

Gula, R. M. *Reason Informed by Faith: Foundations of Catholic Morality* (Mahwah: Paulist, 1989).

Janssens, L. 'Artificial Insemination: Ethical Considerations', *Louvain Studies* 8 (1980), 3–29.

John Paul II. *Evangelium Vitae* (1995). <http://w2.vatican.va/content/john-paul-ii/en/encyclicals/documents/hf_jp-ii_enc_25031995_evangelium-vitae.html> [accessed 25 May 2019].

Kelly, K. T. *New Directions in Moral Theology: The Challenge of Being Human* (London: Geoffrey Chapman, 1992).

Nussbaum, M. C. and Levmore, S. *Aging Thoughtfully: Conversations about Retirement, Romance, Wrinkles & Regret* (Oxford: Oxford University Press, 2017).

Pontifical Council for Justice and Peace. *Compendium of the Social Doctrine of the Church* (2006). <http://www.vatican.va/roman_curia/pontifical_councils/justpeace/documents/rc_pc_justpeace_doc_20060526_compendio-dott-soc_en.html#Meaning%20and%20primary%20implications> [accessed 25 May 2019].

Rudman, S. *Concepts of Person and Christian Ethics* (Cambridge: Cambridge University Press, 1997).

U.S. Department of Defense. *News Transcript* (February 12, 2002). <https://archive.defense.gov/Transcripts/Transcript.aspx?TranscriptID=2636> [accessed 25 May 2019].

Vatican II Council. *Gaudium et Spes* (1965). <http://www.vatican.va/archive/hist_councils/ii_vatican_council/documents/vat-ii_const_19651207_gaudium-et-spes_en.html> [accessed 25 May 2019].

West, C. 'Prophetic Religion and the Future of Capitalist Civilization', in Eduardo Mendieta and Jonathan Vanantwerpen (eds.), *The Power of Religion in the Public Square* (New York: Columbia University Press, 2011): 92–110.

Žižek, S. *Living in the End Times* (London: Verso, 2011).

CHAPTER 2

Standards and continuing professional development for chaplains: Learning pathways for aged care chaplains

Peter Carblis

Abstract

Aged care chaplaincies operate at the intersections of faith, religion, belief, and spirituality within contexts defined by the fourth stage of life, culture, and healthcare. Often a form of civil chaplaincy, aged care chaplaincies commonly serve in institutions subject to government scrutiny and regulation. Furthermore, they are subject to increasing calls for professionalisation as spiritual-care practitioners, recognition as allied health professionals, and to the adoption of formal standards of practice. This chapter considers the development of a framework that will enable the critical evaluation, specification, and continual improvement of the attributes of assistant, practising, accomplished, and lead practitioners. This will enable consideration of faith-based distinctives, specifications of regulatory bodies, professional associations and peak bodies, research on spiritual care in aged care, and research on inter-cultural and inter-faith practices.

Introduction

For many years, there has been a consistent call for the professionalisation of chaplaincy across a wide range of settings.[1] Chaplaincy is increasingly recognised as a challenging and important ministry that is valued locally and internationally. It uniquely engages the issues of ultimate concern in a person's life through the exercise of spiritual care. Those who serve effectively in any of its settings are greatly respected by both the people they serve and the communities of practice within which they serve.

Chaplaincy is an essential service that is provided in both short-term crisis situations and through long-term accompaniment. Its settings include aged care, civil (government institutions), community, corporate, educational, emergency services, healthcare, military, police, prison, and sports settings. While each setting determines the nature of the practice of chaplaincy within it, there is also much that is common to all chaplaincies.

Like other professions, chaplaincy has a common core of knowledge and skills essential for those entering the service. It also has a body of advanced and specialised knowledge and skills that apply variously across its settings, which are constantly under development. Therefore, chaplaincy requires the constant improvement of curricula to meet agreed-upon standards for its entry and advanced levels, specialisations and continuing professional development (CPD).

This chapter considers how professional standards for chaplaincy in general may be described in sufficient detail to guide precise CPD. This is then applied to aged care chaplaincy in particular by applying the methodology used for The Australian Professional Standards for Teachers. This was developed for a similar purpose for a similarly complex profession.[2] This methodology enables the effective search, identification and curation of training and development resources across the intersections encountered by the profession. In the case of aged- care chaplaincy, these include the intersections of faith, religion,

---

1 Orton, 'Transforming Chaplaincy', 128; Timmins et al., 'The Role of the Healthcare Chaplain: A Literature Review', 101; Timmins et al., 'The Role of the Healthcare Chaplain'.
2 NESA, *Australian Professional Standards for Teachers*.

belief, and spirituality within contexts defined by the fourth stage of life, culture, and healthcare.

What follows first considers the professional standards for chaplaincy in general and may be described in sufficient detail to guide precise CPD. This initially involves consideration for the nature of the chaplaincy profession, the need for professional standards, the purpose of standards, and the levels of service. Six standards are then proposed and related to the three domains of professional knowledge, practice and engagement. Focus areas for each standard are then proposed for each level of service and consideration of each standard then concludes with examples of sources from which knowledge may be accessed for practising chaplains in aged care.

The Profession of Chaplaincy

The distinguishing feature of the chaplaincy profession in all its settings is its disciplined focus on the ultimate concerns of the person rather than the circumstance or setting in which they are found. This is the essence of what is now described as spiritual care. This focus enables the other professions within their communities of practice to focus on their role within the setting. Medical professionals must focus on healing, educators on teaching, emergency services on emergencies and so on. Just as such services need to be aware of the spiritual needs of those they serve, chaplains must be aware of how the professionals with whom they serve provide and understand the services they deliver. In all of this, chaplains must be able to provide spiritual care to those who deliver such services in each setting as well as those who receive the services.

Spiritual care has become an umbrella term that incorporates both 'religious care' and 'pastoral care'.[3] Within spiritual care, how a person relates to their ultimate concerns is called their spirituality. MacKinlay uses the language of ultimate concern or meaning to define spirituality. In her study of the spiritual dimension of ageing, she writes:

---

3   Meaningful Ageing, 'National Guidelines for Spiritual Care in Aged Care', 8.

The definition of spirituality is: that which lies at the core of each person's being, an essential dimension which brings meaning to life. Constituted not only by religious practices, but understood more broadly, as relationship with God, however God or ultimate meaning is perceived by the person and in relationship with other people.[4]

Professional Standards for Chaplains

Like any profession, chaplaincy requires standards to ensure quality in its practice. Properly set, standards define, provide boundaries, and set performance criteria for any profession; properly declared, standards are public statements regarding what is deemed to constitute professional quality. The capacity to serve in any profession, then, requires the demonstration of capabilities thus prescribed. Development of such capacity first requires an initial foundation that introduces the developing practitioner to the common core of the profession, and then consideration of practice aspects congruent with the context and domain of the community in which they may serve.

The development of the professional standards for chaplaincy is an integral part of ensuring quality spiritual care is delivered in the institutions and communities in which chaplaincies are found. These standards draw on and build the significant work undertaken previously in Australia and elsewhere.

There have been several attempts to fully or partially define chaplaincy practice and to prescribe standards of practice for it. In their discussion of what chaplains do, Mowat and Swinton identified the core tasks of chaplaincy as those that seek people who need them, identifying the nature of the need and responding to the need through theological and spiritual praxis (see Figure 1). Standards of practice include the *Spiritual Care Australia Standards of Practice*,[5] the

---

[4] MacKinlay, *The Spiritual Dimension of Ageing*, 52. See also McSherry and Smith, 'Spiritual Care', 118; Puchalski et al., 'Improving the Spiritual Dimension of Whole Person Care', 6.
[5] SCA, 'Spiritual Care Australia Standards of Practice'.

Essential Capabilities of the Civil Chaplaincies Advisory Committee of New South Wales,[6] the *Capabilities Framework for Pastoral Care and Chaplaincy* of Spiritual Health Victoria,[7] and the *Common Qualifications and Competencies for Professional Chaplains* of the North American Board of Chaplaincy Certification.[8] These are broad statements of general principles but, as a rule, do not contain explicit detail. What is developed in what follows suggests such detail.

Purpose of the Standards

The standards developed closely follow the structure of the Australian Professional Standards for Teachers (APST).[9] Like teaching, chaplaincy can be seen as a diverse set of practices organised around a common core. Teaching begins with a common core related to pedagogical practice and, taking human development into account, specialises in subjects such as English, science and languages. Similarly, chaplaincy begins with a core of pastoral practice and, taking human development into account, specialises in the various ways it is practiced (e.g., aged care, corrective services, hospital, police, and school).

The APST are designed to state and organise in explicit detail the constituent parts of high-quality, effective practice. Such standards also provide a common means of accurate communication and accountability between practitioners, educators, institutions served, organisations, professional associations, regulators and the public. Furthermore, they are invaluable in allowing for accurate self-assessment: they allow practitioners to recognise both current and developing capabilities, their personal goals and attainments.

---

6 CCAC, 'Education, Qualification and Registration - Civil Chaplaincies Advisory Committee'.
7 Spiritual Health Victoria, 'Capabilities Framework for Pastoral Care and Chaplaincy'.
8 BCC, 'Common Qualifications and Competencies for Professional Chaplains'.
9 NESA, *Australian Professional Standards for Teachers*.

Figure 1. Core Tasks of Chaplaincy.[10]

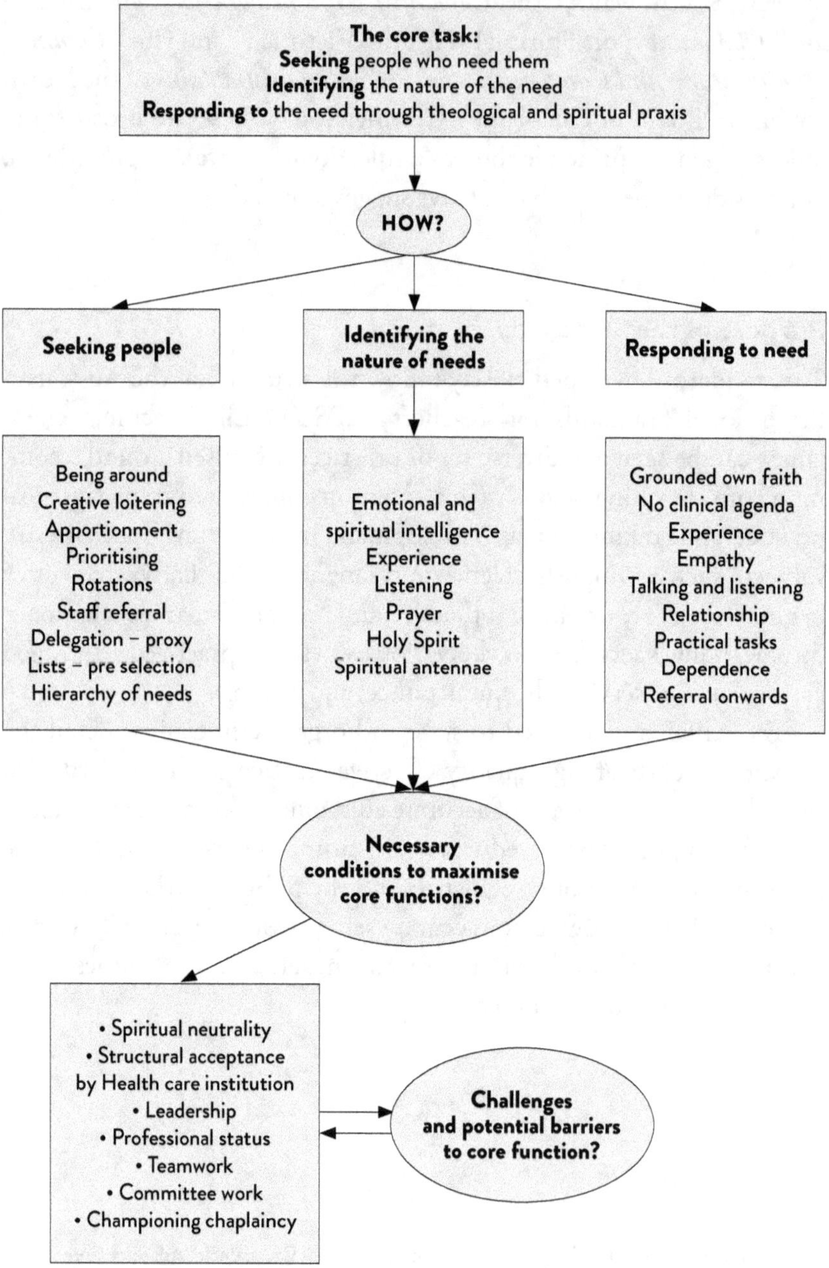

The core task:
Seeking people who need them
Identifying the nature of the need
Responding to the need through theological and spiritual praxis

HOW?

Seeking people

- Being around
- Creative loitering
- Apportionment
- Prioritising
- Rotations
- Staff referral
- Delegation – proxy
- Lists – pre selection
- Hierarchy of needs

Identifying the nature of needs

- Emotional and spiritual intelligence
- Experience
- Listening
- Prayer
- Holy Spirit
- Spiritual antennae

Responding to need

- Grounded own faith
- No clinical agenda
- Experience
- Empathy
- Talking and listening
- Relationship
- Practical tasks
- Dependence
- Referral onwards

Necessary conditions to maximise core functions?

- Spiritual neutrality
- Structural acceptance by Health care institution
- Leadership
- Professional status
- Teamwork
- Committee work
- Championing chaplaincy

Challenges and potential barriers to core function?

---

10   Mowat and Swinton, 'What Do Chaplains Do?', 34.

Development of the Standards

The six standards proposed here are informed by the *Essential Capabilities for Chaplains and Pastoral Care Workers* prescribed by the Civil Chaplaincies Advisory Committee (CCAC) of New South Wales,[11] the *Standards of Practice of Spiritual Care Australia* and the allied health staff expectations of chaplaincy roles and tasks as tabulated by Carey, Swinton and Grosshoeme.[12] They are organised into an overlapping framework that enables the domains of professional knowledge, practice and engagement to be explored and addressed by considering focus areas related to each standard in a manner appropriate to each of the four levels of service.

Levels of Service

The four levels of service are labelled 'Assistant Chaplain', 'Practising Chaplain', 'Accomplished Chaplain' and 'Lead Chaplain'. The specifications relating to each level incorporate and deepen what is required at the previous level. *See Table 1. Chaplaincy Levels of Service*

---

11 CCAC, 'Education, Qualification and Registration'.
12 SCA, 'Spiritual Care Australia Standards of Practice', 8–19.

Table 1. Chaplaincy Levels of Service.

Level of Development	Service provided	Knowledge and Skills	Accountability	AQF Attributes[13]
Assistant Chaplain	• Pastoral visitation • Non-anxious affirming presence • Conducts spiritual need assessment • Spiritual conversation	• Listening skills • Essential Capabilities of Chaplaincy • Ethics of chaplaincy • Faith-based mission • Referral skills • Setting-based mission	• Acts autonomously with limited responsibility. • Guided by and reports to Associate chaplain or higher.	• Level 4
Practising Chaplain	• Conduct appropriate liturgies and rituals • Sacramental ministry • Response to crises • Integration with other professionals in chaplaincy setting	• Leadership skills relating to assistant chaplains. • Crisis management • Knowledge of responsibilities and capabilities of other professionals in chaplaincy setting	• Exercises autonomy and judgement. • Responds to contingencies within broad but established parameters.	• Level 5
Accomplished Chaplain	• Supervises and coordinates activities of assistant and associate chaplains. • Provides spiritual mentoring.	• Leadership skills relating to assistant and associate chaplains. • Detailed understanding of responsibilities and capabilities of other professionals in chaplaincy setting	• Provides specialist advice and functions to other stakeholders in chaplaincy settings.	• AQF Level 6 or 7
Lead Chaplain	• Supervises and coordinates activities of assistant chaplains, associate chaplains and chaplains. • Evaluates spiritual care practices	• Management skills relating to the employment and deployment of teams of chaplains.	• Exercise well-developed judgement, adaptability and responsibility as a practitioner or learner.	• AQF Level 8 or above

---

13 Garland, 'AQF Levels'.

The four levels of service provide benchmarks that recognise the professional growth of chaplains throughout their service. The levels of service represent increasing levels of knowledge, practice and professional engagement. Progression through the stages results in growth in understanding and application across an increasingly broad and complex range of situations.

Assistant Chaplains

Assistant chaplains will have completed a qualification that meets the minimum requirements of a nationally accredited program of basic chaplaincy education. As a minimum, this is expected to match the attributes of Level 4 of the Australian Qualification Framework (AQF).

Appropriately qualified assistant chaplains will be considered as possessing sufficient knowledge and skills to provide spiritual care services under the supervision of a chaplain.

They will have been assessed as possessing sufficient knowledge and skills to engage with the basic cultural, intellectual, life-stage, physical, religious, and social characteristics of their clients. They will have a basic understanding of the principles of inclusion and of strategies for differentiating their actions to meet the specific spiritual care needs of their clients. Finally, assistant chaplains will have a basic understanding of the ethics of their practice.

Practising Chaplains

Those recognised as practising chaplains will have completed a qualification that provides a foundation of specialised knowledge and skills appropriate for one recognised as a skilled practitioner. This qualification will also provide a grounding for further learning. As a minimum, this is expected to match the attributes of Level 5 of the AQF.

Appropriately qualified practising chaplains will be considered as possessing sufficient knowledge and skills to competently provide spiritual care services either as a sole practitioner or within team settings.

They will have been assessed as possessing sufficient knowledge and skills to engage autonomously with the broad cultural, intellectual, life-stage, physical, religious, and social characteristics of their clients. They will have a broad understanding of the principles of inclusion and of strategies for differentiating their actions to meet the specific spiritual care needs of their clients. Finally, practising chaplains will have a broad understanding of the ethics of their practice.

Accomplished Chaplains

Those recognised as accomplished chaplains will have completed a qualification that provides a foundation of broad and coherent knowledge and skills appropriate for one recognised as a professional practitioner. This qualification will also provide a grounding for further learning. As a minimum, this is expected to match the attributes of Level 7 of the AQF.

Appropriately qualified accomplished chaplains will be considered as possessing sufficient knowledge and skills to competently provide spiritual care services and consultancy either as a sole practitioner or within team settings.

They will have been assessed as possessing sufficient knowledge and skills to engage autonomously with the detailed cultural, intellectual, life-stage, physical, religious, and social characteristics of their clients. They will have a detailed understanding of the principles of inclusion and of strategies for differentiating their actions to meet the specific spiritual care needs of their clients. They will also possess the capacity to anticipate, respond to and solve unforeseen problems and issues, and to provide leadership wherever necessary to guide and transmit knowledge and skills in and to others. Finally, accomplished chaplains will have a comprehensive and detailed understanding of the ethics of their practice.

Lead Chaplains

Those recognised as lead chaplains will have completed a qualification that provides a foundation of advanced knowledge and skills appropriate for one recognised as a leading professional practitioner. This qualification will also provide a grounding for further learning. As a minimum, this is expected to match the attributes of Level 8 or higher of the AQF.

Appropriately qualified and recognised chaplains will be considered as possessing advanced knowledge and skills to competently provide spiritual care services and consultancy within supervisory and/or team settings.

Lead chaplains must be recognised and respected by colleagues, clients and the community as exemplary chaplains. They will have demonstrated consistent and insightful spiritual care practice over time. They establish inclusive professional environments in which ongoing learning of the cultural, intellectual, life-stage, physical, religious, and social characteristics of their clients is valued. Lead chaplains must also be skilled in mentoring other spiritual care practitioners at all levels. Finally, they will promote creative and insightful thinking among their colleagues.

Professional Standards for Chaplains

The six standards are as follows:

1. Understand clients and respond to their needs
2. Understand spiritual care
3. Provide spiritual care
4. Create and maintain supportive and safe spiritual care environments
5. Engage in professional development
6. Engage professionally with colleagues, relatives, carers and the community

The sub-components of each standard are referred to as focus areas. These itemise components of capability at each level of service and reflect characteristics of the complex process of providing spiritual care. Effective chaplains will integrate and apply what is outlined in the descriptors to both increase the spiritual well-being of those they serve as well as contribute to the development of care environments in which spiritual care is exercised.

As each standard is addressed, focus areas are identified that enable further detail in the specification of the knowledge, practice and professional engagement needed for the effective practice of chaplaincy. Descriptors for each focus area are then provided for the four levels of Assistant Chaplain, Practising Chaplain, Accomplished Chaplain and Lead Chaplain (see Table 2).

Table 2. Domains of Chaplaincy Standards.

Domain of Chaplaincy	Standards	Focus Areas and Descriptors
Professional Knowledge	1. Understand clients and respond to their needs 2. Understand spiritual care	Vary according to level of service. Listed on tables of standards.
Professional Practice	3. Provide spiritual care 4. Create and maintain supportive and safe spiritual care environments	
Professional Engagement	5. Engage in professional development 6. Engage professionally with colleagues, relatives, carers and the community	

Professional Knowledge

In order to provide effective spiritual care, chaplains must draw on a body of professional knowledge and research related to the nature of spiritual care and the needs of those they serve within the relevant contexts.

Chaplains must know their clients well. This involves an in-depth understanding of the diverse linguistic, cultural and religious backgrounds their clients bring. It also involves understanding the specific, immediate and situated circumstances and contexts of those they serve and in which they serve. Chaplains must be insightful and alert to the experiences of their clients and how such experiences affect their well-being. They must know how to engage with their clients in ways that meet their cultural, intellectual, life-stage, physical, religious, and social characteristics.

The tables below have been developed for standards 1 and 2. They illustrate how the sources, from which CPD learning programs might be developed, might be accessed in an aged care context.

Standard 1: Understand clients and respond to their needs

Focus	Assistant Chaplain	Practising Chaplain	Accomplished Chaplain	Lead Chaplain
1.1 Evaluate individual spiritual care needs	1.1.1 Establish empathetic rapport with individual centred on their well-being.	1.1.2 Deepen empathetic rapport with individual centred on identifying their ultimate concerns as they emerge in and from their experience, journey and story.	1.1.3 Expresses appropriate curiosity to assist individuals to relate their ultimate concerns to spirituality and/or their opposition to it.	1.1.4 Guide development of listening and communications skills required to establish empathetic rapport with individuals
1.2 Use spiritual care assessment tools	1.2.1 Conducts spiritual care assessments.	1.2.2 Interprets spiritual care assessments.	1.2.3 Conduct on-going assessments and modify care as required.	1.2.4 Ensure appropriate spiritual care assessments are made.
1.3 Respect human diversity	1.3.1 Engages with all individuals regardless of race, gender, gender expression, or religion with unconditional positive regard.	1.3.2 Listens non-anxiously and non-judgementally to individual understandings of life, meaning, morality and spirituality et cetera.	1.3.3 Expresses appropriate curiosity to assist individuals relate their ultimate concerns about life, meaning and spirituality to their sense of well-being.	1.3.4 Ensures that all individuals, regardless of race, gender, gender expression, or religion are received and responded to with competent understanding, empathy and unconditional positive regard.

Focus	Assistant Chaplain	Practising Chaplain	Accomplished Chaplain	Lead Chaplain
1.4 Multi- and inter-cultural issues	1.4.1 Engages positively with all individuals regardless of ethnicity, race, socio-economic status or culture	1.4.2 Recognises and responds appropriately to expressions of dimensions of culture in individuals.	1.4.3 Expresses appropriate curiosity to assist individuals relate their cultural concerns about life, meaning and spirituality to their sense of well-being.	1.4.4 Ensures that all individuals, regardless of culture, are received and responded to with competent understanding, empathy and unconditional positive regard.
1.5 Multi- and inter-faith issues	1.5.1 Engages positively with all individuals regardless of faith, denomination or personal philosophy.	1.5.2 Recognises and responds appropriately to expressions of faith or personal philosophy dimensions of culture in individuals.	1.5.3 Expresses appropriate curiosity to assist individuals to relate their faith or personal philosophy related concerns about life, meaning and spirituality to their sense of well-being.	1.5.4 Ensures that all individuals, regardless of faith, denomination or personal philosophy are received and responded to with competent understanding, empathy and unconditional positive regard.
1.6 Life-stage	1.6.1 Engages appropriately with individuals in accord with their stage of life.	1.6.2 Recognises and responds appropriately to each individual in a manner that is appropriate to their life stage.	1.6.3 Expresses appropriate curiosity to assist individuals to relate their stage-related concerns about life, meaning and spirituality to their sense of well-being.	1.6.4 Ensures all individuals are served appropriately in accord with their stage of life.
1.7 Client circumstances and condition	1.7.1 Relates to individuals with a general understanding of their condition or concerns arising from the circumstances in which they are being served.	1.7.2 Relates to individuals with a basic understanding of their condition or concerns arising from the circumstances in which they are being served.	1.7.3 Relates to individuals with a detailed understanding of their condition or concerns arising from the circumstances in which they are being served.	1.7.4 Ensures individuals are served appropriately in accord with a thorough understanding of their condition or concerns arising from the circumstances in which they are being served.

Standard 2: Understand spiritual care

	Assistant Chaplain	Practising Chaplain	Accomplished Chaplain	Lead Chaplain
2.1 Engage in theological/ spiritual reflection	2.1.1 State theological foundation of spiritual /pastoral care in terms of religious tradition.	2.1.2 Apply theological foundation of spiritual/pastoral care in context of religious tradition.	2.1.3 Advise on application of theological foundation of spiritual/pastoral care principles to problems in context of religious tradition.	2.1.4 Supervise the application of theological foundation of spiritual/pastoral care principles to problems in context of religious tradition.
2.2 Define and apply concept of spirituality	2.2.1 Awareness of traditional, clinical and popular definitions of spirituality.	2.2.2 Respond to clients in accord with their understandings of spirituality.	2.2.3 Explore understandings of spirituality expressed by clients.	2.2.4 Guide responses to and exploration of spirituality in chaplaincy settings.
2.3 Promote spiritual well-being	2.3.1 Awareness of relationship of spirituality to well-being.	2.3.2 Support the spiritual and well-being of clients.	2.3.3 Encourage the development of spiritual well-being in clients.	2.3.4 Guide the promotion of spiritual well-being in chaplaincy settings.
2.4 Practice appreciative action and reflection	2.4.1 Awareness of principles of appreciative enquiry and reflection.	2.4.2 Support clients through the practices of appreciative enquiry and reflection	2.4.3 Exercise appreciative inquiry and reflection in practice settings.	2.4.4 Promote and guide the exercise of appreciative inquiry and reflection in practice settings.
2.5 Promote continuity of care	2.5.1 Awareness of the importance of continuity of spiritual care.	2.5.2 Encourage continuity of spiritual care in clients.	2.5.3 Include strategy for continuity of spiritual care in the spiritual care plan	2.5.4 Promote and guide continuity of spiritual care in practice settings.
2.6 Understand grief and loss	2.6.1 Awareness of how individuals experience grief and loss.	2.6.2 Identify and respond appropriately to individuals experiencing grief and loss	2.6.3 Provide advice on helping those experiencing grief and loss.	2.6.4 Supervise the provision of help to those experiencing grief and loss.

Professional Knowledge in Aged-Care

Standard 1: Understand clients and respond to their needs – examples of sources

Focus	Practising Chaplain	Examples of sources from which knowledge may be accessed
1.1 Evaluate individual spiritual care needs	1.1.2 Deepen empathetic rapport with individual centred on identifying their ultimate concerns as they emerge in and from their experience, journey and story.	Joint Commission. 'Evaluating Your Spiritual Assessment Process'. *The Source*, Joint Commission on Accreditation of Healthcare Organizations, 3, no. 2 (2005), 7–8. MacKinlay, Elizabeth. 'Assessment of Spirituality and Spiritual Needs: A Developmental Approach' in *Spiritual Growth and Care in the Fourth Age of Life*, (London and Philadelphia: Jessica Kingsley Publishers, 2006), 43–55.
1.2 Use spiritual care assessment tools	1.2.2 Interprets spiritual care assessments.	LaRocca-Pitts, Mark. 'FACT, A Chaplain's Tool for Assessing Spiritual Needs in an Acute Care Setting', *Chaplaincy Today* 28, no. 1 (March 2012), 25–32. Meaningful Ageing. 'ConnecTo'. Meaningful Ageing Australia, 2017. http://meaningfulageing.org.au/connecto/.
1.3 Respect human diversity	1.3.2 Listens non-anxiously and non-judgementally to individual understandings of life, meaning, morality and spirituality, et cetera.	Carr, Ashley, Simon Biggs, and Helen Kimberley. 'Ageing, Diversity and the Meaning(s) of Later Life: Cultural, Social and Historical Models to Age By', *Contemporary Readings in Law and Social Justice* 7, no. 1 (1 January 2015), 7. AGDH. *Aged Care Diversity Framework*. (Canberra: Australian Government Department of Health, 2017).
1.4 Multi-and inter-cultural issues	1.4.2 Recognises and responds appropriately to expressions of dimensions of culture in individuals.	Hofstede, Geert, Gert Jan Hofstede, and Michael Minkov. *Cultures and Organizations: Software of the Mind.* (3rd edn. New York: McGraw-Hill Education, 2010). MacKinlay, Elizabeth. 'Models of Spirituality in Ageing - Multifaith and Multicultural Perspectives', in *The Spiritual Dimension of Ageing* (2nd edn. London and Philadelphia: Jessica Kingsley Publishers, 2017).
1.5 Multi-and inter-faith issues	1.5.2 Recognises and responds appropriately to expressions of faith or personal philosophy dimensions of culture in individuals.	Davie, Grace, and John Vincent. 'Religion and Old Age'. *Ageing & Society* 18, no. 1 (January 1998), 101–10. Volf, Miroslav. 'Mindsets of Respect, Regimes of Respect', in *Flourishing: Why We Need Religion in a Globalized World*, Chapter 3 (New Haven: Yale University Press, 2015).

Focus	Practising Chaplain	Examples of sources from which knowledge may be accessed
1.6 Life-stage	1.6.2 Recognises and responds appropriately to each individual in a manner that is appropriate to their life stage.	Erikson, Erik H., and Joan M. Erikson. *The Life Cycle Completed*. Extended Version (New York: W. W. Norton & Company, 1998). Erikson, Erik H., Joan M. Erikson, and Helen Q. Kivnick. *Vital Involvement in Old Age. Reissue edition* (New York London: W. W. Norton & Company, 1994).
1.7 Client circumstances and condition	1.7.2 Relates to individuals with a basic understanding of their condition or concerns arising from the circumstances in which they are being served,	Healthdirect Australia, 'Elder Abuse Concerns', text/html, My Aged Care, 4 June 2018, https://www.myagedcare.gov.au/legal-information/elder-abuse-concerns; Healthdirect Australia. 'Dementia', 1 May 2018. https://www.myagedcare.gov.au/getting-started/health-conditions/dementia. Posner, Richard A. *Aging and Old Age* (Chicago and London: University of Chicago Press, 1997).

Standard 2: Understand spiritual care – examples of sources

Focus	Practising Chaplain	Examples of Sources from which knowledge may be accessed
2.1 Engage in theological/spiritual reflection	2.1.2 Apply theological foundation of spiritual/pastoral care in context of religious tradition.	Caperon, John, Andrew Todd, and James Walters. *A Christian Theology of Chaplaincy* (London and Philadelphia: Jessica Kingsley Publishers, 2018). Geyer, Richard E., and Patricia M. Geyer. *Chaplains of the Bible: Inspiration for Those Who Help Others in Crisis* (Ambassador International, 2012).
2.2 Define and apply concept of spirituality	2.2.2 Respond to clients in accord with their understandings of spirituality.	McSherry, Wilfred, and Keith Cash. 'The Language of Spirituality: An Emerging Taxonomy', *International Journal of Nursing Studies* 41, no. 2 (1 February 2004), 151–61. Schneiders, Sandra M. 'Biblical Spirituality', *Interpretation* 70, no. 4 (1 October 2016), 417–30.
2.3 Promote spiritual well-being	2.3.2 Support the spiritual well-being of clients.	Jackson, David, Colleen Doyle, Hannah Capon, and Elizabeth Pringle. 'Spirituality, Spiritual Need, and Spiritual Care in Aged Care: What the Literature Says', *Journal of Religion, Spirituality & Aging* 28, no. 4 (October 2016), 281–95. Meaningful Ageing Australia. *National Guidelines for Spiritual Care in Aged Care.* (Melbourne: Meaningful Ageing Australia, 2016). www.meaningfulageing.org.au.
2.4 Practice appreciative action and reflection	2.4.2 Support clients through the practices of appreciative enquiry and reflection.	Börjesson, Ulrika, Elisabet Cedersund, and Staffan Bengtsson. 'Reflection in Action: Implications for Care Work', *Reflective Practice* 16, no. 2 (4 March 2015), 285–95. James, Inger, Karin Blomberg, Elisabeth Liljekvist, and Annica Kihlgren. 'Working Together for a Meaningful Daily Life for Older Persons: A Participatory and Appreciative Action and Reflection Project', *Action Research* 13, no. 4 (1 December 2015), 336–53.
2.5 Promote continuity of care	2.5.2 Encourage continuity of spiritual care in clients.	Clare, J., and A. Hofmeyer. 'Discharge Planning and Continuity of Care for Aged People: Indicators of Satisfaction and Implications for Practice', *The Australian Journal of Advanced Nursing: A Quarterly Publication of the Royal Australian Nursing Federation* 16, no. 1 (1998), 7–13. Gonnella, Joseph S., and Mary W. Herman. 'Continuity of Care', *Journal of the American Medical Association* 243, no. 4 (25 January 1980), 352–54.
2.6 Understand grief and loss	2.6.2 Identify and respond appropriately to individuals experiencing grief and loss.	McCall, Junietta B. *Grief Education for Caregivers of the Elderly.* (New York and Hove: Routledge, 2014). WorkCover NSW. *Managing Loss and Grief in the Aged-Care Industry.* (Sydney: WorkCover NSW, 2000).

Professional Practice

At the core of their practice, chaplains must contribute to the creation (and maintenance of) inclusive, welcoming, and safe care environments, in which spiritual care is properly integrated into care plans and support strategies. Furthermore, they must be skilled in effective and appropriate communication techniques.

Chaplains must regularly evaluate all aspects of their practice to ensure they maximise the efficacy of spiritual care provided to clients. They must be able to interpret basic information about the condition and profile of their clients, identify ethical boundaries, and develop strategies that enable their clients to receive the maximum benefit possible from their service.

Chaplains must also be able to operate effectively at all stages of the processes needed for the provision of care. This includes planning, development, serving clients, evaluation, and reporting.

The tables below have been developed for standards 3 and 4, and how they might be developed in an aged care context follows.

Standard 3: Provide spiritual care

Focus	Assistant Chaplain	Practising Chaplain	Accomplished Chaplain	Lead Chaplain
3.1 Pastoral visitation	3.1.1 Initiate pastoral contact.	3.1.2 Participate in pastoral conversations.	3.1.3 Direct and develop the art of the pastoral conversation.	3.1.4 Develop and maintain sense of connectedness in which pastoral conversations are welcomed and valued.
3.2 Spiritual conversations	3.2.1 Initiate spiritual conversations.	3.2.2 Conduct on-going spiritual mentoring through conversations.	3.2.3 Direct and develop the art of spiritual mentoring through the conversation.	3.2.4 Develop and maintain a welcoming and safe environment in which spiritual conversations are valued.
3.3 Ministry of presence	3.3.1 Provide non-anxious presence.	3.3.2 Provide non-intrusive immediate caring accompaniment as appropriate to clients.	3.3.3 Direct and develop the skills of presence and accompaniment.	3.3.4 Develop and maintain a culture in which non-anxious presence and accompaniment is valued.
3.4 Thanatology	3.4.1 Awareness of the event and processes of dying and their effects on families and significant others.	3.4.2 Accompany clients, families and significant others through the event and processes of death and dying.	3.4.3 Support care-givers, clients' families and significant others through the event and processes of death and dying.	3.4.4 Supervision of and support for care-givers, clients' families and significant others through the event and processes of death and dying.
3.5 Liturgy, prayer, reflection and/or ritual.	3.5.1 Conducts appropriate spiritual conversations.	3.5.2 Conducts liturgies and rituals including sacramental services as appropriate to the faith or worldview of both client and chaplain.	3.5.3 Provides spiritual mentoring related to the appreciation of liturgies, rituals and sacraments as appropriate to the faith or worldview of both client and chaplain as appropriate.	3.5.4 Supervision of practices ensuring practises of prayer, reflection, ritual and/or spiritual mentoring are appropriate to the faith or worldview of both client and chaplain.

Focus	Assistant Chaplain	Practising Chaplain	Accomplished Chaplain	Lead Chaplain
3.6 Spiritual care plan	3.6.1 Interprets spiritual care plan.	3.6.2 Makes accurate entries on spiritual care plan.	3.6.3 Develops spiritual care plans for specific individuals.	3.6.4 Ensures spiritual care plans for individuals are developed ethically and accurately.
3.7 Response to critical incidents	3.7.1 Provide prompt non-anxious reassuring presence.	3.7.2 Observe and assess well-being of individuals subject to a critical incident including victim and responders.	3.7.3 Follow up well-being of individuals subject to a critical incident including victim and responders.	3.7.4 Guides response of chaplains to individuals subject to a critical incident including victim and responders.
3.8 Supporting the disempowered	3.8.1 Identify imbalances of power.	3.8.2 Provide spiritual support as appropriate for disempowered clients as appropriate.	3.8.3 Develops prudent responses to remedy disempowerment and injustice in client circumstances.	3.8.4 Assesses risks and benefits involved in responses to remedy disempowerment and injustice in client circumstances.
3.9 Respect for traditions, worldviews, and/or affiliations	3.9.1 Awareness of basic tenets of faith traditions, worldviews and/or affiliations of clients.	3.9.2 Conducts conversations related to client tradition, worldview, or affiliation.	3.9.3 Maintains respectful and ethical multi- and inter-faith environment.	3.9.4 Ensures client traditions, worldviews and/or affiliations are responded to ethically and accurately.
3.10 Referral to appropriate faith tradition	3.10.1 Refers those whose faith and worldview is not best served by a person of the faith or worldview of the chaplain to an appropriate chaplain or pastoral care worker.	3.10.2 Develops network of chaplains and pastoral care workers of faiths and worldviews other than their own to whom referrals may be made.	3.10.3 Guides the ethical recognition of and referrals to practitioners of other faiths and worldviews.	3.10.4 Ensures appropriate and ethical referrals are made by chaplains to practitioners of other faiths and worldviews.

Standard 4: Create and maintain supportive and safe spiritual care environments

Focus	Assistant Chaplain	Practising Chaplain	Accomplished Chaplain	Lead Chaplain
4.1 Maintain appropriate personal boundaries	4.1.1 Establish professional boundaries with clients, their families, significant others and colleagues.	4.1.2 Establish non-intrusive caring boundaries with clients, families and significant others.	4.1.3 Deal ethically and effectively with violations of appropriate boundaries.	4.1.4 Ensure that a culture of respect for personal boundaries is established and maintained.
4.2 Ensure confidentiality and privacy	4.2.1 Awareness of confidentiality and privacy ethics and policies.	4.2.2 Interpret, maintain and apply confidentiality and privacy ethics and policies with clients, their families, significant others and colleagues.	4.2.3 Solve problems and deal with ethical dilemmas relating to confidentiality and privacy.	4.2.4 Ensure that a culture of respect for confidentiality and privacy is established and maintained.
4.3 Adherence to codes of conduct	4.3.1 Awareness of appropriate codes of conduct.	4.3.2 Interpret, maintain and apply ethical practices arising from codes of conduct with clients, their families, significant others and colleagues.	4.3.3 Solve problems and deal with ethical dilemmas relating to codes of conduct.	4.3.4 Ensure that a culture of respect for adherence to codes of conduct is established and maintained.
4.4 Mandatory reporting responsibilities	4.4.1 Comply with mandatory reporting ethics and policies.	4.4.2 Disclose and exercise mandatory reporting ethics and policies with clients, their families, significant others and colleagues.	4.4.3 Solve problems and deal with ethical dilemmas arising from mandatory reporting requirements.	4.4.4 Ensure that a culture of respect and diligence is established and maintained with respect to mandatory reporting responsibilities.
4.5 Ensure no proselytising or inappropriate personal views	4.5.1 Understand what proselytising is and avoid it.	4.5.2 Distinguish between proselytising, evangelism and appropriate personal disclosure.	4.5.3 Solve problems and deal with ethical dilemmas arising from the distinctions between proselytising, evangelism and appropriate personal disclosure.	4.5.4 Ensure guidelines that distinguish between proselytising, evangelism and appropriate personal disclosure are developed and maintained.

Professional Practice in Aged Care Context

Standard 3: Provide spiritual care – examples of sources

Focus	Practising Chaplain	Examples of sources from which knowledge may be accessed
3.1 Pastoral visitation	3.1.2 Participate in pastoral conversations.	Boyd, Glenn E. 'Pastoral Conversation: Relational Listening and Open-Ended Questions', *Pastoral Psychology* 51, no. 5 (1 May 2003), 345–60. Miller, Andrew J. 'The Spiral Staircase: A Narrative Approach to Pastoral Conversation', *Journal of Pastoral Care & Counseling* 70, no. 1 (1 March 2016), 26–33.
3.2 Spiritual conversations	3.2.2 Conduct on-going spiritual mentoring through conversations.	Pickering, Sue. *Listening and Spiritual Conversation: Singing God's Songs in a Noisy World.* (Canterbury Press, 2017). Schaller, Mary, and John Crilly. *The 9 Arts of Spiritual Conversations: Walking Alongside People Who Believe Differently.* (Carol Stream, Illinois: Tyndale Momentum, 2016).
3.3 Ministry of Presence	3.3.2 Provide non-intrusive immediate caring accompaniment as appropriate to clients.	Nolan, Steve. *Spiritual Care at the End of Life: The Chaplain as a 'Hopeful Presence'.* (London and Philadelphia: Jessica Kingsley Publishers, 2011). Pennel Jr., Joel E. *The Gift of Presence: A Guide to Helping Those Who Suffer.* (Nashville Tennessee: Abingdon Press, 2010).
3.4 Thanatology	3.4.2 Accompany clients, families and significant others through the event and processes of death and dying.	Grewe, Fred. *Time to Talk about Dying: How Clergy and Chaplains Can Help Senior Adults Prepare for a Good Death.* (London and Philadelphia: Jessica Kingsley Publishers, 2018). Kübler-Ross, Elisabeth. *On Death and Dying: What the Dying Have to Teach Doctors, Nurses, Clergy and Their Own Families.* (New York: Scribner, 2014).
3.5 Liturgy, prayer, reflection and/or ritual.	3.5.2 Conducts liturgies and rituals including sacramental services as appropriate to the faith or worldview of both client and chaplain as appropriate.	Mitchell, Kenneth R. 1989. 'Ritual in Pastoral Care', *Journal of Pastoral Care* 43 (1), 68–77. Mowat, Harriet, and Maureen O'Neill. 2013. *Spirituality and Ageing: Implications for the Care and Support of Older People.* Evidence Summaries to Support Social Services in Scotland 19. IRISS: Institute for Research and Innovation in Social Services
3.6 Spiritual care plan	3.6.2 Makes accurate entries on spiritual care plan.	Hilsman, Gordon J. *Spiritual Care in Common Terms: How Chaplains Can Effectively Describe the Spiritual Needs of Patients in Medical Records.* (Jessica Kingsley Publishers, 2016). Thomas, Keri, Ben Lobo, and Karen Detering (eds). *Advance Care Planning in End of Life Care.* (2nd ed. Oxford: Oxford University Press, 2017).

Focus	Practising Chaplain	Examples of sources from which knowledge may be accessed
3.7 Response to critical incidents	3.7.2 Observe and assess well-being of individuals subject to a critical incident including victim and responders.	Australian Government Department of Health. 'Guide for Reporting Reportable Assaults: Ageing and Aged Care', Accessed 4 July 2018. https://agedcare.health.gov.au/ensuring-qual-ity/aged-care-quality-and-compliance/guide-for-reporting-reportable-assaults. Janes, Nadine, Mary Fox, Mandy Lowe, Kathy McGilton, and Lori Schindel-Martin. 'Facilitating Best Practice in Aged Care: Exploring Influential Factors through Critical Incident Technique', *International Journal of Older People Nursing* 4, no. 3 (15 June 2009), 166–76.
3.8 Supporting the disempowered	3.8.2 Provide spiritual support as appropriate for disempowered clients as appropriate.	Kaplan, Daniel, and Barbara Berkman. *The Oxford Handbook of Social Work in Health and Aging.* (Oxford University Press, 2015). Schindler, Ruben. 'Empowering the Aged—A Postmodern Approach', *The International Journal of Aging and Human Development* 49, no. 3 (1 October 1999), 165–77.
3.9 Respect for traditions, worldviews, and/or affiliations	3.9.2 Conducts conversations related to client tradition, worldview, or affiliation.	Dolan, Simon L., and Kristine Marin Kawamura. *Cross Cultural Competence: A Field Guide for Developing Global Leaders and Managers.* (Emerald Group Publishing, 2015). MacKinlay, Elizabeth, ed. *Ageing and Spirituality Across Faiths and Cultures.* (London and Philadelphia: Jessica Kingsley Publishers, 2010).
3.10 Referral to appropriate faith tradition	3.10.2 Develops network of chaplains and pastoral care workers of faiths and worldviews other than their own to whom referrals may be made.	Janssen, Janine. *Weaving Social Networks: Tips for Police Officers and Other Professionals about Building and Maintaining Networks in a Multi-Ethnic Society.* (The Hague: Eleven International Publishing, 2012). Stoll, Louise, and Karen Seashore Louis. *Professional Learning Communities: Divergence, Depth and Dilemmas.* (Maidenhead: McGraw-Hill Education (UK), 2007).

Standard 4: Create and maintain supportive and safe spiritual care environments – examples of sources

Focus	Practising Chaplain	Examples of Sources from which knowledge may be accessed
4.1 Maintain appropriate personal boundaries	4.1.2 Establish non-intrusive caring boundaries with clients, families, significant others.	Cloud, Henry, and John Sims Townsend. *Boundaries: When to Say Yes, When to Say No to Take Control of Your Life*. (Grand Rapids, Michigan: Zondervan, 1992). McKie, Linda, Sarah Cunningham-Burley, and Jo Campling. *Families in Society: Boundaries and Relationships*. (Bristol: Policy Press, 2005).
4.2 Ensure confidentiality and privacy	4.2.2 Interpret, maintain and apply confidentiality and privacy ethics and policies with clients, their families, significant others and colleagues.	Bernoth, Maree, Elaine Dietsch, Oliver Kisalay Burmeister, and Michael Schwartz. 'Information Management in Aged Care: Cases of Confidentiality and Elder Abuse', *Journal of Business Ethics* 122, no. 3 (1 July 2014), 453–60. Hughes, Mark. 'Privacy in Aged Care', *Australasian Journal on Ageing* 23, no. 3 (n.d.), 110–14.
4.3 Adherence to codes of conduct	4.3.2 Interpret, maintain and apply ethical practices arising from codes of conduct with clients, their families, significant others and colleagues.	Council on Collaboration. 2004. 'Common Code of Ethics for Chaplains, Pastoral Counselors, Pastoral Educators and Student'. Association of Professional Chaplains. http://www.professionalchaplains.org/files/professional_standards/common_standards/common_code_ethics.pdf. Salvation Army. 2016. 'Chaplains Code of Conduct'. Salvation Army: Australian Southern Territory. https://www.salvationarmy.org.au/Global/State%20pages/Victoria/Crossroads/Spiritual%20Care/Chaplains%20Code%20of%20Conduct.pdf.
4.4 Mandatory reporting responsibilities	4.4.2 Disclose and exercise mandatory reporting ethics and policies with clients, their families, significant others and colleagues.	Australian Government Department of Health. 'Compulsory Reporting for Approved Providers of Residential Aged Care Services'. Other. Ageing and Aged Care, 5 July 2018. https://agedcare.health.gov.au/ensuring-quality/aged-care-quality-and-compliance/compulsory-reporting-for-approved-providers. Australian Government Department of Health. 'Guide for Aged Care Staff – Compulsory Reporting'. Other. Ageing and Aged Care, 5 July 2018. https://agedcare.health.gov.au/ensuring-quality/aged-care-quality-and-compliance/compulsory-reporting-for-approved-providers/guide-for-aged-care-staff-compulsory-reporting
4.5 Ensure no proselytising or inappropriate personal views	4.5.2 Distinguish between proselytising, evangelism and appropriate personal disclosure.	Longenecker, Dwight, 'Evangelize, Don't Proselytize – And There's a Difference', *Aleteia — Catholic Spirituality, Lifestyle, World News, and Culture*, 2013 <http://aleteia.org/2013/10/03/evangelize-dont-proselytize-and-theres-a-difference/> [accessed 5 July 2018] Thiessen, Elmer J., *The Ethics of Evangelism* (Milton Keynes: Authentic Media Inc, 2014).

Professional Engagement

A chaplain engages those served first by being a non-anxious, approachable and caring presence. Alert to their own spiritual needs and capabilities, they must consistently and mindfully analyse, evaluate and expand their professional learning both collegially and individually. In particular, chaplains must demonstrate respect and professionalism in all their interactions with clients, colleagues, managers, and the community. Chaplains must also value engagement with the diverse communities within and beyond which they serve.

The tables below have been developed for standards 5 and 6, and how they might be developed in an aged care context follows.

Standard 5: Engage in professional development

Focus	Assistant Chaplain	Practising Chaplain	Accomplished Chaplain	Lead Chaplain
5.1 Provide feedback and report on practice	5.1.1 Comply with reporting requirements and responsibilities.	5.1.2 Construct descriptive oral and written reports that reflect on practice.	5.1.3 Construct evaluative oral and written reflective reports on practice.	5.1.4 Evaluate and respond to oral and reflective reports by practitioners.
5.2 Receive feedback and report on practice	5.2.1 Participate in formal external appraisal of practice.	5.2.2 Participate in self- and external appraisal of practice.	5.2.3 Conduct and report on appraisal of other practitioners.	5.2.4 Evaluate and respond to appraisal of other practitioners.
5.3 Pastoral supervision	5.3.1 Participate willingly in supervision of practice at the level of Assistant Chaplain.	5.3.2 Participate willingly in supervision of practice at the level of Practising Chaplain.	5.3.3 Participate willingly in supervision of practice at the level of Accomplished Chaplain.	5.3.4 Supervise practice of other chaplains.
5.4 Self-care	5.4.1 Practise self-care.	5.4.2 Develop and implement self-care plan.	5.4.3 Evaluate self-care needs and risks of self and other practitioners.	5.4.4 Ensure that self-care needs and risks of practitioners are diligently addressed in their work environment.

Standard 6: Engage professionally with colleagues, relatives, carers and the community

Focus	Assistant Chaplain	Practising Chaplain	Accomplished Chaplain	Lead Chaplain
6.1 Work in multi-disciplinary teams	6.1.1 Aware of the nature and mission of other professionals and workers.	6.1.2 Participates in inter- and multi-disciplinary consultations and conferences with individuals and groups.	6.1.3 Initiates inter- and multi-disciplinary consultations and conferences with individuals and groups.	6.1.4 Establishes and oversees a culture of collegiality and collaboration in the services in which chaplaincy is offered.
6.2 Conduct referrals	6.2.1 Identify issues in clients for whom referral to a practitioner in another discipline of practice may be warranted.	6.2.2 Provide referrals to a practitioner in another discipline of practice might when a client issue warrants it.	6.2.3 Reviews and reports on referrals made to other disciplines.	6.2.4 Establishes and oversees processes and procedures by which referrals are made to practitioners of other disciplines.
6.3 Receive referrals	6.3.1 Respond to referrals from practitioners of other disciplines or other sources under guidance of practising, accomplished or lead chaplain.	6.3.2 Respond autonomously to referrals from practitioners of other disciplines or other sources.	6.3.3 Review and report on responses to referrals received from other disciplines or other sources.	6.3.4 Establishes and oversees processes and procedures by which referrals are received from other disciplines or other sources.
6.4 Collaborate with other practitioners	6.4.1 Participate in learning, collaborative and coordination processes, and events with colleagues from other disciplines.	6.4.2 Contributes to learning, collaborative and coordination processes, and events with colleagues from other disciplines.	6.4.3 Initiates learning, collaborative and coordination processes and events with colleagues from other disciplines.	6.4.4 Establishes and oversees processes and procedures by which learning, collaborative and coordination processes, and events take place with colleagues from other disciplines.
6.5 Organisational reporting requirements	6.5.1 Contributes to reports as requested.	6.5.2 Provides regular and complete reports in accordance with organisational requirements.	6.5.3 Reviews and responds to reports submitted by other chaplains in accordance with organisational requirements.	6.5.4 Establishes and oversees processes and procedures by which reports are completed, received and responded to.

Focus	Assistant Chaplain	Practising Chaplain	Accomplished Chaplain	Lead Chaplain
6.6 Organisational policies and guidelines	6.6.1 Comply with relevant organisational policies and guidelines as required.	6.6.2 Interprets and comply with organisational policies and guidelines.	6.6.3 Provides evaluative feedback on organisational policies and guidelines.	6.6.4 Ensures that organisational policies and guidelines support the delivery of quality chaplaincy and pastoral care services.
6.7 Integrate spiritual care into allied disciplines and services.	6.7.1 Cooperates with practitioners of other disciplines under guidance.	6.7.2 Initiates collaborative contribution of spiritual care into the delivery of allied disciplines and services.	6.7.3 Advocates and guides the incorporation of spiritual care practices into the practice of allied disciplines and services.	6.7.4 Provides advocacy for a holistic and integrated approach to spiritual care.

Professional Engagement in Aged Care Context

Standard 5: Engage in professional development – examples of sources

Focus	Practising Chaplain	Examples of Sources from which knowledge may be accessed
5.1 Provide feedback and report on practice	5.1.2 Construct descriptive oral and written reports that reflect on practice.	Fitchett, George, Kelsey White, and Kathryn Lyndes. *Evidence-Based Healthcare Chaplaincy: A Research Reader.* (London and Philadelphia: Jessica Kingsley Publishers, 2018). Spiritual Health Victoria. 'Guidelines for Writing in Patient Notes: A Resource for Chaplaincy and Pastoral Care'. Spiritual Health Victoria.
5.2 Receive feedback and report on practice	5.2.2 Participate in self- and external appraisal of practice.	Cooperrider, David, Diana D. Whitney, and Jacqueline M. Stavro. *The Appreciative Inquiry Handbook: For Leaders of Change.* (San Francisco: Berrett-Koehler Publishers, 2008). ACTPS. 'The Art of Feedback: Giving, Seeking and Receiving Feedback'. ACT Government. Accessed 7 June 2018. https://www.cmtedd.act.gov.au/__data/assets/pdf_file/0003/463728/art_feedback.pdf. Samuels, Neil. 'An Appreciative Performance Appraisal Conversation'. David L. Cooperrider Center for Appreciative Inquiry at Champlain College and Case Western Reserve University's Weatherhead School of Management. https://appreciativeinquiry.champlain.edu/educational-material/an-appreciative-performance-appraisal-conversation/.
5.3 Pastoral supervision	5.3.2 Participate willingly in supervision of practice at the level of practising chaplain.	DeLong, William R. *Courageous Conversations: The Teaching and Learning of Pastoral Supervision.* (Lanham, Maryland: University Press of America, 2009). Steere, Dr David A. *The Supervision of Pastoral Care.* (Eugene, Oregon: Wipf and Stock Publishers, 2002).
5.4 Self-care	5.4.2 Develop and implement self-care plan	Figley, Charles R. *Compassion Fatigue: Coping with Secondary Traumatic Stress Disorder In Those Who Treat The Traumatized.* (London: Routledge, 2013). Ziguras, Christopher. *Self-Care: Embodiment, Personal Autonomy and the Shaping of Health Consciousness.* (London: Routledge, 2004).

Standard 6: Engage professionally with colleagues, relatives, carers and the community – examples of sources

Focus	Practising Chaplain	
6.1 Work in multi-disciplinary teams	6.1.2 Participates in inter- and multidisciplinary consultations and conferences with individuals and groups.	Beers, Robin L. *Organizational Learning in Multidisciplinary Teams: Knowledge Brokering Across Communities of Practice*. (San Franciso: Alliant International University, California School of Organizational Studies, 2003). Housley, William. *Interaction in Multidisciplinary Teams*. (Abingdon: Routledge, 2018).
6.2 Conduct referrals	6.2.2 Provide referrals to a practitioner in another discipline of practice might when a client issue warrants it.	Lee, Ronald R. 'Referral as an Act of Pastoral Care', *Journal of Pastoral Care* 30, no. 3 (1 September 1976), 186–97. Leeuwen, René Van, and Bart Cusveller. 'Nursing Competencies for Spiritual Care', *Journal of Advanced Nursing* 48, no. 3 (2004), 234–46.
6.3 Receive referrals	6.3.2 Respond autonomously to referrals from practitioners of other disciplines or other sources.	Moran, Michael, Kevin J. Flannelly, Andrew J. Weaver, Jon A. Overvold, Winifred Hess, and Jo Clare Wilson. 'A Study of Pastoral Care, Referral, and Consultation Practices Among Clergy in Four Settings in the New York City Area', *Pastoral Psychology* 53, no. 3 (1 January 2005), 255–66.
6.4 Collaborate with other practitioners	6.4.2 Contributes to learning, collaborative and coordination processes and events with colleagues from other disciplines.	Mellon, Brad F. 'Faith-to-Faith at the Bedside: Theological and Ethical Issues in Ecumenical Clinical Chaplaincy', *Christian Bioethics* 9, no. 1 (April 2003), 57–67. Moran, Michael, Kevin J. Flannelly, Andrew J. Weaver, Jon A. Overvold, Winifred Hess, and Jo Clare Wilson. 'A Study of Pastoral Care, Referral, and Consultation Practices Among Clergy in Four Settings in the New York City Area', *Pastoral Psychology* 53, no. 3 (1 January 2005), 255–66.
6.5 Organisational reporting requirements	6.5.2 Provides regular and complete reports in accord with organisational requirements.	Donatelle, E. P. 'Administrative Communication by Written Correspondence', in *Written Communication in Family Medicine*, 81–122. Springer, New York, NY, 1984. 'Maintaining Documentation in an Aged Care Environment - It Doesn't Need to Be Hard'. *Frontline Care Solutions*, 5 June 2017. https://www.frontlinecaresolutions.com/maintaining-documentation-aged-care-environment/.
6.6 Organisational policies and guidelines	6.6.2 Interprets and complies with organisational policies and guidelines.	Croft, Helen. 'Responding to the Aged-Care Operational Environment', in *The Experienced Carer: Frontline Leaders in Australia's Aged Care Workplaces*, (Frenchs Forest: Pearson Higher Education AU, 2012), 253–300. 'Workplace Policies and Procedures'. Guidelines. NSW Government Industrial Relations, 29 August 2011. http://www.industrialrelations.nsw.gov.au/oirwww/Employment_info/Managing_employees/Workplace_policies_and_procedures.page.

6.7 Integrate spiritual care into allied disciplines and services.	6.7.2 Initiates collaborative contribution of spiritual care into the delivery of allied disciplines and services.	Edwards, A., N. Pang, V. Shiu, and C. Chan. 'The Understanding of Spirituality and the Potential Role of Spiritual Care in End-of-Life and Palliative Care: A Meta-Study of Qualitative Research', *Palliative Medicine* 24, no. 8 (December 2010), 753–70.
		Holmes, Cheryl. 'Stakeholder Views on the Role of Spiritual Care in Australian Hospitals: An Exploratory Study', *Health Policy* 122, no. 4 (1 April 2018), 389–95.

Conclusion

The methodology of *The Australian Professional Standards for Teachers* provides a sound means by which standards for professional chaplains might be specified, contextualised and applied to the various settings in which chaplaincies are found. As illustrated with respect to *Practising Chaplains* in aged care, a most helpful aspect of this methodology is its provision of a framework that enables the search, identification and curation of training and development resources across the intersections encountered by the profession. This also enables the evaluation of resources available for each area, the identification of gaps, and the setting of research agendas.

Bibliography

BCC. 'Common Qualifications and Competencies for Professional Chaplains'. Board of Chaplaincy Certification, 2017. www.professionalchaplains.org

'Capabilities Framework for Pastoral Care and Chaplaincy'. Spiritual Health Victoria, 2011. www.spiritualhealthvictoria.org.au/LiteratureRetrieve.aspx?ID=198497.

Carey, L. B., Swinton, S. and Grosshoeme D. H. 'Chaplaincy and Spiritual Care', in Lindsay B. Carey and Bernice A. Mathisen (eds.), *Spiritual Care for Allied Health Practice: A Person- Centered Approach*, (Philadelphia: Jessica Kingsley Publishers, 2018).

CCAC. Education, Qualification and Registration—Civil Chaplaincies Advisory Committee', 14 March 2018. https://sites.google.com/a/ccacnsw.org.au/public/endorsement/registration-of-hs- chaplains-and-pastoral-care-workers.

Garland, A. 'AQF Levels', 6 February 2015. https://www.aqf.edu.au/aqf-levels. MacKinlay, E. *The Spiritual Dimension of Ageing* (1st edn; London and Philadelphia: Jessica Kingsley Publishers, 2001).

McSherry, W. and Smith, J. 'Spiritual Care', in Wilfred McSherry, Robert McSherry, and Roger Watson, (eds.) *Care in Nursing: Principles, Values and Skills*, (Oxford; New York: Oxford University Press, 2012), 117–34.

Meaningful Ageing. 'National Guidelines for Spiritual Care in Aged Care'. Meaningful Ageing Australia, 2016. http://meaningfulageing.org.au/downloads/ms_7526.pdf.

Mowat, H. and Swinton, J. *What Do Chaplains Do? The Role of the Chaplain in Meeting the Spiritual Needs of Patients* (Aberdeen: University of Aberdeen Centre for Spirituality, Health and Disability, February 2007).

NESA. Australian Professional Standards for Teachers. (Sydney: NSW Education Standards Authority, 2012).

Orton, M. J. 'Transforming Chaplaincy: The Emergence of a Healthcare Pastoral Care for a Post-Modern World', *Journal of Health Care Chaplaincy* 15, no. 2 (2008), 114–31.

Puchalski, C. M., Vitillo, R. Hull, S. K. and Reller, N. 'Improving the Spiritual Dimension of Whole Person Care: Reaching National and International Consensus', *Journal of Palliative Medicine* 17, no. 6 (2014): 642–56.

SCA. 'Spiritual Care Australia Standards of Practice'. Spiritual Care Australia, 2014. https://www.spiritualcareaustralia.org.au/SCA/Documents/SCA_Standards_of_Practice_Document.pdf.

Timmins, F. et al. 'The Role of the Healthcare Chaplain: A Literature Review', *Journal of Health Care Chaplaincy* 24, no. 3 (2018), 87–106.

CHAPTER 3

In providing aged care with compassion and respect, what role can spirituality play?

Carol Flanagan and Jack Flanagan

Abstract

How do we ensure that older Australians can live life to the full? Too many people are afraid of old age or dementia, or nursing homes, yet we will all be carers or cared for one day. It is important to treat our ageing population with respect and compassionate, insightful care. Relatives, friends, nurses, even strangers can provide sensitive care. Decisions about where an ageing person should live, what care they should receive and how to arrange and finance access to the most compassionate and appropriate care are critical elements for bringing hope to the lives of those older Australians in our care.

Introduction

On average, the majority of us are living much longer than a century ago. The illnesses and diseases that killed many people in the not so distant past can now be cured, but they often leave many with one or more chronic conditions requiring ongoing care. In the past, that care would have been provided by family members, but with increasingly fragmented families, with children and relatives often living elsewhere or unable to cope with the care required, more elderly people find themselves having to live in aged care homes.

A major issue for older people moving into an aged care home is that, whatever the quality of the home, the meals and the staff, it is not the same as living in their own home. All aged care providers emphasise the quality of the service they offer, but even the best aged care services can be delivered without much compassion or respect and, furthermore, little or no spirituality. Yet, these are key values that can make a significant difference to the quality of life experienced by residents in aged care facilities.

Who Will Need Care?

The care needs of older Australians vary. Care needs depend on people's functional capacities, physical and mental health, culture and language, and the environment in which they live. Many live with declining health and older Australians need access to care services that address their current and ongoing needs to maintain or restore a relatively healthy lifestyle.

Aged care is now one of the largest industries in Australia servicing the needs of over 1.3 million people. The Commonwealth Government funds approximately 70 per cent of the costs associated with residential aged care, with residential care fees making up the remainder. In 2016–2017, Commonwealth funding of home support was $2.4 billion, home care $1.6 billion and residential aged care $11.9 billion. Consumer expenditure on aged care was $4.8 billion (excluding accommodation deposits).[1] These are significant figures and growing at approximately 8 per cent each year.

The age composition of Australia's population is projected to change dramatically over the next half-century. In 2017, 3.8 million people aged 65 years and over comprised 15 per cent of Australia's population and it is estimated the proportion of the population over 65 years will

---

1   Aged Care Financing Authority, *Sixth Report on the Funding and Financing of the Aged Care Sector*, xv.

grow steadily. In 2015, 473,000 people (or 2 per cent of the population) was 85 years or older and this number is expected to grow rapidly.[2]

The ageing of Australia's population is the result of smaller families with fewer children, combined with an increase in average life expectancy. However, with more people living longer, the prevalence of dementia is expected to rise from an estimated 459,000 Australians living with dementia in 2020 to around 1,076,000 by 2058 if there is no medical breakthrough.[3] These projections will place considerable financial pressure on the Commonwealth budget, which any government would look to reduce.

According to the Productivity Commission, in 2008, given that people are living longer, the lifetime risk of requiring some aged care for those over 65 years of age, was 68 per cent for females and 48 per cent for males.[4] The discrepancy between these figures was accounted for because, on average, women live longer than men and, once alone, need more care. In 2014, the likelihood of entering an aged care facility for those over 65 was 55 per cent for females and 38 per cent for males.[5] These percentages have grown significantly since 2000.

Health Issues as We Get Older

Aged care facilities often promote the quality of the food they serve, boasting of sophisticated, varied or rotating menus, wide choice, and regular variations or special celebrations. However, so many factors affect what happens next. Many older people have fixed views on what sort of foods they are willing to eat. Their cultural background, the way food was served in their family, their perceptions of what is appropriate to eat at particular times of the day, and their own mobility or other physical limitations can all dramatically affect what a person ultimately eats and, consequently, many end up malnourished.

---

2   Australian Institute of Health and Welfare [AIHW], *Older Australia at a Glance*, 5. Australian Bureau of Statistics [ABS], *Australian Demographic Statistics*.
3   Dementia Australia, *Dementia Statistics*, 1.
4   Productivity Commission, 'Caring for Older Australians', xxxv.
5   Royal Commission into Aged Care Quality and Safety, *Background Paper 2, Medium and Long-Term Pressures on The System*, 16.

As we age, it becomes increasingly common for a number of symptoms consistent with chronic conditions to be present. A growing number of drugs may be prescribed for an aged care resident and all will inevitably be accompanied by risks and side effects. Not all drugs combine effectively and, in combination, some may be harmful.

At present, approximately 53 per cent of nursing-home residents have some form of dementia.[6] There is a conventional view that people with dementia have lost their entire self, but recent research indicates many parts of the brain of a person living with dementia light up when exposed to music, the ability to express themselves, and in the presence of domestic animals such as dogs, cats and chickens. As Oliver Sacks put it:

> In particular, the response to music is preserved, even when dementia is very advanced [...] musical perception, musical sensibility, musical emotion and musical memory can survive long after other forms of memory have disappeared. Music of the right kind can serve to orient and anchor a patient when almost nothing else can.[7]

Older people are frailer. Their sense of balance and muscle strength both deteriorate with age. Poor vision, osteoporosis and physical obstacles all contribute to an escalating risk of falling. When an older person falls and fractures a hip, it is a major and potentially catastrophic event. Many will suffer infections and other complications of surgery as a result. Many will not walk again and 30 per cent will die within a year. Quite literally, it is often the beginning of the end.[8]

Only in recent years has it been understood that, where a person has even mild memory loss before surgery, a general anaesthetic may trigger or worsen dementia. Post-operative cognitive decline can occur in anyone, and while many people experience confusion after waking from operations, approximately one in five patients over 65 still suffer mentally three months later.

---

6   AIHW, *Dementia Among Aged Care Residents*, vi.
7   Sacks, *Musicophilia – Tales of Music and the Brain*, 336.
8   Brennan-Olsen, 'Why Hip Fractures in the Elderly are Often a Death Sentence', 1.

The aged are no less likely than any other population of people to suffer from mental illness. It has been estimated that, in the USA, psychotropic medications (i.e., medications that affect the mind, such as tranquilisers, sedatives, and antidepressants) are prescribed for 35 per cent of the population over 65 and that the rate is even higher in the case of nursing-home residents. The Royal Commission into Aged Care heard that up to 80 per cent of dementia patients were taking some form of psychotropic drug but these drugs were only useful in 10 per cent of cases. Furthermore, such drugs put seniors at greater risk of death, stroke, disability and pneumonia.[9]

Confronting the Challenges

Many people are reluctant to face not only their own mortality, but that of parents and other loved ones. When a parent is severely ill, there may be a desire to ask doctors to do everything to keep the person alive, even where the quality of their life may be severely impaired.

Families today are shrinking (with one or, at most, two children) with no relatives living close by. Siblings and children may be unavailable to help an older parent or family member in need of care.

Older people with care needs have trouble identifying reliable advice, especially when it comes to a possible move to an aged care facility. At the same time, they may need to look at the need to sell the family home or borrow funds to meet the refundable accommodation deposit (RAD) or the alternative daily accommodation payment (DAP) before weighing up the impact of their decision on ongoing pension payments.

---

9   Martin, 'Nursing Homes Turning Residents into 'Zombies'', 1.

Loneliness

Too many elderly people are suffering from loneliness. They can be in a nursing home, yet still be extremely lonely. As Mother Teresa described:

> In the West, there is loneliness, which I call the leprosy of the West. In many ways, it is worse than our poor in Calcutta. The poverty of being unwanted, unloved and uncared for is the greatest poverty. We must start in our own homes to remedy this kind of poverty. There is a terrible hunger for love. We all experience that in our lives—the pain, the loneliness. We must have the courage to recognize it. These poor you may have right in your own family. Find them. Love them.[10]

In a speech to the National Press Club, the Minister for Ageing, Ken Wyatt, stated that up to 40 per cent of aged care residents received no visitors at all.[11]

Many people living in aged care facilities once said they would never do so, and many of them have families who promised never to allow them to be moved into one. Such statements are often made on the basis of emotion and fear, but they can cause a lot of pain. Times and circumstances change and sometimes there is no other reasonable choice but to find the best possible facility. Moving to an aged care facility is not necessarily bad. As psychogeriatrician Neil Jeyasingam explained:

> I see previous patients who have discovered entirely new levels of functioning (in a nursing home). There are patients with severe dementia whose families struggled for years to accommodate them at home—in the last few times I see them, they are usually smiling.[12]

---

10 See Palladino, 'Mother Teresa Saw Loneliness as Leprosy of the West'.
11 Owen, '40 Per Cent of People in Aged-Care Facilities Have No Visitors', 1.
12 Jeyasingam, 'Nursing Homes can be the Best Place to Grow Old', 1.

> **Figure 1: Aged Care Provider Advertising**
>
> Our Bupa Model of Care is an industry-leading service model. It provides you with greater and more immediate access to medical services and increased choice in how and where you receive care, creating better health and well-being outcomes [...] You can receive medications in your room at a time that suits your needs. (BUPA)
>
> At Opal Aged Care, our residents and families are at the centre of every decision we make [...] With over 70 homes across Australia, we provide exceptional care to more than 6,000 residents. (Opal)
>
> At Uniting, we take pride in offering warm and welcoming residential care options that are tailored to your wants, not just your care needs. It's our job to help you to live the most active and fulfilled life possible. (Uniting Care)
>
> Our highly skilled residential care services staff are dedicated to enhancing your quality of life. (Catholic Healthcare)

Spirituality

All aged care facilities through their advertising indicate a caring approach to residents (see Figure 1). In their advertising, the two not-for-profit providers quoted in Figure 1 focus on residents leading a better quality of life than may have been possible outside their care facilities, yet there is no direct focus on the spiritual aspect of life in their promotional material (although not-for-profit providers created from a Christian tradition tend to do this in practice through the provision of pastoral care).

From a religious perspective, spirituality firmly focuses on the divine and transcendental. In recent years, medicine and nursing research has focused on the spiritual aspects of a patient's life, taking the transcendental aspect of spirituality as a starting point and applying it to all people irrespective of whether they have a religious affiliation. In the nursing literature, one well-accepted definition of spirituality states it has several component parts: 1) the power within a person that gives meaning and purpose, as well as fulfillment to life, suffering and death; 2) a person's will to live; and 3) a person's belief and faith in self, others and God.[13]

Renetzky believed that belief in God most affected a person's spiritual well-being. This is not surprising considering nursing emerged from religious orders and Florence Nightingale asserted that the living body was the temple of God's spirit.[14] Nursing research on spiritual care is still developing, and assessing it is difficult due to definitional issues, small sample sizes and somewhat rudimentary research tools. However, nursing education in the United Kingdom requires that nurses assess and implement care that meets the spiritual needs of the patient and their family and friends.[15]

The World Health Organisation indicated this change in perspective for patients and medical practitioners when it reported the following:

> Until recently, the health professions have largely followed a medical model, which seeks to treat patients by focusing on medicines and surgery, and gives less importance to beliefs and to faith. This reductionism or mechanistic view of patients as being only a material body is no longer satisfactory. Patients and physicians have begun to realise the value of elements such as faith, hope and compassion in the healing process. The value of such 'spiritual' elements in health and quality of life has led to research in this field in an attempt to move towards a more holistic view of health that includes a non-material dimension, emphasising the seamless connections between mind and body.[16]

There is still some confusion between religion and spirituality, with the two often seen as synonymous. However, there appears to be an understanding that spirituality encompasses more than simply religious affiliation, as the following quotes indicate:

---

13   Renetzky, 'The Fourth Dimension', 215.
14   Ross, 'The Spiritual Dimension', 461.
15   Ross, 'The Spiritual Dimension', 461.
16   World Health Organisation, 'Social Change and Mental Health Cluster', 7.

> In every human being there seems to be a spiritual dimension, a quality that goes beyond religious affiliation, that strives for inspiration, reverence, awe, meaning and purpose, even in those who do not believe in God. The spiritual dimension tries to be in harmony with the universe, strives for answers about the infinite, and comes into focus when the person faces emotional stress, physical (and mental) illness, loss, or death.[17]
>
> Spirituality is part of health, not peripheral but core and central to it. It pervades our every thought and action, each caring moment. Spirituality and health are bonded to each other, inseparable companions in the dance of joy and sadness, health and illness, birth and death.[18]

A publication in the USA that analysed 1,200 studies on religion, spirituality and health found substantial evidence to support the notion that spiritual and religious beliefs can be used to cope with illness and result in positive outcomes.[19] The studies indicated a positive relationship between better health and religion (or spirituality) and issues such as heart disease, hypertension, cerebrovascular disease, immunological dysfunction, cancer, mortality, pain and disability.[20]

In a 2010 survey of 4,000 United Kingdom nurses, 83 per cent identified that meeting patients' spiritual needs was extremely important and improved overall quality of nursing care. However, only five percent of respondents felt they achieved this goal.[21]

The embracing of spirituality in medicine and nursing should be of great interest to carers in aged care facilities. Many residents may be suffering from psychiatric issues such as psychoses, depression, anxiety, suicidal thoughts, and personality problems. From the nursing literature we know spiritual care can aid prevention of illnesses, speed recovery from illnesses, and help foster equanimity in the face of ill

---

17 Murray and Zenter, *Nursing Concepts for Health Promotion*, 259, cited in Culliford, 'Spirituality and Clinical Care', 1435.
18 Wright, *Reflections on Spirituality and Health*, 15.
19 Koenig, McCullough and Larson, *Handbook of Religion and Health*, 32-44.
20 Reviewed in Williams and Sternthal, 'Spirituality, Religion and Health', 47.
21 McSherry, 'RCN Spirituality Survey 2010', 21-22.

health.[22] Additionally, in a review of 850 studies, religious beliefs were shown to be a positive influence on mental health outcomes such as suicidal behaviour, substance misuse and well-being.[23]

In the area of nursing, where there appears to be a lack of clear definitions around spirituality and practical guidance for dealing with it, nurses are often uncertain about how spiritual needs can and should be addressed. Sartori suggests what is needed in the training of nurses (which includes aged care nurses and employed care givers), is the following:

- Respect for privacy, dignity and religious and cultural beliefs;
- taking time to give patients support and reassurance, especially during times of need;
- showing kindness, concern and cheerfulness when giving care; and
- allowing patients to discuss anxieties or fears.[24]

These are aspects of carer training that could be readily implemented in all aged care facilities rather than simply those faith-based aged care services and hospitals that offer pastoral care. Faith-based services draw on the Gospels and the mission and ministry of Jesus for their pastoral care approach to spirituality to connect with residents, witness their struggles, be their companions and offer support throughout their declining years. Pastoral carers attempt to transcend cultures, beliefs and other spiritual practices. The philosophy adopted is that each person is important and that understanding their stories and spirituality is important to the restoration of their well-being.[25] Accordingly, good spiritual care is the responsibility of all staff in an aged care service.

---

22 Koenig, McCullough and Larson, *Handbook of Religion and Health*, cited in Culliford, 'Spirituality and Clinical Care', 1434.
23 Moreira-Almeida, Neto and Koenig, 'Religiousness and Mental Health', 242-50, cited in Sartori, 'Spirituality 1', 14-17.
24 Sartori, 'Spirituality 1', 14.
25 Confoy, *Welcome, Inclusion, Attentive Presence*, 5-30.

Why Focus on Spirituality?

In their document *Spiritual Care Matters* the Scottish Inter-Faith Council stated that human creativity, relationships, hopes, fears, guilt, happiness, religion, beliefs, life, death and spirituality encompass all of life.[26]

Carers require greater understanding of the nature and importance of our shared humanity and to help staff, residents, relatives and other carers to behave kindlier when dealing with each other, all in the belief that people who are valued experience improved health and well-being.

There is, however, strong evidence that when the human elements of compassion, hope, understanding and the relationship between carer and those cared for are ignored, carers in aged care services ignore a crucial element in the wellness process. Several aged care scandals were publicised in 2017, where ongoing abuse of some residents at Oakden, a South Australian state-run nursing home, and poor resident care at Opal Aged Care in Victoria was noted. ABC television broadcast further complaints on its *Four Corners* program in 2018.

A major problem for aged care providers is the need to reduce costs—the major one being staffing—as government money per resident has fallen in recent years. The analysis of the operating performance of 974 aged care facilities for the year to the 30th of June, 2018, by accounting firm StewartBrown revealed a continuing decline in their overall profitability. In 2018, more than 45 per cent of aged care facilities reported an operating loss (up from 34 per cent in 2017) and, even more alarming, over 21 per cent reported an effective cash loss.[27]

Declining revenues for home-care operators have led to a reduction in staff hours provided as well as a reduction in profits by around 30 per cent. The financial performance of aged care providers in 2018 indicates the current funding model is not sustainable, with forecasts of an increasing number of facilities being in jeopardy in the near future unless the Government provides additional funding.[28]

---

26 Scottish Inter-Faith Council, *Spiritual Care Matters*, 12.
27 StewartBrown, 'Aged Care Financial Performance Survey', 4.
28 StewartBrown, 'Aged Care Financial Performance Survey', 4.

There has also been a decline in the average level of qualifications of staff in nursing homes over the past 15 years. The majority of care staff are classified as personal care assistants (PCAs), who hold minimum qualifications and who work in conjunction with a decreasing number of qualified nurses.

Nursing home staff are increasingly required to deal with the multiple ailments of ageing and, ultimately, death. More than 80 per cent of residents require high care and nearly one-third of these individuals die each year. These people need expensive clinical care, yet the Commonwealth Government has been reducing the amount of funding per resident and only spending more in total as demand increases.

Until 2017, there were good profits to be made in aged care for the larger operators. Alarmed at the increases in government expenditure on aged care, the Commonwealth Government in 2017 announced cuts of $1.2 billion over four years to the Aged Care Funding Instrument (ACFI) subsidy used to fund providers for individual aged care places. In recent years, the ACFI subsidy has been frozen and the recalibration of ACFI scoring has seen reductions in subsidies to new entrants to aged care facilities. Allied to this reduction in real funding subsidies are rising staff salaries and electricity costs, leading to aged care provider profit margins being squeezed. The ongoing reports of poor care for too many residents have raised concerns the industry is putting profit before people.[29]

What can be observed from over the last decade is a creeping form of industrial aged care where a few operators run larger, more efficient aged care homes, with 90 or more residents in each rather than the historical 20 to 30 residents. To run these efficiently and to achieve an acceptable return for the providers, every operating aspect is managed from the acquisition of materials, laundry, food acquisition and preparation, drug acquisition and dissemination and minimum requirements for staffing (i.e., in effect, the commodification of residents and staff).

Whilst such an operating model can efficiently keep costs from escalating, there are bound to be problems when it fails to work properly—which will always be the case when the major resource to be

---

29 Lane, 'Six Big Players Dominate Australia's Scandal-hit Aged Care Sector', 1.

managed efficiently is human labour. The Federal Government's solution has been twofold in 2019: first, to establish an Aged Care Quality and Safety Commission and, second, a Royal Commission into Aged Care.

The Royal Commission's main task has been to examine evidence of substandard aged care, abuse and systematic failures, and to draw up recommendations for improvement. The controversial practice of physical and chemical restraints in aged care homes has also be examined, with some alarming disclosures of systematic abuse of residents.

Increasingly, it would appear many nursing-home residents have limited to no access to relatives or friends who can care for them and, therefore, end up selling the family home to move to a nursing home, which, on the surface, may appear to be a haven for older people. Additionally, with the high cost involved in making this move, there may be an assumption that the care provided by the aged care facility must be good. However, the scandals revealed by the Royal Commission indicate that only those residents with someone to advocate on their behalf receive the care they need. As Maree Duffy-Moon explains:

> We would not leave our children alone in a place foreign to them, with untrained and seemingly uncaring staff to supervise them, yet we do this to the many people who have nurtured us, made massive contributions to the country we live in.[30]

We suspect that conditions in nursing homes appear so bad to relatives because they have never previously encountered a situation where the majority of residents around their loved family member have dementia and require a high level of care. We believe turning this situation around is not a mammoth task; rather, it requires a change in the mindsets of operators and staff regarding what constitutes residents' major needs. As well as being cared for with good food and excellent physical care, residents also need to be valued for who they are, irrespective of the level of dementia or other chronic ailments from which they may be suffering.

30 Duffy-Moon, 'Out of Sight Out of Mind', 1.

An alternative to the industrial model will be necessary to ensure nursing homes meet their residents' and carers' needs. It requires nursing-home providers to integrate the needs of the human spirit into the care they offer. Such a model would generate significant gains in the effectiveness of care and towards the satisfaction of all parties, especially for the residents and those close to them, and would also be cost-effective for the providers.

The Scottish Inter Faith Council report suggests there are four reasons for focusing on spiritualty in the care of nursing-home residents. First, there is an ethical consideration: it is the right thing to do, to treat people with compassion irrespective of their faith, belief, gender, age, ability/disability, sexual orientation or life stance. Prospective residents will be attracted to those nursing homes that can demonstrate they treat all residents with compassion and will be put off by those who cannot demonstrate such compassion.

Second, there is a legal consideration, because there is a regulatory framework and the new Aged Care Quality and Safety Commission will be alert to charges of discrimination and will promote the equal and fair treatment of all from any culture or background.

Third, there is a financial consideration. Specifically, if residents experience greater satisfaction and better outcomes, such as a reduction in the use of psychotropic drugs, and there is less stress and absenteeism among staff, then costs will go down.

Finally, there is a clinical consideration. Specifically, there is increasing evidence that when people are well cared for, their health improves because their immune system appears to work more efficiently.[31]

Why is Spirituality Important in Nursing Homes?

All people have spiritual needs and in many not-for-profit aged care providers, a pastoral care team helps residents and their relatives deal with both spiritual and religious needs. Spirituality relates to the major questions in life. These include questions such as why is this happening

---

31 Scottish Inter Faith Council, 2008.

to me? How do I make sense of it? How do I feel about changes in my life? What do I believe is important in my life? What gives me comfort and hope? What do I trust? Who do I trust? And who loves me and is loved by me, no matter what?[32]

To identify and deal with spiritual needs, nursing-home staff (not only the pastoral care workers, where they exist) need to take a genuine interest in each resident as a person. They need to demonstrate concern and kindness towards residents, have empathy with them, and take the time to listen to them and respect their point of view. However, this may be difficult in the short-term. As one witness at the Aged Care Royal Commission stated:

> Aged care facilities should be staffed with compassionate caring staff, they shouldn't be staffed with people who have been forced to do an aged care course by Centrelink because they can't find work somewhere else.[33]

Aged care providers can give their staff access to a broad range of spiritual resources such as the traditional religious rituals and symbolic practices, space for prayer and meditation, availability of relevant holy writings and access to supportive communities from a local church, mosque or synagogue. However, spiritual resources can include, for example, activities such as deep reflection, yoga, tai chi, cooking, gardening, engaging with nature, reading, poetry, engaging in art classes and other group activities and sports, as well as going on pilgrimages and retreats.

The benefits that accrue when spiritual needs are effectively met include improvements to pain management and an improved sense of well-being, as well as improved management of psychological and cardiovascular needs.[34]

---

32 University of Maryland Medical Centre, *What is Spiritual Care?*, 1.
33 Martin, 'Nursing Homes Turning Residents into "Zombies"', 1.
34 University of Maryland Medical Centre, *What is Spiritual Care?*, 1.

Importance of Spirituality in Aged Care

We argue the spiritual well-being of residents in aged care facilities is as important (if not more important) than that in hospital settings. Loneliness, illness, falls and the extensive use of psychotropic drugs threaten the lived experience of many residents in aged care facilities. A focus on spirituality in research into aged care could indicate the very positive impact of an integrated spiritual model on all aspects of a resident's life in an aged care facility. We should consider spirituality as integral to the care of the elderly and not an optional add-on:

The provision of spiritual care by NHS (National Health Service) staff is not yet another demand on their hard-pressed time. It is the very essence of their work and it enables and promotes healing in the fullest sense to all parties, both giver and receiver, of such care.[35]

In an increasingly corporatised aged care industry, a focus on spiritual care is a necessary antidote to the tendency to view relationships with residents as essentially contractual rather than relational, where it is the latter that really matters.

---

35 Levison, *Spiritual Care Matters*, 4.

Bibliography

Aged Care Financing Authority. *Sixth Report on the Funding and Financing of the Aged Care Sector*, (July 2018) < https://www.health.gov.au/resources/publications/sixth-report-on-the-funding-and-financing-of-the-aged-care-sector-july-2018> [accessed 8 March 2020].

Australian Bureau of Statistics. *Australian Demographic Statistics*, (June 2016) <https://www.abs.gov.au/AUSSTATS/abs@.nsf/Previousproducts/3101.0Feature%20Article1Jun%202016> [accessed 8 March 2020].

Australian Institute of Health and Welfare. 'Dementia Among Aged Care Residents: First Information from the Aged Care Funding Instrument', *Aged Care Statistics Series no. 32.* (Cat. no. AGE 63. Canberra: AIHW May, 2011), < https://www.aihw.gov.au/getmedia/6d160b74-621b-4e08-b193-bc90d5b7f348/11711.pdf.aspx?inline=true>, [accessed 9 March 2020].

Australian Institute of Health and Welfare. *Older Australia at a Glance* (Cat. no. AGE 87. Canberra: AIHW 2018) <https://www.aihw.gov.au/reports/older-people/older-australia-at-a-glance> [accessed 9 March 2020].

Brennan-Olsen, S. 'Why Hip Fractures in the Elderly are Often a Death Sentence', *The Conversation* (4 June 2018) <https://theconversation.com/why-hip-fractures-in-the-elderly-are-often-a-death-sentence-95784> [accessed 9 March 2020].

Confoy, M. *Welcome, Inclusion, Attentive Presence: The Central Role of Pastoral Care in Catholic Health and Aged Care*, (Canberra: Catholic Health Australia, 2015).

Culliford, L. 'Spirituality and Clinical Care', *British Medical Journal* 325: 1434 (2002). <https://www.bmj.com/content/325/7378/1434.full> [accessed 9 March 2020].

Dementia Australia. *Dementia Statistics* (North Ryde, January 2020) <https://www.dementia.org.au/statistics> [accessed 9 March 2020].

Duffy-Moon, M. 'Out of Sight Out of Mind. I Despair at How We Treat Our Elderly', *The Guardian*, (6 January 2019) <https://www.theguardian.com/global/commentisfree/2019/jan/06/out-of-sight-out-of-mind-i-despair-at-how-we-treat-our-elderly> [accessed 9 March 2020].

Flanagan, C. A. and Flanagan, J.   *Happily Ever After: A Guide to the Best Aged Care for the People You Love* (Sydney, The Rocks Practice, 2016) <http://www.happilyeverafterthebook.com.au> [accessed 9 March 2020].

Jeyasingam, N.   'Nursing Homes can be the Best Place to Grow Old', *The Sydney Morning Herald,* (27 March, 2016) <https://www.smh.com.au/opinion/nursing-homes-can-be-the-best-place-to-grow-old-20160327-gnrrf1.html> [accessed 9 March 2020].

Koenig H.G., McCullough M.E., and Larson D.B.   *Handbook of Religion and Health* (New York: Oxford University Press, (2001 and 2012).

Koenig, H. G.   'Religion, Spirituality and Medicine in Australia: Research and Clinical Practice', *Medical Journal of Australia* 186: 10 (2007): S45–S46.

Lane, I.   'Six Big Players Dominate Australia's Scandal-hit Aged Care Sector', *The New Daily,* (September 2018) <https://thenewdaily.com.au/money/retirement/2018/09/19/aged-care-profits-players/> [accessed 9 March 2020].

Levison, C.   Foreword to *Spiritual Care Matters,* (NHS Education for Scotland, February 2009). <https://www.nes.scot.nhs.uk/media/3723/spiritualcaremattersfinal.pdf> [accessed 9 March 2020].

Martin, L.   'Nursing Homes Turning Residents into 'Zombies', Aged Care Royal Commission to Hear', *The Guardian,* (15 January 2019) <https://www.theguardian.com/australia-news/2019/jan/15/nursing-homes-turning-residents-into-zombies-aged-care-royal-commission-to-hear> [accessed 9 March 2020].

Martin, L.   'Aged Care Inquiry Told up to 80% of Dementia Patients Prescribed Psychotropic Drugs', *The Guardian,* (13 February 2019)   <https://www.theguardian.com/australia-news/2019/feb/13/aged-care-inquiry-told-up-to-80-of-dementia-patients-prescribed-psychotropic-drugs> [accessed 9 March 2020].

McSherry, W.   *RCN Spirituality Survey 2010,* Royal College of Nursing (2010).

<https://www.merseycare.nhs.uk/media/1863/rcn-spirituality-survey.pdf> [accessed 9 March 2020].

Moreira-Almeida, A., Neto, F. L., Koenig, H. G. 'Religiousness and Mental Health: A Review', *Revista Brasileira de Psiquiatria* 28 (2006): 242–250.

<http://www.scielo.br/scielo.php?script=sci_arttext&pid=S1516-44462006000300018> [accessed 9 March 2020].

Murray, R. B. and Zenter, J. P. *Nursing Concepts for Health Promotion* (London: Prentice Hall, 1975).

Owen, M. '40 Per Cent of People in Aged-Care Facilities Have No Visitors', *The Australian*, (25 October, 2017) <https://www.theaustralian.com.au/nation/health/unannounced-assessment-visits-for-aged-care-under-new-reforms/news-story/637c682f4b6389cfec91501cf0fd7c84> [accessed 9 March 2020].

Palladino, K. 'Mother Teresa Saw Loneliness as Leprosy of the West', *The News-Times*, (April 17, 2004) <https://www.newstimes.com/news/article/Mother-Teresa-saw-loneliness-as-leprosy-of-the-250607.php> [accessed 9 March 2020].

Productivity Commission, 'Caring for Older Australians', *Report No. 53, Final Inquiry Report*, Canberra (2011). < https://www.pc.gov.au/inquiries/completed/aged-care/report/aged-care-volume1.pdf> [accessed 9 March 2020].

Renetzky, L. 'The Fourth Dimension: Applications to the Social Services', in D. O. Moberg (ed.), *Spiritual Well-being: Sociological Perspectives* (Lanham, Maryland: University Press of America 1979): 215–254.

Ross, L. 'The Spiritual Dimension: its Importance to Patients' Health, Well-Being and Quality of Life and its Implications for Nursing Practice', *International Journal of Nursing Studies* 32 (October 1995), 457-468.

Royal Commission into Aged Care Quality and Safety. *Background Paper 2, Medium and Long-Term Pressures on The System: The Changing Demographics and Dynamics of Aged Care*, Canberra, May 2019, <https://agedcare.royalcommission.gov.au/publications/Documents/background-paper-2.pdf> [accessed 6/3/2020].

Sacks, O. *Musicophilia – Tales of Music and the Brain* (New York: Alfred A. Knopf, 2007).

Sartori, P. 'Spirituality 1: Should Spiritual and Religious Beliefs Be Part of Patient Care?', *Nursing Times* 106 (2010), 28. <https://www.nursingtimes.net/roles/nurse-managers/spirituality-1-should-spiritual-and-religious-beliefs-be-part-of-patient-care/5017359.article> [accessed 9 March 2020].

Scottish Inter Faith Council. *Spiritual Care Matters* (NHS Education for Scotland 2008) <https://www.nes.scot.nhs.uk/media/3723/spiritualcaremattersfinal.pdf> [accessed 9 March 2020].

StewartBrown. 'Aged Care Financial Performance Survey', Sydney (2018) <http://www.stewartbrown.com.au/images/documents/StewartBrown---ACFPS-Sector-Report-June-2018.pdf> [accessed 9 March 2020].

University of Maryland Medical Centre. *What is Spiritual Care?* (2019) <https://www.umms.org/ummc/patients-visitors/for-patients/pastoral-care/what-is-spiritual-care> [accessed 9 March 2020].

Williams, D. R. and Sternthal, M. J. 'Spirituality, Religion and Health: Evidence and Research Directions', *Medical Journal of Australia* 186 (2007) <https://www.mja.com.au/journal/2007/186/10/spirituality-religion-and-health-evidence-and-research-directions> [accessed 9 March 2020].

World Health Organisation. 'Social Change and Mental Health Cluster', *WHOQOL and Spirituality, Religiousness and Personal Beliefs*. (1998) <http://apps.who.int/iris/bitstream/handle/10665/70897/WHO_MSA_MHP_98.2_eng.pdf;jsessionid=848C9866BA5A300229405BA1B3557E6E?sequence=1> [accessed 9 March 2020].

Wright, S. G. *Reflections on Spirituality and Health* (London: Whurr, 2005).

PART 2

The Theology of Ageing

CHAPTER 4

Human biological ageing: Creation or curse? Exploring two foundational models

David James Hooker

Abstract

The claim that human biological ageing is 'good' in the Biblical creation sense is challenged by the enduring doctrine of the Cosmic Fall (a fallen creation). However, this doctrinal model has critical deficiencies as it neglects theology rooted in Deuteronomy, the prophets, Psalms and Romans, and fails to appropriate the contribution of ongoing sin to creation's damage. An alternative model, which we have designated Cosmic Disintegration, is able to make up for the shortcomings of the Cosmic Fall model while also stressing the fundamental and persistent goodness of God's creation, with biological ageing as an organically original and theologically good component of it. To recognise human ageing as 'good' is to provide a strong foundation for the perspective in practical theology of 'embracing life' in our older years.

Introduction

Upon what foundation do we build a practical theology of human ageing? Is human ageing 'good' in the Biblical creation sense? Or is it one of the hallmarks of a fallen creation—a consequence of humanity's first sin? Answering these questions is pivotal. Specifically, adopting an understanding of human ageing as belonging to God's good handiwork or, conversely, as a consequence of the tragedy of sin can form highly polarised theological foundations and, therefore, highly divergent practical and pastoral theologies.

The claim that sin has affected the very fabric of creation is central to the Christian theological doctrine of the Cosmic Fall. Stated briefly, this doctrine proposes the disobedience of the first humans not only affected a break in humanity's relationship with God, but also directly caused an intrinsic physical change in all creation, leading to decay and degeneration (including ageing), disease, sickness and suffering, violence and predation, and even death (whether natural or unnatural). The emphasis here is not on an extrinsic change brought to bear over and against creation, but on an intrinsic and enduring change in the fabric of creation—to the point where the 'good' in creation is twisted, disfigured, ruined, and even obliterated. A brief preliminary overview in this chapter will show that this doctrine still figures prominently in contemporary theological commentary on key scriptural texts.

Yet, this chapter also illustrates the doctrine of the Cosmic Fall has critical deficiencies as it neglects the theology rooted in Deuteronomy, the prophets, Psalms and Romans, and fails to appropriate the contribution of ongoing sin to creation's damage. Taken together, this means the traditional model of a cosmic fall errs in several regards, not least for the purposes of this chapter when it includes human biological ageing (and ageing in creation generally) in the post-fall consequences of primeval human sin.

A model that may well be known as Cosmic Disintegration rather than Cosmic Fall can explain the way ongoing and overt human sin is the actual mechanism whereby damage to creation is caused while also stressing the fundamental and persistent goodness of God's creation, with biological ageing as an organically original and theologically good component of it. Therefore, this chapter hopes to contribute towards a theological foundation that comprehends human biological ageing as 'good' in the Biblical creation sense. To recognise human ageing as 'good' is to provide a strong foundation for the perspective in practical theology of 'embracing life' in our older years.

Positioning Our Argument within the Perspective of Medical Science

It is important to place our argument within a medically and scientifically reasonable picture of human ageing. Medical science distinguishes between life-span and life-expectancy[1] (see Figure 1).

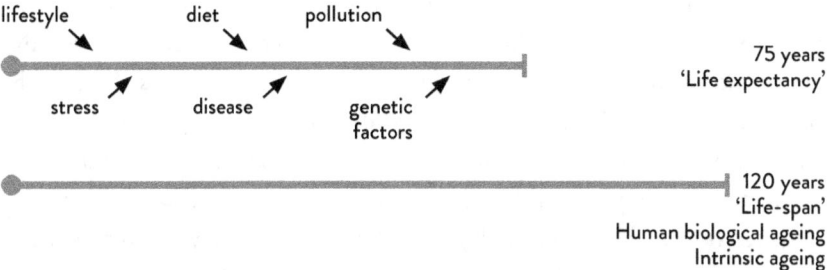

Figure 1: Distinguishing life-expectancy from life-span.

Medical science attributes an approximate 120-year limit to human life-span, determined by intrinsic ageing factors. It is this ageing process that is the focus of this chapter. Actual length of life (life-expectancy) may have a modulated ageing process determined in part by many more factors that are not the subject of this chapter. In Figure 1 above, extrinsic factors (e.g., pollution and disease) are examples only and not intended to be exhaustive. Our argument focuses on human ageing as determining life-*span*, but at the chapter's end we briefly comment on how extrinsic factors[2] may fit theologically into the two foundational models discussed.

---

1 Dong, Milholland, and Vijg, 'Evidence for a Limit to Human Lifespan', 538.
2 Examples of the influence of extrinsic factors on ageing in the literature: Kennedy et al., 'Geroscience: Linking Aging to Chronic Disease', 159; Epel et al., 'Accelerated Telomere Shortening in Response to Life Stress', 101; Vermeij et al., 'Restricted Diet Delays Accelerated Ageing and Genomic Stress. Kim et al., 'Obesity and Weight Gain'. 18; Effros et al., 'Aging and Infectious Diseases'.

The Doctrine of the Cosmic Fall in Historical Theology

The two key scriptures that consistently surface in the doctrine's historicity, and that exegetically ground it, are Genesis 1–3 and Romans 8:18–22, texts to which we shall subsequently turn. Most commentators regard the latter passage as Paul's own comment on Genesis 3:17–19.

This doctrine has a long history—almost as long as Christian theology itself. As Bimson has noted, Theophilus of Antioch (c. 115–185) argued human sin not only affected humanity but transferred its effects to the remainder of the created order.[3] The doctrine continues and develops through the centuries with such influential and prolific thinkers as the post-Nicene John Chrysostom (349–407AD), the Reformer John Calvin (1540) and several influential contemporary Biblical theologians.[4] Calvin speaks of the world's 'degeneration' and 'corruption', Barth of the 'present misery' of every 'particle of the world', Godet of the 'sombre hue' of nature, and Fitzmyer of creation's present 'lack of beauty, vitality, and strength'.

Due to its contemporary persistence, the doctrine must still be considered a force to be reckoned with. To help our investigations it is worth weaving the common doctrinal threads together into a Cosmic Fall model (see Figure 2).

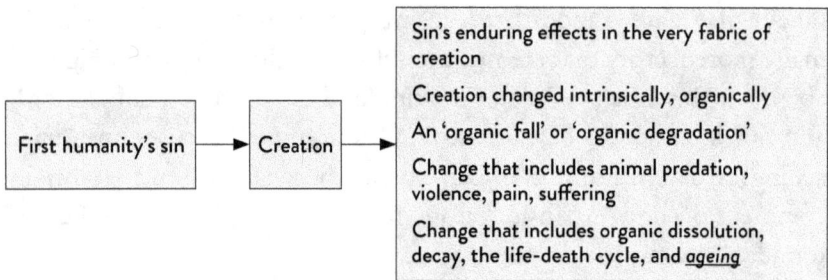

Figure 2. Model 1: The Cosmic Fall outlining key doctrinal points.

---

3   Bimson, 'Reconsidering a "Cosmic Fall"'.
4   Calvin, *A Commentary on Genesis*, 174. Chrysostom, *Saint Chrysostom*, 444. Other more contemporary commentators writing of a cosmic fall include: Von Rad, *Genesis: A Commentary*, 93–94; Cassuto, *A Commentary on the Book of Genesis*, 163–69; Mathews, *Genesis 1-11:26*, 249ff; Calvin, *The Epistles of Paul to the Romans and Thessalonians*, 173–74; Barth, *The Epistle to the Romans*, 308–309; Murray, *The Epistle to the Romans*, 302–304; Godet, *Commentary on Romans*, 314; Beker, *Paul the Apostle*, 149, 232; Bruce, *Romans*, 170; Ziesler, *Paul's Letter to the Romans*, 219–221; Fitzmyer, *Romans: A New Translation*, 505, 507, 509; Moo, *The Epistle to the Romans*, 517; Moo, *Romans 1–8*, 554; Kruse, *Paul's Letter to the Romans*, 347–348; Merrill, 'Pre-Human Death', 14; Barth changes his perspective on ageing, creation and death in his Church Dogmatics.

This model conveys the following: (a) an *intrinsic* physical change, one that has occurred to change the very fabric of creation and has warped or even removed the goodness of creation; (b) an *enduring* change affected by the first Adamic fall (on this point, though humanity's ongoing sin is acknowledged, it is not by this model considered to be the cause of the imperfections in a post-fall creation); (c) though not always explicitly listed as an effect, the ageing of humans and of all creation is an essential aspect/dimension of this view as it is a major manifestation of nature's 'dissolution' or 'decay'; and (d) human biological ageing, which is particularly relevant to this chapter, is posited within the effects of sin from the original fall.

We stress this model has a covert mechanism as an explanation. Specifically, no answer is given to the question, *how* did the first human's sin organically change the fabric of creation? The mechanism is encapsulated in mystery. The phenomenon of a 'shrouded' explanation may alone be considered enough to question the validity of such a model.[5]

However, it is certainly not the only model to try to explain sin's consequences for all creation. At this point, it would be appropriate to introduce and to develop an alternative model to the Cosmic Fall, a model we term Cosmic Disintegration, which is the main focus of this chapter. In this model, the overt, specific and ongoing evil of all unbelieving humanity acts against a good creation to ruin and damage it. This fundamentally contrasts with the Cosmic Fall model above and is outlined in Figure 3.

---

5   We are no closer to removing the mystery from the mechanism when many commentators on passages relevant to this model (e.g., Rom. 8:18–25) seem to simply reiterate what the text says. For example, Ziesler is not explanatory: 'it is taken for granted that the created world is not at present free to be its true self'. Here he gives no explanation for how this may be other than to argue that God has subjected creation to this condition. Ziesler, *Paul's Letter to the Romans*, 219–220. Nor is Moo helpful: '[Paul says] the sub-human creation itself is not what it should be, or what God intended it to be. It has been subjected to frustration'. 'Humanity's fall into sin marred the 'goodness' of God's creation, and creation has ever since been in a state of "frustration"'. Moo, *The Epistle to the Romans*, 515.

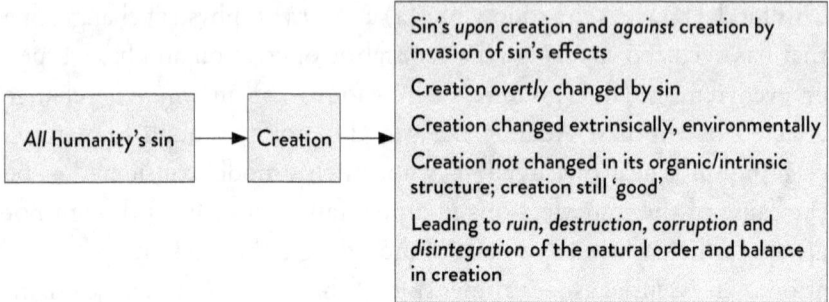

Figure 3. Model 2: Cosmic Disintegration outlining key doctrinal points.

In the model above, italicised words draw out the key features to which we shall return in subsequent analyses. Critically, (a) in contrast to the shrouded explanation of the Cosmic Fall model, this model contains an overt mechanism to robustly and openly explain the suffering of creation; (b) the dire effect of all humanity's overt sin upon creation is acknowledged while advocating the concurrent continuing goodness of creation after the fall; (c) for this chapter, this model provides an explanation that covers the possibility that human biological ageing (and ageing in creation more generally) is not included in the consequences of human sin.

Although perhaps not as widespread among biblical theologians as the Cosmic Fall model, the Cosmic Disintegration model also has a significant history in Christian theology, favoured in various forms by patristic and contemporary theologians. In his *City of God*, Augustine (354–430AD) rejects certain arguments that could be used to favour a cosmic fall while promoting the concept of a currently good creation. To Augustine, the 'defects' and 'dissolution' of creation belong to the creatures' 'mode of being' given by the Creator. This supports a view that the post-fall creation is indeed good and has not been changed intrinsically by the fall.[6] Rimbach links Paul's 'groaning' of creation in Romans 8 to human overt sin, citing modern humanity's woeful exploitation

---

6   Augustine, *City of God*, 453, 455, 475–476.

of creation's resources.⁷ In his commentary on Romans, Jewett shows an articulate appreciation for Roman imperial practices and the honour system in both Jewish and Graeco-Roman cultures. An honoured ruler in imperial Rome claimed a god-like power to 'restore the world to a paradisiacal condition by his piety and military dominance'.⁸ Commenting on Romans 8:18–22, Jewett writes that Paul claims the very antithesis of this: humans have overtly ruined the world and now creation's hope lies in the revealing of Christ's followers, most of whom (in the Roman church) have no honour and hail from poor and slave classes. However, the significant point for us is that here we have a perspective that sees sin's effects on creation as *non-intrinsic, ongoing and overt*, which clearly accords with a Cosmic Disintegration model. For other contemporary Christian thinkers, the answer to the question of which model is most valid is either ambiguous or unresolved.⁹

We contend in this chapter that Cosmic Disintegration (Model 2) indeed offers the best explanation for sin's effects on creation from humanity's first sin onward and is most consistent with sound interpretations not only of the key texts Genesis 1–3 and Romans 8:18–22, but scripture's overall perspective on creation and the sin-creation nexus. In the succeeding sections we formulate detailed arguments to support this contention.

Deuteronomy's Covenantal Blessing/Curse Theology Reveals and Helps to Explain a Cosmic Principle between Human Sin and God's Creation: Model 2 is Supported

In the Deuteronomic setting, a solemn yet simple choice is placed before Israel: to walk with God, to manifestly be His people, to be obedient or to follow other gods (Deut. 28:14), to walk away from

---

7   Rimbach, '"All Creation Groans"', 385. Rimbach however muddies the waters when he also appears to support Model 1: 'there is more to the futility of creation than its endless cyclic repetition of flowering and decay, its "redness in tooth and claw" (Lipsius), its beauty and catastrophe, and its mindless exploitation'.
8   Jewett, *Romans*, 512–513.
9   Jewett, *Romans*, 170; Longenecker, *The Epistle to the Romans*, 22–24; Surburg, 'Good Stuff!', 245, 248, 257.

Him and be disobedient. The consequences of Israel's response to Yhwh's covenant are laid down in great detail in Deuteronomy 28 with further solemn commentary in chapters 29 to 32 (30:1; 'when all *these* blessings and curses' הַדְּבָרִים הָאֵלֶּה הַבְּרָכָה). Their response will incur blessings for obedience and curses for disobedience (Deut. 28:9,15). The blessings include peace, prosperity and success in health, childbirth, harvesting, animal husbandry, work, travel, defeat of enemies and inter-national recognition (Deut. 28:1–14). Curses encompass the opposite: illness, disease, turmoil, confusion, failure, scorn, derision, defeat, slavery, injustice and abuse (Deut. 28:15–68). This can be perceived as a choice between two polarised domains of life: 'life with God' or the 'God-less life'. The following observations form an argument claiming that, in Deuteronomic theology, the curses due to sin—the consequences of overt sin—overtly affect creation as well as humanity.

First, there is certainly a 'personal' element to both blessings and curses (i.e., the covenantal pronouncements apply directly to Israel's own persons, both individually and as a people). The consequence of sin flows directly from their relationship with Yhwh and sin against Yhwh's covenant is overt: it is a specific transgression of specific, revealed decrees and laws (e.g., Deut. 5:6–22). Likewise, the blessings and curses are overt, being direct and living pronouncements from Yhwh to Israel's immediate and more distant future (Deut. 31:15–22; 4:25–26). Therefore, here there is only a link with personal, overt and specific sin and no explicit link with the original fall.

Second, it is also essential to illuminate the effect of Israel's life on creation. The same sins of God's people have consequences for creation as they do personally. Covenant violation brings creation's disintegration and destruction; covenant faithfulness brings the peace, fruitfulness and prosperity of creation. Some appropriate examples are as follows:

- Israel's crops, her livestock's young, her harvested grain, will be cursed (28:17,18).
- Scorching heat and drought, blight and mildew are promised (28:22–24).

- Seed, grape, oil harvests will fail or be destroyed (28:38–42).
- Disaster on the 'watered land as well as the dry' (29:19)[10]; 'calamities' on the land, the land to become a 'burning waste' devoid of any fruitfulness (29:22,23).
- The Lord's fire of wrath 'will devour the earth and its harvests, and set afire the foundations of the mountains [...] I will reap calamities upon them, and spend my arrows against them. I will send wasting famine against them, consuming pestilence and deadly plague' (32:22–24).

Of the land's destruction, Merrill puts it well: 'Nothing could be more ironic than for the land of Canaan, a land "flowing with milk and honey" [...] to become one divested of any sign of fertility and productivity'.[11]

Third, the curses—and necessarily those that involve creation—are also invoked against other nations (Deut. 30:7) 'who hate and persecute [Israel]' (cf. Deut. 7:15). This extension of curses to any nation that sets itself up against Yhwh reveals a kind of cosmic dimensionality to the sin-creation nexus: it matters not whether the sin comes from the chosen people but whether or not a people (anyone, anywhere) align themselves with Yhwh (see Figure 4).

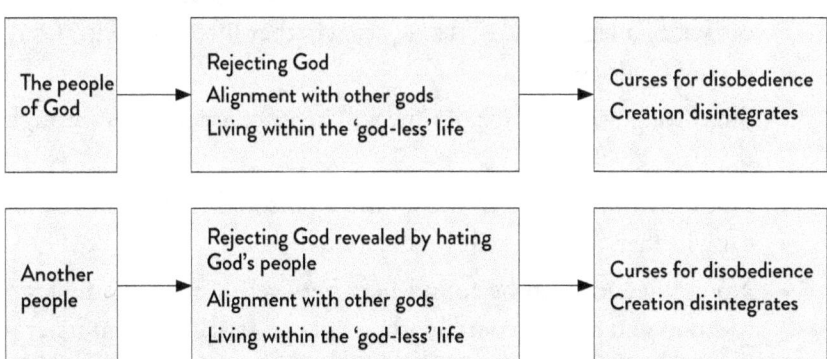

Figure 4. Deuteronomy's theology reveals a cosmic dimensionality to the sin-creation nexus.

---

10 A merism denoting totality. Merrill, *Deuteronomy*, 382.
11 Merrill, *Deuteronomy*, 384.

The cosmic dimensionality of sin's effect on creation reflects Yhwh's cosmic reign. As the Lord of all people and all creation, He has explicit authorship of both blessings and curses, of prosperity or destruction (Deut. 28:63).

Fourth, the curses for disobedience to Yhwh's covenant are not due to Israel's aimless yet innocent wandering, as if they had simply lost their way; rather, they are linked back to their abandonment of Yhwh *and* their attachment to other 'gods' (Deut. 4:25–28; 5:7–10; 8:19–20; 11:13–17; 11:26–28; 29:24–27; 30:15–18). Other nations and the gods of other nations were enticements away from a pure devotion to Yhwh and enticements towards many 'detestable' practises that incur the curses of judgement (Deut. 12:29–31). We observe here an 'either-or' concept: either Israel was following Yhwh and receiving His blessings for covenantal faithfulness, or it was following other gods and incurring His curses for disobedience.

In summary we note the following:

- In Deuteronomic theology, human sin and the consequence of sin is specific and overt.
- Whether or not a human being belongs to God's chosen people does not determine Yhwh's invocation of blessings and curses.
- The consequences of sin are always rooted in personal allegiance or lack of allegiance to Yhwh (i.e., whether life is 'life with God' or 'the God-less life').
- Sin through the passage of time will incur consequences through the passage of time.
- Not only does overt sin incur curses personally, but also cosmically in that creation will be affected.
- No connection can be found here between humanity's first sin in Eden and some general cosmic change (fall) that haunts creation down the ages; nevertheless, there is support for Model 2.

As shown in the following section, the theology of the Hebrew prophetic traditions is highly consistent with the Deuteronomic sin-creation nexus.

The Covenantal Blessing/Curse Theology of the Hebrew Prophets also Reveals and Helps to Explain a Cosmic Principle between Overt Human Sin and God's Creation: Model 2 is Supported

In Isaiah 1–39, the pre-exilic eighth-century BC prophet Isaiah records oracles of judgement against the disobedience of Israel and other nations. Table 1 comprehensively lists from 1 Isaiah those elements of creation involved in Yhwh's judgement due to covenant violation.

Table 1. Elements of creation in 1 Isaiah's oracles of judgement.

Reference	Creation category	God's judgement involving creation
Isa. 13:13 Isa. 24:4 Isa. 24:18 Isa. 34:4	Heavens	The heavens tremble The heavens languish Heaven's floodgates opened The heavens roll up like a scroll
Isa. 24:21	Powers in the heavens	The powers in the heavens punished
Isa. 13:10	Heaven's stars, constellations	Will not show their light
Isa. 13:10 Isa. 24:23	Sun	Sun darkened Sun ashamed
Isa. 13:10 Isa. 24:23	Moon	Moon does not give its light Moon dismayed
Isa. 8:21–22 Isa. 13:13 Isa. 24:1; 24:3 Isa. 24:3 Isa. 24:4 Isa. 24:5 Isa. 24:6 Isa. 24:11 Isa. 24:19–20	Earth	Distress, darkness, fearful gloom seen on the earth The earth shaken The earth laid waste and devastated The earth plundered The earth dries up and withers The earth defiled The earth consumed by a curse Joyful sounds banished from the earth The earth broken up, split asunder, violently shaken, swaying and reeling
Isa. 24:1	Earth's face	Earth's face ruined
Isa. 24:18	Earth's foundations	Earth's foundation shaken
Isa. 24:1 Isa. 24:6	Earth's inhabitants	Earth's inhabitants scattered Earth's inhabitants burned up
Isa. 13:11 Isa. 24:4	World	The (people of the) world punished The world languishes and withers
Isa. 24:13 Isa. 34:2–3	Nations	Nations with cities ruined and unprotected Nations totally destroyed
Isa. 1:7	Country	Country desolate

Reference	Creation category	God's judgement involving creation
Isa. 7:24 Isa. 8:21–22 Isa. 9:2 Isa. 10:23 Isa. 13:9 Isa. 32:13 Isa. 34:9	Land	Land covered with briers and thorns Distressed and hungry roam the land Land of deep darkness Destruction upon whole land Land desolate Land overgrown with briers and thorns Land turned to blazing pitch
Isa. 7:25 Isa. 42:15	Hills	Hills uncultivated, filled with briers and thorns Hills laid waste
Isa. 10:18–19	Forests	Forest's trees and splendour completely destroyed
Isa. 1:7 Isa. 14:23 Isa. 17:9 Isa. 32:14	Cities	Cities burned with fire Babylon turned to swampland Cities abandoned to thickets and undergrowth City turned to wasteland
Isa. 1:7 Isa. 10:18 Isa. 16:8 Isa. 19:7	Fields	Fields stripped by foreigners Field's fertility destroyed Fields wither Sown fields parched and destroyed
Isa. 7:23–25 Isa. 17:9	Places	Places become briers and thorns Places abandoned to thickets and undergrowth and desolation
Isa. 15:6	Waters	Waters dry up
Isa. 19:5	River	River waters dry up
Isa. 19:6	Riverbed and canals	Riverbed parched, dry; canals stink
Isa. 19:6 Isa. 34:9	Streams	Streams dwindle and dry up Streams turned to pitch
Isa. 19:8	Fishermen	Fishermen fail to catch fish and groan
Isa. 10:19	Trees	Forest trees reduced to a few
Isa. 34:4	Fig tree	Shrivelled figs
Isa. 15:6	Grass	Grass withered
Isa. 15:6 Isa. 42:15	Vegetation	Vegetation destroyed Vegetation dried up
Isa. 19:6	Reeds	Reeds wither
Isa. 19:6	Rushes	Rushes wither
Isa. 17:10–11 Isa. 19:7	Plants	Plants fail to grow Plants wither
Isa. 17:11 Isa. 32:10	Harvests	Harvest fails Grape harvest fails
Isa. 16:10	Orchards	No more joy and gladness in them
Isa. 5:10 Isa. 16:10	Vineyards	Vineyards produce very little No more singing and shouting in them

Reference	Creation category	God's judgement involving creation
Isa. 7:23	Vine	Vines given over to briers and thorns
Isa. 16:8		Vines wither and are trampled
Isa. 24:7		Vines wither
Isa. 5:10	Seed	Seeds produce a poor yield of grain

Additionally, the same connection between creation's destruction/disintegration and humanity's violation of Yhwh's will is to be found in the judgement oracles of the minor prophets.[12]

Compared to 1 Isaiah, however, Deutero-Isaiah's use of the creation motif is strikingly different. Writing to the Hebrews during the Sixth Century BC Babylonian exile, the author of Deutero-Isaiah records oracles of comfort, redemption and salvation. The mood changes from 1 Isaiah's one of judgement to one of 'exaltation and confidence',[13] while the role of creation categories also changes—creation is now strongly linked with power, glory and praise of YHWH as creator in order to encourage trust (40:25–26; 43:1,14–21; 44:3,23,24; 45:5–7,11–13,18; 48:12–13; 50:2–3).[14]

From 1 Isaiah (Table 1) and the minor prophets, we are able to form a surprisingly comprehensive picture of creation (from the stars' constellations to the smallest seed), covering a great many categories with which the prophets' hearers were familiar. Furthermore, creation is pictured as disintegrating in direct consequence of YHWH's specific oracles of judgement upon the overt and specific sin of the people.[15] The highly prevalent creation-disintegration theme of 1 Isaiah's judgement oracles ceases almost completely in 2 and 3 Isaiah's words of comfort and salvation, where creation is a motif for YHWH's restorative power.

---

12 Hos. 2:9–12; 4:1–3; Joel 1:5–20; Amos 8:8,9,13,14; Mic. 6:13–16; 7:13; Nah. 1:3–6; Zeph. 1:18; 2:8,9; 2:13–15; Hag. 1:7–11; 2:16–19; Zech. 7:13; 14:12–15; Mal. 1:2–5; 4:6.
13 Whybray, *The Second Isaiah*, 3.
14 The laying waste of mountains and hills and the drying up of vegetation, et cetera in Isa. 42:15 is not to be seen as a direct invocation of covenantal curses because it rests within a song of praise for YHWH's restoration and commitment to his people, and describes simply YHWH's power over creation to do as he pleases.
15 The overt and specific sin of humanity is exemplified in Isa. 24:5 (NIV): 'the earth is defiled by its people; they have disobeyed the laws'.

In 1 Isaiah, the oracles that involve creation are against many countries and peoples (e.g., Assyria, 10:18–19; 13:13; Moab, 15:1 to 16:14; Damascus, 17:1–14; Cush, 18:1–7; Egypt, 19:1–25). In applying to any nation or people that lives against God, it is shown there is a general principle applying to creation: due to human overt and specific sin, God subjects creation to change as a component of His judgement.

Overall, the theology of the pre-exilic prophets is thoroughly consistent with Deuteronomic theology on the consequences of overt sin that involve creation. On the matter of consistency, there is more to be said for the pervasiveness of the sin-creation nexus in Israel's theology. We find it has a long tradition (being spoken from ancient Job in a setting of the Second Millennium BC) and a broad one (occurring in the Wisdom literature as well as the aforementioned genres). In Job 24:18, Job calls the land belonging to the rebellious, the murderers, the adulterers, and the thieves as 'cursed', and in 31:38–40 he invokes judgement upon his own land if he has been unjust to his fellow human beings: 'let briers come up instead of wheat, and weeds instead of barley'.[16] Moreover, we would claim Genesis 3:17–19, a passage that has become a key support for the Cosmic Fall model, is in fact thoroughly consistent with the creation-disintegration theme in Deuteronomy, the prophets and Job—by symbolically encapsulating[17] Israel's covenantal blessing-curse theology.[18]

Importantly for this chapter and as with Deuteronomy's theology, against Model 1 but supporting Model 2, there is no evidence for causation between primeval human sin and a general and intrinsic Cosmic Fall.

---

16 Jewett, *Romans*, 516.
17 With Jewett, who speaks of the thorns and thistles of Gen. 3:18 as 'symbols' of 'endless frustration in the human interaction with the natural environment'. Jewett, *Romans*, 513.
18 Against an interpretation favouring the Cosmic Fall model, Braaten notes the LXX reads, 'cursed is the ground *in your works*' [my italics] indicating that the effect on creation is tied up with humanity's interaction with it, and the curse is not of the earth *per se*. Braaten, 'All Creation Groans', 28. Moreover, Walsh notes that the Hebrew בַּעֲבוּרֶךָ is not to be rendered as causal 'because of you', but relational, 'in regard to you'. He says, 'the ground is not cursed absolutely, but only as insofar as it impinges upon the existence of Adam'. Walsh, 'Genesis 2:4b–3:24', 96.

The Psalm's Confessional and Doxological Theology of Creation is God-Affirming and Life-Affirming and is Not Consistent with a Warped, Twisted, Changed Creation which, Due to a Cosmic Fall is Subject to Degradation, Ageing and Death: Model 1 is Not Supported

Twenty-four of the one hundred and fifty Psalms explicitly reflect on creation, marking it as a significant theme in this prayer book. We may delineate the Psalms' creation themes as the following:

God Has Acted by Creating

Creation is God's personal property (24:1,2; 50:9–12) and handiwork (Ps. 8:3,4; 19:1–6) formed by His word (33:6–9), comprehensively referred to as the (celestial) heavens (8:3,4; 33:6–9), the earth (33:6–9; Ps. 104), the skies, mountains, seas and dry land (36:5,6; 95:4,5), domesticated and wild creatures (50:9–12), day and night, sun and moon, summer and winter and earth's boundaries (74:13–17; Ps. 104), the clouds, wind and lightning (135:5–7), and the human body (94:9; 119:73; 139:13–16). Together, these declarations appropriately echo the Genesis 1 narrative of the original creation.

God is Still Acting in Creation

Yet God has not merely formed and established His handiwork, He also reigns over it (47:7,8), doing as He pleases (135:5–7), even overruling the normal creation processes as He sees fit (77:16–20). The characteristics of this reign are unmistakeable: God provides, enriches, blesses and cares for His creation (65:5–13; 145:15,16,21; 147:4,5,8,9,16–18), and in truth His creation is 'full of His unfailing love' (33:6–9; 119:64).

God's Faithful People Can See God's Character in Creation

Can we see anything of God's attributes from all of this? As the Psalmist sees the existing, present creation in his life, God formed and established it all (24:1,2). God's wonders, faithfulness, might, unique power (36:5,6; 89:5–13), His righteousness and justice (36:5,6), His glory (97:1–6) and His love (Ps. 136) can all be seen in creation.

Our Appropriate Response is to Love and Praise Him

From such a magnificent and consistent portrayal of God's past and present action and from His attributes from creation, the right response is the evocation of awe (8:3,4), joy in heart and song (65:5–13), praise and worship (145:15,16,21; 147:4,5,8,9,16–18; Ps. 148; 150:6), and to proclaim emphatically 'His love endures forever!' (Ps. 136). Even creation rejoices in its Maker (Ps. 96:4–13). Indeed, it is fitting and right that every living thing—all of creation—praise the Creator for its creation (Ps. 148; 150:6).

Yet we cannot neglect another of the Psalmist's reflections on creation. Psalmist theology also acknowledges that heaven and earth will 'wear out like a garment' and 'perish' (102:25–27), and that the life-death cycle is part of God's activity in creation (104:27–30). We stress this point: the life-death cycle is also a work of God in this Psalm (104:24), together with many other examples of God's creativity (104:1–23), all of which evoke praise to God and a prayer that God Himself will take pleasure in them (104:31).

The Psalmists' portrait of a contemporary creation—we stress creation as it presently stands—is not one that is projected by Model 1 (i.e., of intrinsic ruin, destruction, decay, corruption, futility, emptiness and purposelessness). It is our contention that the Psalms' portrayal of God's present creation is so positive, uplifting, life-affirming and God-affirming that it makes little sense to dovetail this with a creation that is changed in its very fabric due to sin.[19] It makes far more sense to agree with the Psalmist that this present creation wonderfully reflects the goodness of Genesis 1's original creation.[20] Yet, importantly, this of course does not exclude an understanding of humanity's interaction with creation where creation can be and is abused and ruined by

---

19 A perspective complimented by other texts: Job 26:7–14; Job 38, 39; Rev. 3:14; Is 6:3. Contra Reuss' 'sombre hue' (quoted by Godet), the 'present misery' (Barth), the 'evils' (Calvin) or 'lack of beauty' (Fitzmyer) (from previously cited commentaries) of creation that, frankly, paint a very depressing picture of our world. Surely this does not do justice to the beauty and goodness of present creation attested in the Psalms and by the Lord Jesus.
20 Foerster, 'κτίζω', 1000–1035. Foerster remarks on how 'remote' the concept is of a fallen creation in the whole OT, saying, 'the seeds laid in these two [Genesis creation] stories for the development of the idea of a fallen creation are not yet brought to fruition in the OT'. (Foerster, 'κτίζω', 1014).

humanity's overt evil against it and its Maker.

Jesus is thoroughly consistent with Psalms' creation perspective. He uses the glorious beauty of the lilies of the field to exhort trust (Matt. 6:28,29). The sun and rain are good gifts from the hand of God to humanity (Matt. 5:45). Food for the birds is God's good gift to them (Matt. 6:26). And what might this food be? Surely the birds in Jesus day—just as in our day—include in their diet the insects and smaller mammals. Though indirect, Jesus is thus attesting to the 'goodness' of the life-death cycle in the food chain and the way it has a purposeful part in the running of creation. Moreover, to Jesus, God's provision for the birds is considered a clear enough example to be a lesson that teaches us to trust in God.

Having briefly referenced the New Testament here, it is appropriate to turn now to Romans 8:18–22, whose interpretation has been instrumental in the development of the Cosmic Fall model.[21]

Exegesis of Romans 8:18–22 and Other Pauline Passages: Model 2 is Supported

In this section, we argue an interpretation of Romans 8:18–22 can be robustly consistent with the pervasive covenantal blessing-curse theology in the Old Testament.

In addition to his explicit Old Testament citations,[22] Paul employs allusions and 'echoes' of OT scripture to build his theology.[23] For example, of the Old Testament allusion to Deuteronomy 28 in Romans 2:5–11 Hays writes: 'The allusion is a trope, inviting the reader to picture the eschatological wrath of God in terms of Deuteronomy's images'. This trope 'is not casually chosen, for Paul sees in the Deuteronomic covenant a prefiguration of the gospel, and he sees the attendant blessings and curses as words addressed to his own

---

21 Space does not permit an examination of inter-testamental literature, but see Gowan, 'The Fall and Redemption of the Material World', 7.
22 Thompson, *Deuteronomy*, 11; Moyise, *The Old Testament in the New*, 75; Moyise, *Paul and Scripture*, 127–131.
23 Hays, *Echoes of Scripture in the Letters of Paul*.

time'.[24] Here we find the very covenantal blessing-curse theology with which we claim Romans 8:18–22 is consistent, and which features (a) the 'either-or' polarity of humanity; (b) blessings for the righteous but the cursed 'trouble and distress' for the evil-doer; and (c) the bringing of all humanity under the law of sin's consequences. We may also point out the three intertwined themes of creation-sin-judgement found in Deuteronomy and the prophets are also intertwined in Paul's fundamental treatise of the human condition in Romans 1:18–32.[25]

In defending Model 2, our argument has two components:

a) Romans 8:18–22 exegesis and consistency with Old Testament blessing-curse theology;

b) Comparison of Psalms' creation theology with Paul's concepts of creation.

Romans 8:18–22 Exegesis and Consistency with Old Testament Covenantal Blessing-Curse Theology: Model 2 is Supported

Romans has a letter structure customary to the day but with an extended letter body. 8:18–22 falls squarely within the letter body, before the paraenetic unit (12:1 to 15:13), being part of Paul's reasoned theological argument for the gospel. I term 8:18–25 'living in freedom by the Spirit'. Against the backdrop of bondage to the law of sin and death (7:21–23; 8:2), Paul explains the new law of the Spirit given through the gospel (8:1–4, the Spirit frees us from condemnation; 8:5–13, the Spirit of life; 8:14–17, the Spirit of sonship; 8:18–27, the Spirit of future glory).

To précis Romans 8:18–25, the weight of our present sufferings (τὰ παθήματα) cannot be compared to the weight of our future glory (8:18). Paul stresses the magnificence of the Christian believer's future glory through the Spirit by also highlighting creation's eager waiting for this glory to happen (8:18–19). Both creation and Christ's believers groan (8:22,23), both wait in hope for change (8:21,22,25), both will be liberated and brought into glory (8:21).

---

24 Hays, *Echoes of Scripture in the Letters of Paul*, 44.
25 The many sins judged by God of which Paul speaks in Rom. 1 have their roots in humanity's aberrant relationship with creation and with its Maker (Rom. 1:18–20).

What Paul says about creation in this context is intriguing and somewhat mysterious: creation presently is subjected to 'frustration' (New International Version [NIV]; ματαιότητι) as it groans as in travail (πᾶσα ἡ κτίσις συστενάζει καὶ συνωδίνει) for liberation from 'bondage to decay' (NIV; ἀπὸ τῆς δουλείας τῆς φθορᾶς). It should be noted the origin of creation's suffering is not specified in this text, implying that even though this passage carries so much weight in the Cosmic Fall argument, that weight may be seen as coming from an assumption, with the Disintegration Model still a distinct possibility to be considered. We now to turn to an analysis of the aforementioned key words.

8:18-22. κτίσις. With many commentators, though κτίσις can adopt a range of meanings—'the act of creating', 'creature' and 'creation generally'—the latter is preferred here particularly in view of 'all creation' in 8:22. Yet there is considerable debate over what Paul's 'all creation' here really includes. With most commentators, the most appropriate meaning is of the sub-human creation.[26]

8:18. παθήμα. Some commentators build a definition of 'suffering' in 8:18-25 by connection with 5:2-4. Doubtless, the 'suffering/glory' themes of 8:18-25 are further developments of those themes expounded in 5:2-4. However, it should be noted 5:2-4's different word for suffering: θλῖψις. Ziesler notes the common NT's application of θλῖψις for Christian persecution;[27] however, Moo is correct to point out its broader meaning to include other kinds of 'pressure' such as illness, circumstantial trials and the like.[28] Thus, at the very least, the Pauline 'suffering' of 8:18-25 will likely include Christian persecution. Jewett agrees, noting the sufferings of the believers specifically included (among other types) 'harassment and deportation'; these are

---

26 For useful discussions see: Cranfield, *A Critical and Exegetical Commentary on the Epistle to the Romans*, 411–412; Moo, *The Epistle to the Romans*, 513–515; Murray, *The Epistle to the Romans*, 301–302; Foerster, 'ktizw', 1000–1035. Foerste (1028–1029) notes the NT's exclusive use of κτίσις for *God's* creation, probably borrowing from the LXX's use of this word to mark a line between a human artisan's simple fashioning of an object and God's fashioning *and command over* his creation. Jonathan Moo also has a sensible overview, arriving at the same conclusion, in Moo, 'Romans 8:19–22 and Isaiah's Cosmic Covenant', 513–515.
27 Ziesler, *Paul's Letter to the Romans*, 138.
28 Moo, *The Epistle to the Romans*, 302–303.

manifestations of suffering in Christ's name and signs of 'eschatological solidarity with Christ'.[29]

However, besides the link to 5:2–4, there is a link to another section that provides clearer guidance on how to define πάθημα in 8:18–25. In the early part of 8:18–25's argument, Paul reiterates topics from closing arguments of the previous section (8:14–17) to build new themes upon them. These topics are glory (8:17, now in 8:18), sons of God (8:14–17, now in 8:19) and sufferings (introduced in the transitional 8:17, now in 8:18). Importantly, the sufferings of 8:17 are those 'shared with Christ' (εἴπερ συμπάσχομεν ἵνα καὶ συνδοξασθῶμεν; i.e., suffering due to being a follower of Christ).[30] This can only mean the sin and evil of unbelievers acting upon Christians because they bear God's name.[31] It is sinful action clearly outside of the will of God and, therefore, overtly against God Himself. Through theme reiteration, Paul carries this kind of suffering into 8:18 (τὰ παθήματα τοῦ νῦν καιροῦ); therefore, I believe 'sufferings' here includes—to a major extent—those brought about by the sin and evil of unbelievers acting against the will of God.[32] It is these sufferings of which believers will be liberated (8:21,23).

This analysis of the contextual meaning of suffering is important for our argument. We have previously remarked that both creation and believers groan, both wait, and both will be delivered into glorious freedom. If believers are groaning and waiting for deliverance from the overt sin and evil that acts against the name of God (the name they bear and for which they suffer), then it is reasonable to argue creation is also groaning and waiting for deliverance from this same overt sin and evil rather than from a covert effect in the fabric of creation.

8:20. τῇ γὰρ ματαιότητι ἡ κτίσις ὑπετάγη ('for the creation was subjected to frustration'; NIV). Paul may have in mind Genesis 3:17–18 here,

---

29 Jewett, *Romans*, 508–510.
30 Jewett agrees: 'This passage in Romans [...] clearly has the sense of believers suffering with Christ'. Jewett, *Romans*, 503.
31 For a useful discussion, see Moo, *The Epistle to the Romans*, 504–506. Also Bauer, Gingrich, and Arndt, *A Greek-English Lexicon of the New Testament*, 602.
32 Ziesler, *Paul's Letter to the Romans*, 218: 'Presumably [...] opposition and persecution'. Paul uses πάθημα for persecution in other letters: 2 Cor. 1:5–7; Phlm. 3:10; Col. 1:24.

though not necessarily as the exclusive object of exegesis.[33] Most commentators find support for Paul's exegesis only of this passage by noting the aorist verbal forms for 'subject' (i.e., the subjection of creation was a one-time past event and, hence, the Cosmic Fall). Contra this view, Greek grammarians note the aorist can indeed refer back to repeated actions taken in a collective sense; hence, this is consistent with our Cosmic Disintegration model.[34] The evidence of the verb tense here, therefore, does not favour one model over another. Importantly, this Old Testament text as we have argued is consistent with Deuteronomy and the pre-exilic prophets by symbolically encapsulating Israel's covenantal blessing-curse theology and is paradigmatic for all humanity.[35]

ματαιότητι ('frustration', NIV). The creation was subjected to 'frustration' not of its own will. 'Frustration' here represents emptiness, futility, purposelessness, transitoriness,[36] and, in scripture, is commonly associated with the overt sins from the minds and words of unbelievers (e.g., Eph. 4:17; 2 Pet. 2:18). Could not this same emptiness and futility arising from an unbelieving life pressure creation itself? The wickedness of humanity acting against the will of God does not listen to the Creator in seeking how to relate to creation or how to care for it in righteous stewardship. Instead, humanity abuses, scars and violates creation for its own ends, forcing short-sighted (transitory) and self-centred endeavours on creation that have little or no godly stewardship intent.

Significantly, this word is used by Paul elsewhere in Romans. Paul writes in Rom 1:21 of the 'futility' of wicked humanity that is darkened in its understanding, becoming 'futile in their thinking' (ἀλλὰ ἐματαιώθησαν ἐν τοῖς διαλογισμοῖς αὐτῶν) fundamentally through rejection of God and idolatry (1:21–23)—precisely the catalyst for the Deuteronomic curse of any people and land as previously discussed. Centring around this important word in Paul's Romans vocabulary we may construct a unifying scheme (see Figure 5).

---

33 With the great majority of commentators.
34 Braaten, 'All Creation Groans', 136.
35 Jewett speaks of the thorns and thistles of Gen. 3:18 as 'symbols' of 'endless frustration in the human interaction with the natural environment'. Jewett, *Romans*, 513.
36 Bauer, Gingrich, and Arndt, *A Greek-English Lexicon of the New Testament*, 495.

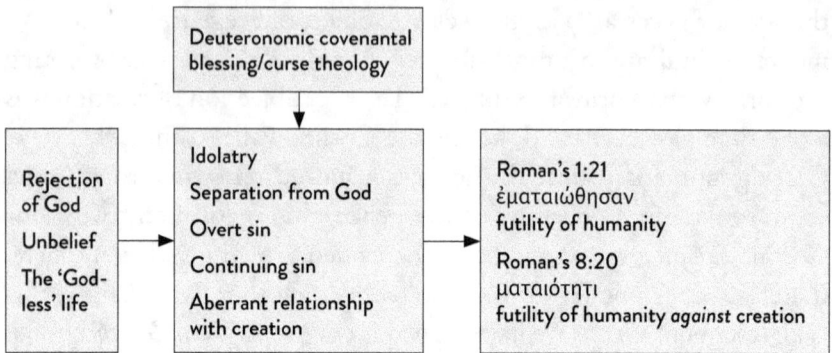

Figure 5. In Romans, 'futility' of humanity affects both humanity and creation generally.

The creation was subjected to frustration 'by the will of the one who subjected it in hope'. Though the agent is not identified, the best explanation is the Creator Himself.[37] Overt human evil and wickedness has damaged creation from the outset and continues to do so, yet the Creator has allowed this in His wisdom and patience, affecting a sovereign subjection by Him. Certainly this would not be the only case of God's subjection of an entity to humanity's sin: examples can be found in His timely and patient relenting of judgement in the face of protracted Amorite sin (Gen. 15:16), His allowance of divorce amongst Israelites (Mark 10:1–9), His giving over of the godless to their sin (Rom. 1:24,26,28), and His consigning of all to disobedience for the sake of His mercy (Rom. 11:32). Moreover, from 1 Isaiah's judgement oracles involving creation, it makes sense to speak of the damage and decay of creation as occurring under Yhwh's subjection.

8:21. ἀπὸ τῆς δουλείας τῆς φθορᾶς 'from bondage to decay' or 'from enslavement to ruin and destruction'. Greek δουλεία means slavery or servitude, including under a person (T. 12 Patr. Joseph 1:5; 10:3), to fear (Rom. 8:15) or the fear of death (Heb. 2:15), or to godless world principles (Gal. 5:1).[38] This implies an authority structure where power

---

37 For an informative discussion of alternatives, see Ziesler, *Paul's Letter to the Romans*, 219–220.
38 Zerwick and Grosvenor, *A Grammatical Analysis of the Greek New Testament*, 476; Bauer, Gingrich, and Arndt, *A Greek-English Lexicon of the New Testament*, 205.

is exerted over the one in bondage. In our passage, the Pauline thought is slavery τῆς φθορᾶς. φθορᾶς can have a range of meanings including ruin, death, destruction, corruption, decay and even pollution.[39] Of note, elsewhere in the NT decay/corruption is the result of overt human evil (an ethical connection[40]): it refers to the corruption in the world caused by evil human desires (2 Pet. 1:4 ἀποφυγόντες τῆς ἐν τῷ κόσμῳ ἐν ἐπιθυμίᾳ φθορᾶς), of the slavery to corruption of false prophets (2 Pet. 2:19 αὐτοὶ δοῦλοι ὑπάρχοντες τῆς φθορᾶς), and the principle of reaping corruption by sowing to one's sinful nature (Gal. 6:8 ὅτι ὁ σπείρων εἰς τὴν σάρκα ἑαυτοῦ ἐκ τῆς σαρκὸς θερίσει φθοράν; φθοράν contrasted with eternal life). Bauer notes that, when it is applied to the world of nature, 'the reason for the destruction is not found in the word itself, but must be made clear by an addition'. It is not clear in our present text what that addition is; therefore, broadly the meaning is slavery to ruin, destruction, dissolution, deterioration or corruption. We note, however, in the majority of examples, the ruin and destruction (whether within nature or in other situations) is of an unnatural, invasive kind,[41] consistent with overt sin acting extrinsically. Moreover, 1 Isaiah's description of creation's disintegration due to humanity's overt sin (Table 1) carries many descriptors that fit soundly into Paul's 'enslavement to ruin and destruction': trembling, languishing, in distress, shaken, laid waste, devastated, drying up and withering, wasting, defiled, consumed, broken up, split asunder, violently shaken, swaying and reeling, ruined, destroyed, made desolate, stripped, parched, shrivelled, and failed.

Thus, it is a reasonable explanation to infer that creation is enslaved under humanity's overt power that invades, ruins and corrupts. That power originates from the lordship given to humanity by the Creator

---

39 Bauer, Gingrich, and Arndt, *A Greek-English Lexicon of the New Testament*, 858.
40 Murray, *The Epistle to the Romans*, 304. Murray is one of the very few who considers this ethical connection but rejects it because 'φθορά itself would not be predicated of the creation'. In disagreement, creation *can* be corrupted (ruined, destroyed) by overt human evil, with this corruption occurring outside the realm of the essence and fabric of creation. Peter's meaning in 2 Pet. 1:4 is similar: 'that you may escape the corruption in the world caused by evil human desires'.
41 Bauer, Gingrich, and Arndt, *A Greek-English Lexicon of the New Testament*, 858. Examples: caught animals destined to be killed, destruction by abortion, seduction of a virgin, the ruin of moral depravity.

(Gen. 1:28), a power now mutated by humanity's evil, and under which it has been decreed by the Creator that the subjected creation does not have the power to negate it.

8:22. οἴδαμεν γὰρ ὅτι 'for we know that'. The phrase is used here and elsewhere by Paul in Romans (2:2; 3:19; 7:14; 8:28) to bring the readers into a point of shared knowledge. To what shared knowledge was Paul referring? Jewett has gathered fascinating support to argue the readers knew of a theory in the Roman civic cult whereby humanity's continual failures and overt evil-doing down the ages had led to nature's corruption, only to be reversed through the Caesars' reigns. Critically for our claim in this chapter, this was not a once-only failure of humanity that cursed all creation and led to intrinsic decline.[42] Another viable possibility is that Paul reminds his readers of the sin-creation nexus found in Old Testament texts.

πᾶσα ἡ κτίσις 'all the creation'. We have already seen such a comprehensive tabulated description of creation in 1 Isaiah's judgement oracles and from other prophets such that, if Paul were borrowing from this sin-creation nexus, we can readily understand him subsuming the many creation categories under his own expression, 'πᾶσα ἡ κτίσις'. Thus, we would say that Paul's 'all creation' need not—indeed, should not—be taken in our modern, literal and scientific sense, but is to be understood as all the created world of which Paul's contemporaries were familiar and of which they had contact.

πᾶσα ἡ κτίσις συστενάζει καὶ συνωδίνει Creation is 'groaning together as in the pains of childbirth'. The personification of creation is expounded by OT authors, a notable example being Isaiah 24 tabulated earlier. This is a sighing or groaning used in connection with an undesirable circumstance or another's behaviour. It expresses a yearning that the situation would change.[43] Though rare in the New Testament, it is far more common in the LXX (Paul's OT source) and consistently carries the context of one crying out for deliverance

---

42 Jewett, *Romans*, 516.
43 For example: 2 Cor. 5:2,4; Heb. 13:17; Mark 7:34. Bauer, Gingrich, and Arndt, *A Greek-English lexicon of the New Testament*, 766.

while under oppression from evil.⁴⁴ Thus, in 8:22, creation groans in its desire to change, and this is explained well by the overt and continual pressure brought to bear against it by the evil of an unbelieving humanity—an intended parallel with Paul's 'groaning' of believers in 8:23. Significantly, the same compound verb, συστενάζει, and the same concept of a personified groaning land due to human overt sin is found in Job 31:38–40 LXX.⁴⁵

All creation groans together (πᾶσα ἡ κτίσις συστενάζει). With contemporary eyes, it is easy to see what may be embedded in Paul's word choice here: creation exhibits in its 'goodness' a remarkable and exquisite balance of inter-connected life processes (i.e., the corruption of one process negatively affects a multitude of processes linked with it). The later section discussing contemporary examples will illustrate this.

Mention must be made of Jonathan Moo's article supporting the hypothesis that Isaiah 24–27 'provides the primary source for Paul's description of the ruin and groaning of creation in Romans 8:19–22', citing thematic and verbal parallels and specifically Paul's citation (though not in Romans) of Isaiah 25:8 to strengthen the case. Moo's study of the thematic parallels (i.e., judgement, glory, suffering, hope, the earth personified) and LXX word parallels have weight;⁴⁶ yet, as shown earlier in this chapter, OT covenant blessing-curse theology involving the sin-creation nexus pervades many more texts than Isaiah 24–27 and is found beyond the Hebrew prophetic tradition. We would see this as adding more weight for the claim that this forms a firm principle in Israelite theology that Paul draws on without being tied down to specific texts. Nevertheless, Moo's conclusion is like ours: creation's slavery to ruin 'is a contingent slavery, such that it remains at the mercy of the effects of ongoing human sin and divine judgement'.⁴⁷

---

44 Moo, *The Epistle to the Romans*, 519.
45 Jewett, *Romans*, 516.
46 Though in Jonathan Moo's own words, this evidence 'cannot be said to provide anything like indisputable proof that Rom 8:19–22 depends on Isaiah 24–27'. Moo, 'Romans 8:19–22 and Isaiah's Cosmic Covenant', 86.
47 Moo, 'Romans 8.19-22 and Isaiah's Cosmic Covenant'. Braaten agrees with Moo in his analysis of Rom. 8:18–22: Creation is 'not redeemed from a fall of nature or a primeval curse on nature by God; rather, she is redeemed from the ongoing effects of human sin'. In Braaten, 'All Creation Groans', 154.

Our exegesis of Romans 8:18–22 demonstrates that it is possible to gather considerable support for Model 2 in Paul's theology. Analysis of other Pauline texts also shows that Paul's understanding of creation supports this model, and it is this to which we now turn.

Paul's Concept of Creation Agrees with Psalms' Confessional and Doxological Theology: Model 2 is Supported

We have seen previously that the Psalmists' portrait of current creation is not one that is projected by Model 1: that of intrinsic ruin, corruption, emptiness and purposelessness; rather, creation wonderfully reflects the goodness of Genesis 1's original creation. Pauline thought repeats just these concepts: a good, life-affirming and God-affirming present creation. In 1 Corinthians 15:40,41 Paul speaks of the 'glory' (here the common Pauline δόξα, also used in Rom. 8:18–26) of heavenly and earthly bodies and in Colossians 1:17 Paul magnifies the Son because he rules in creation and makes all created things 'cohere' (RSV). And significantly in Romans 1:20, he asserts that 'since the creation of the world'[48] (our post-Fall, present creation) 'the things that have been made' reveal God's eternal power and divine nature (exactly as in Psalms)—a revelation so distinct that humanity has no excuse for not seeing these qualities. In Romans 1:20, here the first human's sin has not infected the organic nature of creation. Here there is no judgement upon creation; there is only judgement pronounced upon the wickedness of humanity. Here, rather, creation stands over against humanity as it loudly testifies to the glory of God. It is humanity, not creation, that falls short of the glory of God (Rom. 3:23). The wrath of God is revealed against humanity; the witness to God is revealed by creation.

---

48 Taking ἀπὸ κτίσεως κόσμου temporally not spatially. With Murray, *The Epistle to the Romans*, 39, and Morris, *The Epistle to the Romans*, 81.

Contemporary Examples of Creation's Disintegration by Humanity: Model 2 is Supported

What of our contemporary world? No doubt the apostle Paul could not have perceived how current humanity has dominated our planet. Does this invalidate any use of the state of our present world to strengthen our argument? No. It makes far more sense to claim these groanings continue to our present day. Paul says 'creation has been groaning right up to the present time'; thus, why would creation's groaning suddenly cease from Paul's day forward? More likely the groanings grow ever louder as the tide of humanity swells and reaches ever further. Contemporary cases abound, but space permits our attention be given to only a few.

Humans Disrupt Trophic Cascades

The stability of creation's ecosystems[49] relies on the balance of predatory and consumptive forces within what biologists term 'trophic cascades'.[50] Pace et al. has defined trophic cascades as 'reciprocal predator–prey effects that alter the abundance, biomass or productivity of a population, community or trophic level across more than one link in a food web'.[51] Cascades are diverse and widespread throughout earth's terrestrial, freshwater and marine ecosystems. In an un-disrupted cascade, an exquisite balance maintains the populations of life-forms and relationships between those forms. An example is the otter–urchin–kelp interaction of coastal North America, where 'otters stabilise a system of abundant kelp forests by reducing urchin grazing'.[52] However, human disruption of cascades can and does lead to ecosystem damage and the death of life-forms.[53]

---

49 Whitmee et al., 'Safeguarding Human Health in the Anthropocene Epoch', 1975. 'Ecosystem' is defined as 'a dynamic complex of plant, animal, and microorganism communities and the non-living environment acting as a functional unit'.
50 Ripple et al., 'What is a Trophic Cascade?'.
51 Pace et al., 'Trophic Cascades Revealed in Diverse Ecosystems', 483.
52 Pace et al., 'Trophic Cascades Revealed in Diverse Ecosystems', 484. For other examples, see https://www.youtube.com/watch?v=6dk0DGCa7ow and https://www.youtube.com/watch?v=M18HxXve3CM
53 Pace et al., 'Trophic Cascades Revealed in Diverse Ecosystems', 486. Ripple et al., 'Saving the World's Terrestrial Megafauna', 807.

Human Pollution Damages the Earth

In 2017, the Lancet Commission on Pollution and Health released its detailed study.[54] The headline figures speak for themselves: Man-made pollution causes disease, and these diseases were responsible in 2015 'for 16 per cent of all deaths worldwide, three times more deaths than AIDS, tuberculosis and malaria combined and 15 times more than from all wars and other forms of violence'.[55] The health of the whole globe is analysed in more depth in the Rockefeller Foundation-Lancet Commission on Planetary Health.[56] Again, the evaluation of a 'deeply concerned' Commission is cause for sober reflection:

> We have been mortgaging the health of future generations to realise economic and development gains in the present. By unsustainably exploiting nature's resources, human civilisation has flourished but now risks substantial health effects from the degradation of nature's life support systems in the future. Health effects from changes to the environment including climatic change, ocean acidification, land degradation, water scarcity, overexploitation of fisheries, and biodiversity loss pose serious challenges to the global health gains of the past several decades and are likely to become increasingly dominant during the second half of this century and beyond.[57]

Humans are Causing Devastating Climate Change

Contemporary climate change is primarily driven by increasing greenhouse gases resulting from fossil fuel emissions. So concerned are expert authors over this situation's gravity that in their abstract they remark, 'continuation of high fossil fuel emissions, given current knowledge of the consequences, would be an act of extraordinary

---

54 Landrigan et al., 'The Lancet Commission on Pollution and Health'.
55 See Figure 5.
56 Whitmee et al., 'Safeguarding Human Health in the Anthropocene Epoch'.
57 For graphical representation of these changes see Figure 2, page 1977 in Whitmee et al., 'Safeguarding Human Health in the Anthropocene Epoch'.

witting intergenerational injustice'.[58] The effects of climate change span a spectrum too broad to cover comprehensively here but include (to name but a few) unpredictable and extreme weather patterns that ravage human and non-human life-forms, loss of biodiversity through species decline and extinction, and loss of agricultural productivity.[59]

It is appropriate to conclude this section by bringing to our attention what many scientists agree on. Scientists are not often given to unrestrained figures of expression, yet in 1992 over 1700 concerned scientists published an article 'World Scientists' Warning to Humanity' saying, 'we the undersigned, senior members of the world's scientific community,[60] hereby warn all humanity of what lies ahead. A great change in our stewardship of the earth and the life on it, is required, if vast human misery is to be avoided and our global home on this planet is not to be irretrievably mutilated'.[61] Twenty-five years later, in November 2017, over 15,000 concerned scientists from over 180 countries signed a published 'second notice' saying that, apart from the reversal of ozone depletion, humanity has failed to address with enough speed or commitment so many of the environmental challenges outlined above.[62] The message heralds forth loudly: the ongoing overt acts of humanity are causing creation's suffering; therefore, Model 2 is supported.

Conclusion

It seems we have travelled far and wide from a simple focus on human ageing. Yet, it is hoped in exploring two fundamentally polarised

---

58   Hansen et al., 'Assessing Dangerous Climate Change'.
59   Hansen et al., 'Assessing Dangerous Climate Change'; Whitmee et al., 'Safeguarding Human Health in the Anthropocene Epoch'.
60   Of the 196 living Nobel Laureates at the time, 99 signed this document.
61   Ripple et al., 'World Scientists' Warning to Humanity: A Second Notice'. The 1992 warning is reproduced in Supplemental File S1. On page 4 of this file we read: 'This 1992 document was sent to governmental leaders all over the world [...] The document asks people to take immediate action to stop the ever-increasing environmental degradation that threatens global life support systems on this planet. The appeal was coordinated by Dr. Henry Kendall, Nobel Laureate (1990, Physics), and former Chairperson of the Union of Concerned Scientists'.
62   Ripple et al., 'World Scientists' Warning to Humanity: A Second Notice'.

models that both evaluate human ageing, one may appreciate that an undergirding foundational theology has the potential to profoundly influence a pastoral theology of ageing.

We opened this chapter by demonstrating that historical theology still has much contemporary commentary advocating a doctrine of the Cosmic Fall and, therefore, far from a discarded doctrine, it is still a force to be reckoned with today. This observation moved us forward to condense the doctrine's attributes into a model that relates sin to creation. This is a vital model for any theological examination of human ageing because it portrays human ageing as an enduring consequence of the effects of primeval sin on the fabric of all creation. According to this model, human biological ageing lies outside the 'goodness' of creation.

However, we have found substantial support for an alternative model that we term 'Cosmic Disintegration', while concurrently directly addressing the weaknesses of the Cosmic Fall model. First, the Cosmic Disintegration model offers greater explanatory integrity by providing a robust explanation to describe how humanity's ongoing, overt and specific sin damages and disintegrates creation. Second, it integrates the complimentary theology from Deuteronomy and the pre-exilic prophets that dovetails creation's damage with the ongoing overt and specific sin of all humanity. Third, it assimilates the Psalms' (and the Lord Jesus') life-affirming and God-affirming portrait of a currently good creation, a portrait that even includes creation's life-death cycle as a phenomenon evoking praise to God. Fourth, it incorporates an exegesis of texts from Romans 1 and 8 that advocates Paul's consistency with OT covenantal blessing-curse theology—that is, based on covenantal theology, a good creation is overtly and extrinsically ruined by acts of unbelief. And finally, the Cosmic Disintegration model encourages a fruitful theology-science dialogue by heeding the cry from multitudes of concerned expert scientists regarding humanity's damage to planetary health.

The collective evidence embraced by the Cosmic Disintegration model confronts us with the possibility that creation's 'deformity', 'present misery' and 'sombre hue' are errant theological constructions placed upon a truly good creation, and, critically, that human biological ageing remains a good part of that creation. The only qualification we make here refers back to Figure 1: extrinsic factors such as negligent lifestyle choice, pollution, and unhealthy diet can accelerate ageing. We do not class these factors as creationally good but as belonging within the milieu of factors that disintegrate creation. Nonetheless, to classify human biological ageing (defined in Figure 1 as the intrinsic ageing process) as creationally good is to lay a foundation upon which a constructive and caring pastoral theology of ageing can be built.

Bibliography

Augustine. *City of God.* Translated by Henry Bettenson. (3rd ed. London, England: Penguin Classics, 2003).

Barth, K. *The Epistle to the Romans.* Translated by Edwyn C. Hoskyns. (6th ed. Oxford, England: Oxford University Press, 1968).

Bauer, W., Gingrich, F. W., and Arndt, W. F. *A Greek-English Lexicon of the New Testament and Other Early Christian Literature* (2nd rev. edn. Chicago, IL and London, England: University of Chicago Press, 1979).

Beker, J. C. *Paul the Apostle: The Triumph of God in Life and Thought* (Philadelphia, PA: Fortress, 1980).

Bimson, J. J. 'Reconsidering a 'Cosmic Fall'', *Science and Christian Belief* 18, no. 1 (2006), 63–81.

Braaten, L. J. 'All Creation Groans: Romans 8:22 in Light of the Biblical Sources', *Horizons in Biblical Theology* 28, no. 2 (2006), 131–59.

Bruce, F. F. *Romans* (Tyndale New Testament Commentaries; 2nd ed. Nottingham, England: Inter-Varsity Press, 1985).

Calvin, J. *A Commentary on Genesis* (Geneva Series Commentary; London, England: The Banner of Truth Trust, 1965).

_____, *The Epistles of Paul to the Romans and Thessalonians* (Calvin's New Testament Commentaries; Grand Rapids, MI: William B. Eerdmans, 1960).

Cassuto, U. *A Commentary on the Book of Genesis. Part One* (Jerusalem, Israel: The Magness Press, 1961).

Chrysostom, Saint John. *Saint Chrysostom: Homilies on the Acts of the Apostles and the Epistle to the Romans.* A Select Library of the Nicene and Post-Nicene Fathers of the Christian Church. Edited by Philip Schaff. Vol. XI (Grand Rapids, MI: William B. Eerdmans, 1979).

Cranfield, C. E. B. *A Critical and Exegetical Commentary on the Epistle to the Romans: Introduction and Commentary on Romans I-VIII* (International Critical Commentary; Edinburgh, Scotland: T & T Clark, 1989).

Dong, X., Milholland, B. and Vijg, J. 'Evidence for a Limit to Human Lifespan', *Nature* 538, no. 7624 (October 13, 2016), 257–59.

Effros, R. B., C. V. Fletcher, K. Gebo, J. B. Halter, W. R. Hazzard, F. M. Horne, R. E. Huebner, *et al.* 'Aging and Infectious Diseases: Workshop on HIV Infection and Aging: What Is Known and Future Research Directions'. [In eng]. *Clinical Infectious Diseases* 47, no. 4 (August 15, 2008), 542–53.

Epel, E. S., E. H. Blackburn, J. Lin, F. S. Dhabhar, N. E. Adler, J. D. Morrow, and R. M. Cawthon. 'Accelerated Telomere Shortening in Response to Life Stress', [In eng]. *Proceedings of the National Academy of Sciences of the United States of America* 101, no. 49 (December 7, 2004), 17312–5.

Fitzmyer, J. A. *Romans: A New Translation with Introduction & Commentary* (The Anchor Bible; New York, NY: Doubleday & Company, 1993).

Foerster, W. 'κτίζω', Translated by Geoffrey W. Bromiley, in Gerhard Kittel (ed.) *Theological Dictionary of the New Testament* (Grand Rapids, MI: William B. Eerdmans 1965).

Godet, F. L. *Commentary on Romans* (Kregel Reprint Library; Grand Rapids, MI: Kregel, 1977).

Gowan, D. E. 'The Fall and Redemption of the Material World in Apocalyptic Literature', *Horizons in Biblical Theology* 7, no. 2 (1985), 83–103.

Hansen, J., P. Kharecha, M. Sato, V. Masson-Delmotte, F. Ackerman, D. J. Beerling, P. J. Hearty, *et al.* 'Assessing Dangerous Climate Change: Required Reduction of Carbon Emissions to Protect Young People, Future Generations and Nature', *PLoS One* 8, no. 12 (2013), e81648.

Hays, R. B. *Echoes of Scripture in the Letters of Paul* (New Haven, CT: Yale University Press, 1989).

Jewett, R. *Romans: A Commentary* (Hermeneia; Minneapolis, Minnesota: Fortress, 2007).

Kennedy, B. K., S. L. Berger, A. Brunet, J. Campisi, A. M. Cuervo, E. S. Epel, C. Franceschi, *et al.* 'Geroscience: Linking Aging to Chronic Disease'. *Cell* 159, no. 4 (November 6, 2014), 709–13.

Kim, S., C. G. Parks, L. A. DeRoo, H. Chen, J. A. Taylor, R. M. Cawthon, and D. P. Sandler. 'Obesity and Weight Gain in Adulthood and Telomere Length'. [In eng]. *Cancer Epidemiol Biomarkers Prev* 18, no. 3 (March 2009), 816–20.

Kruse, C. G. *Paul's Letter to the Romans* (The Pillar New Testament Commentary; Grand Rapids, Michigan: William B. Eerdmans, 2012).

Landrigan, P. J., R. Fuller, N. J. R. Acosta, O. Adeyi, R. Arnold, N. N. Basu, A. B. Balde, *et al.* 'The Lancet Commission on Pollution and Health'. *Lancet* 391, no. 10119 (February 3, 2018), 462–512.

Longenecker, R. N. *The Epistle to the Romans: A Commentary on the Greek Text* (New International Greek Testament Commentary; Grand Rapids, Michigan: William B. Eerdmans, 2016).

Mathews, K. A. *Genesis 1-11:26* (New American Commentary; Nashville, Tennessee: Broadman & Holman, 2002).

Merrill, E. H. *Deuteronomy.* (New American Commentary, Nashville, Tennessee: Broadman & Holman, 1994).

———, 'Pre-Human Death and the Effect of the Fall', *Criswell Theological Review* 14, no. 1 (Fall 2016), 15–22.

Moo, D. J. *The Epistle to the Romans* (New International Commentary on the New Testament; Grand Rapids, Michigan: William B. Eerdmans, 1996).

———, *Romans 1-8* Wycliffe Exegetical Commentary (Chicago, Illinois: Moody, 1991).

Moo, J. 'Romans 8.19-22 and Isaiah's Cosmic Covenant', *New Testament Studies* 54, no. 1 (2008): 74–89.

Morris, L. L.   *The Epistle to the Romans* (The Pillar New Testament Commentary; Grand Rapids, Michigan/Leicester, England: William B. Eerdmans/Inter Varsity Press, 1988).

Moyise, S.   *The Old Testament in the New: An Introduction* (Continuum Biblical Studies; London, England: Continuum, 2001).

———,   *Paul and Scripture* (Grand Rapids, Michigan: Baker Academic, 2010).

Murray, J.   *The Epistle to the Romans* (New International Commentary on the New Testament ; Grand Rapids, Michigan: William B. Eerdmans, 1968).

———.   *The Epistle to the Romans* (New International Commentary on the New Testament; Grand Rapids, Michigan: William B. Eerdmans, 1965).

Pace, M. L., J. J. Cole, S. R. Carpenter, and J. F. Kitchell.   'Trophic Cascades Revealed in Diverse Ecosystems', *Trends in Ecology & Evolution* 14, no. 12 (December 1999), 483–88.

Rimbach, J. A.   '"All Creation Groans": Theology/Ecology in St Paul', *The Asia Journal of Theology* 1, no. 2 (1987), 379–91.

Ripple, W. J., G. Chapron, J. V. Lopez-Bao, S. M. Durant, D. W. Macdonald, P. A. Lindsey, E. L. Bennett, et al.   'Saving the World's Terrestrial Megafauna', *Bioscience* 66, no. 10 (October 1, 2016), 807–12.

Ripple, W. J., J. A. Estes, O. J. Schmitz, V. Constant, M. J. Kaylor, A. Lenz, J. L. Motley, et al.   'What Is a Trophic Cascade?', *Trends in Ecology & Evolution* 31, no. 11 (November 2016), 842–49.

Ripple, W. J., C. Wolf, T. M. Newsome, M. Galetti, M. Alamgir, E. Crist, M. I. Mahmoud, and W. F. Laurance. 'World Scientists' Warning to Humanity: A Second Notice', *BioScience* 67, no. 12 (2017), 1026–28.

Surburg, M. P.   'Good Stuff!: The Material Creation and the Christian Faith', *Concordia Journal* 36, no. 3 (2010), 245–62.

Thompson, J. A.   *Deuteronomy: An Introduction and Commentary* (Tyndale Old Testament Commentaries; Leicester, England: Inter Varsity Press, 1974).

Vermeij, W. P., M. E. Dolle, E. Reiling, D. Jaarsma, C. Payan-Gomez, C. R. Bombardieri, H. Wu, *et al.* 'Restricted Diet Delays Accelerated Ageing and Genomic Stress in DNA-Repair-Deficient Mice', *Nature* 537, no. 7620 (September 15, 2016), 427–31.

Von Rad, G. *Genesis: A Commentary* (Old Testament Library; Rev. ed. Philadelphia, Pennsylvania: The Westminster Press, 1972).

Walsh, J. T. 'Genesis 2:4b-3:24: A Synchronic Approach', *Journal of Biblical Literature* 96, no. 2 (1977), 161–77.

Whitmee, S., A. Haines, C. Beyrer, F. Boltz, A. G. Capon, B. F. de Souza Dias, A. Ezeh, *et al.* 'Safeguarding Human Health in the Anthropocene Epoch: Report of the Rockefeller Foundation-Lancet Commission on Planetary Health', *Lancet* 386, no. 10007 (November 14, 2015), 1973–2028.

Whybray, R. N. *The Second Isaiah* (Old Testament Guides; Sheffield, England: JSOT Press, 1983).

Zerwick, M., and M. Grosvenor. *A Grammatical Analysis of the Greek New Testament* (5th rev ed. Rome, Italy: Editrice Pontificio Istituto Biblico, 1996).

Ziesler, J. A. *Paul's Letter to the Romans* (TPI New Testament Commentaries; London, England/Philadelphia, PA: SCM/Trinity, 1989).

CHAPTER 5

Theologies of ageing: A review of the literature

Michelle Eastwood

Abstract

Ageing is a growing area of concern, and this chapter argues that theologies of ageing are not well-developed within the literature. A critical review of key texts within the areas of biblical theologies, and experiential and theological treatises on ageing is presented. Gaps in the current literature are identified and some suggestions for future research are made. It is proposed future theologies of ageing must focus on ageing as a distinct life stage with specific challenges and opportunities and, furthermore, they must be clearly theological. Third, this area of research would benefit from a number of sustained discourses that develop a deep theology of ageing that considers the intersectional impacts of race, gender, culture, wealth, nutrition and particular life experiences.

Introduction

There has been a marked increase of interest in ageing over the last few years and this has been reflected in a growing amount of literature connecting ageing with various elements of faith, community and pastoral care. The Human Ageing Project, a research centre of the University of Divinity based at Catholic Theological College, East

Melbourne, has focused on ageing in the areas of spirituality, ethics, pastoral care and theology. Of these topics, theology is the one that is least well covered in the literature both in terms of depth and breadth. Therefore, it would seem the time is ripe to develop more systematic theologies of ageing.

The aim in this chapter is to highlight key texts and discuss their contribution to the field of theologies of ageing. The literature is split into three main approaches: biblical, experiential and theological (while being acknowledged this is just one way to divide the material). The benefits of this division are that most texts fall neatly into one of these three categories. A further category may be pastoral theologies, although this distinction often has marked overlap with the other categories.

Theology, as Anselm famously described it, is 'faith seeking understanding'. Therefore, a theology of ageing may be considered in terms of faith seeking an understanding of ageing. Alternatively, a theology conceptualised as 'God-talk' may focus on the idea of what God thinks of ageing, or even what is God's purpose for the ageing body. These foundations are important to consider as they inform both the process and the outcome of a theology of ageing. Furthermore, the theological preferences and emphases of an author direct choices about the focus of the selected discourse, whether that be Trinitarian, ecclesial, Christological, practical or via other such lenses. In turn, this influences the potential outcomes and conclusions.

Why is it important to develop a theology of ageing specifically? As the proportion of older people in our society grows, so to do the conversations about ageing. These conversations range from economic considerations in terms of healthcare, pensions and a diminishing tax base through to discussions and laws related to dying. These important conversations can be enhanced through a diversity of voices, experiences and lenses. Theology can add to these discussions by encouraging foci such as the inherent value of each individual life, and what flourishing looks like, even in the face of senescence and death. The development of multiple theologies of ageing will help to reflect the heterogeneity of experiences that are informed by the cumulative and intersectional effects of gender, race, culture, class, health, and nutrition that are found in the lives of older individuals.

Biblical Theologies

Biblical theologies of ageing take two main approaches: older characters in the Bible and thematic understandings of ageing. The literature in each of these categories is limited by the small number of specific references to ageing within the biblical text and their limited length. Jesus, as the incarnational embodiment of God, did not live beyond early middle age and, therefore, Christological theologies of ageing must be inferred from his teaching. The image of God the Father as an old man does not come directly from the biblical text; rather, it has been developed through artistic representations and implied characteristics throughout history. The writers of the gospel and the epistles all seem unconcerned with ageing per se due to their eschatological focus on the imminent return of Jesus. Despite these difficulties, Carol Stockhausen and John Painter have written articles that aim to develop Pauline theologies of ageing.

Stockhausen in *Paul's Theology of Aging* argues that the apostle does not speak about ageing because he is living for the eschaton; however, we are able to develop a theology through his writings on human frailty that are taken as 'analogous statements'.[1] Stockhausen then focuses on statements regarding death and the power of God to overcome death. The other option to death (as presented in the article) is service to others. The inference that can be drawn is that ageing is limited to a precursor to death, during which the general Pauline injunction is to first serve others. While it is important not to shy away from discussions of death as the inevitable end of the ageing process, it should not be seen as the extent of the ageing experience.

Stockhausen implies that Paul lived in a culture that always valued older people as per the instruction in the Hebrew Bible, and that this was enshrined in laws. Therefore, there was no reason for him to make special considerations for this group. However, there is an argument to be made that, if older people are being looked after, there is no need to create laws to enforce it. It can be tempting to idealise the past in terms of ageing individuals, but this does not do justice to

---

[1] Stockhausen, *Paul's Theology of Aging*, 343.

the historical records on ageing.[2]

Finally, Stockhausen links Paul's attitude to old things generally—the old world, the old self—with potential understandings of older people that Paul may hold. The discussion about how 'old' is used to convey negative meanings and how this plays into our ideas about ageing is valuable and deserves consideration. However, in the context of Paul's writing, it is unfair to attribute negative feelings towards older individuals from illustrations of unrelated transformations from old to new.

Alternately, in *Outward Decay and Inward Renewal: A Biblical Perspective on Aging and the Image of God,* Painter bases his Pauline theology of ageing within the early chapters of 2 Corinthians with a particular focus on 4:16: 'So we do not lose heart. Even though our outer nature is wasting away, our inner nature is being renewed day by day'.[3] He argues that Paul sees humans as earthen vessels created from the dust of the earth, in the image of God. This image connotes the fragility of the human body, which is exacerbated through the ageing process. This is contrasted with inner renewal and transformation that comes from being in relationship with God.

Painter suggests that, in a contemporary context, old people are not valued because wisdom and experience are not valued. He contrasts this with the capacity of physically sound individuals to extend their working life. This places the value of the aged person within their ability to contribute economically, which, in itself, undervalues the benefit of the wisdom of older individuals as a gift to their families and wider communities.

Furthermore, Painter states that 'a sound, healthy, fit body provides a great basis for a vigorous spirituality [...] Physical fitness has its impact on spirituality'.[4] The implication of this statement may be read as, older people who are not physically fit will have a diminished or listless faith. In this conception, those in the fourth age who are facing physical decrepitude and imminent death are dismissed as incapable and lacking

---

[2] For more information about the diversity of perspectives on ageing throughout history see Thane, *Long History of Old Age*; and Minois, *History of Old Age*.
[3] The NRSV translation has been used throughout this chapter.
[4] Painter, *Outward Decay, Inward Renewal*, 51.

even the potential for growth. This is in contrast to those in the third age, who, while considered old, may still have the capacity for spiritual growth. In this way, the generative image of God who is making all things new is limited to the healthy elderly who are able to contribute in some way. There is a paradox within this article that argues for a positive inner transformation in spite of the negative outward degeneration, which is illustrated through images of physical capacity.

These are two articles demonstrating some of the difficulties of developing a theology of ageing generally and extrapolating a theology on the basis of scant references to ageing within the New Testament text and Pauline corpus specifically. Rachel Dulin's *A Crown of Glory* and Harris' *Biblical Perspectives on Aging* develop theologies of ageing based on a broader consideration of ageing within the biblical text. As Dulin notes, 'the issue of old age is not treated systematically or comprehensively in any part of the biblical literature'[5] and, therefore, she adopts a phenomenological approach to determine characteristic features within the text. Both authors use examples such as the reported ages of the forefathers in Genesis, examples of older characters such as Abraham and Sarah, as well as commandments, laws and wisdom sayings related to the elderly. This results in the notions that old age is a blessing for a life well lived and that old age should be a time of honour.

Old age as a time of honour is connected to the command from the Decalogue to honour one's parents (Exod. 20:12; Deut. 5:16) and is reflected in the idea that children and grandchildren are evidence of blessings in one's later years (Job 42:16–17). It is also reflected in phrases such as 'length of days' (Deut. 30:20; Job 12:12; Ps. 21:4; Prov. 3:2) and 'good old age' (Gen. 15:15, 25:8; Judg. 8:32; 1 Chr. 29:28), which indicate the hope that death will be postponed for those who serve the Lord. Honour for aged persons is often idealised as a biblical ideal; however, as Harris notes, 'although the Hebrew Bible does not record a history of treatment for the elderly, it contains indirect evidence that implies that in Israel practices toward the elderly often fell short of its ideals'.[6] Of course, this is also the reality within many

---

5   Dulin, *Crown of Glory*, 5.
6   Harris, *Biblical Perspectives on Aging*, 41.

modern contexts and perhaps reminds us that how to deal with ageing is a perennial problem.

Dulin focuses mainly on the positive examples of ageing, while Harris notes the elderly are also portrayed as intransigent, impotent and senile. For example, Isaac, in his senility, is tricked by Jacob into bestowing the blessing on the 'wrong' son (Gen. 27), and there is also the picture of David on his deathbed unable to be 'warmed' by his nubile young companion—warmed, in this case, meaning unable to be sexually aroused (1 Kgs. 1:1–4). There is also the bareness of Sarah's womb, which takes an intervention from Yhwh to rectify the issue of Abraham having no suitable heirs (Gen. 18). Similarly, Hannah's older and barren state is the cause of much grief for her, which impacts on her husband, Peniniah (1 Sam. 1–2:21). For women in the Bible, ageing is often associated with being no longer able to bear children. The Bible does give us instances of the problems of old age (Eccl. 12), but theologians have tended to avoid these pictures in favour of instances of veneration for the elderly.

It is also worth noting that anthropological and other historical data that has emerged from this period suggests the subsistence lifestyle of the ancient Near East meant that not many people lived to old age as we know it. The Hebrew Bible uses such terms as זָקֵן (zaqen; 'grey haired'), or שֵׂיבָה (se'bah; 'elders'), both of which can be translated as 'old'; however, it is plausible these terms may refer to anyone from middle age onwards. The elders are the patriarchs of the family rather than an age-based qualification; therefore, drawing specific links to a theology of ageing from their circumstance is somewhat tenuous. Furthermore, the specific references to ageing and old age are relatively rare and, therefore, may be insufficient from which to develop an extended biblical theology. Joel Ajayi in his *Biblical Theology of Gerassapience* gives an overview of the Hebrew lexicography of words relating to ageing and wisdom in the Hebrew text, arguing these two conceptions form a dyad in the biblical literature. This is an interesting proposition; however, he spends most of the book discussing wisdom with little consideration for ageing. This makes his argument of a dyad unconvincing as a whole, but this is not to say that the two words are wholly unrelated. This argument encourages the idea that, in the biblical text, wisdom is synonymous with ageing, even though this is not borne out in his analysis.

A biblical theology of ageing provides evidence that many of the issues of ageing and the aged today are not so far from the experience of the biblical authors who spanned a wide breadth of historical, social and cultural contexts. Given the primacy of the biblical text as a basis for doctrine, theology and liturgy (particularly in evangelical contexts), there is a need to dig deeper into the little known or considered examples of ageing within the Bible. This would generate a movement away from an idealised or sainted idea of ageing and, instead, allow for grappling with ageing from a variety of perspectives and understandings.

Understanding the Experience of Ageing

There are two books that explore a more empirical approach to theology and ageing. Robert M. Gray and David O. Moberg interviewed a selection of aged persons within the church to discern how the church could better deal with older people This is detailed in their book *The Church and the Older Person*, published in 1977. This book reflects many notions of its time (including understandings of gender) that may seem outdated to the contemporary reader. However, the question of what the church can do to support older people and what can be expected of the them individually is still relevant.

Ian Knox, author of *Older People and the Church*, undertook similar research published in 2002. Despite the gap between these two publications, the findings are strikingly similar. Knox suggests one of the reasons the needs of older people are forgotten is they are not significantly different from any others needs within the church—that is, the need to alleviate anxiety about death, giving support in difficult circumstances, providing opportunities to participate and companionship, and meeting basic socio-psychological needs are all needs expressed by all people and not just aged individuals.[7] The needs Knox identified are related to the five Principles for Older Persons, developed

---

7   Knox, *Older People and the Church*, 214.

by the United Nations in 1999 (The Year of Older People). The principles are *independence, participation, care, self-fulfilment and dignity*, all of which Knox observes are relevant to all members of the community. In terms of theologies of ageing, this should prompt the question of how these principles apply specifically to older people, particularly those within our faith communities. Additionally, are there other special considerations that need to be kept in mind when considering the needs of older people?

Gray, Moberg and Knox show us the best way to answer this question is to ask elderly people themselves. These issues can be addressed by building a community that listens and values older people and is willing to act on their behalf. Furthermore, these are questions that need to be asked continually and consistently lest we fall into the trap of assuming we know the needs of our elderly members and overlook issues that have not yet emerged within our own contexts.

There are also a number of texts that reflect on personal experiences of ageing, either of the author or of their loved ones. Anecdotal experience, as with all case studies, gives us important information and often a more detailed examination of experiences. However, anecdotal experience is always limited to the individual and requires further validation before being accepted as normative. It offers hints about where to look for more information and perspectives that have been left out, ignored, or otherwise not represented. It also comes with narrative perspectives that may infer causation where none exists. It is the nature of the human brain to connect our experiences into coherent stories that colour our memories and the re-telling of them. This reinforces the idea that we need to continue to ask older people their experience to be able to develop consistent themes and understandings. Theologies based on the actual experience of ageing remains an undeveloped area of the literature and has the potential for further investigation. This is particularly true in seeking understandings of how intersections such as gender, culture, race, and class impact the experience of ageing.

Theological Approaches

The final and largest category is theological approaches, both practical and systematic. When we look at the theological categories there are number of themes that arise, such as ageing as suffering, death and decline; ageing as a time of growth and spiritual development; ageing as a catalyst to consider embodiment, creation theology and the imago Dei; ageing as a foretaste of heaven; and the effect of ageing on relationships. Each theme leads the author in a different direction as they grapple with the effects of physical decline and the potential for spiritual and/or emotional growth. The texts selected in this chapter reflect key ideas as well as some of the diversity within this field.

Earl Dahlstrom in *Toward a Theology of Aging* presents ageing through the theological concerns of time, creation, man, vocation, and salvation. He argues ageing is part of God's creative design and, therefore, should be valued as part of God's will for humanity. He also explains 'there is no special theology for the aging' and that time is only a human concept antithetical to a timeless God.[8] It strikes me as interesting and perhaps problematic that you would write a piece on the theology of ageing when you think it does not exist as a meaningful category. However, his idea of old age as an accomplishment or climax of 'God's intent in the creation of persons' is worthy of further consideration.[9] Is old age in and of itself an accomplishment? Or is it the nature of what someone does in their old age that is important? These questions are important given the knowledge the impact of poverty and other hardships demonstrably reduce average longevity; therefore, a theology of ageing that privileges number of years may implicitly contain classist assumptions.

David Tracy's *Eschatological Perspectives on Ageing* presents the idea ageing is 'our most concrete existential encounter with our own peculiarly human reality as historical and temporal beings'.[10] Tracy explains that learning to understand and even reverence the experience of ageing allows us to learn about authentic humanity, which is what

---

8   Dahlstrom, *Toward a Theology of Aging*, 12.
9   Dahlstrom, *Toward a Theology of Aging*, 8.
10 Tracy, *Eschatological Perspectives on Aging*, 120.

both Christian and Jewish theologies call us to do. He presents this argument in terms of traditional, prophetic, and apocalyptic models that encourage us to focus on the enduring nature of the discussion of ageing. He also considers the way our vision of temporality—past, present and future—impacts our understanding of ageing. Drawing on Tracy's ideas of temporality, Dale M. Schlitt argues memory embodies the experience of ageing, and 'the way in which we come to terms with the present so as to be able to live for the future, which for the ageing means especially living for others, is by making reference to and depending upon a mediating past'.[11] Tracy's conception of ageing is the closest one comes to a systematic discussion of the theology of ageing, and it would be beneficial to have the ideas he presented explored in a longer text.

Drew Christiansen in *And Your Elders Will Dream Dream's* argues the cultural focus on the model of free, uncommitted, self-indulgent early adulthood flattens our understanding of the natural life-course and denies the experience of progressive loss and diminishment of ageing. As he notes, 'aging is a process that transpires over a long period of years, comprising a succession of transitions and crises that over time force attention to ultimate realities and profoundly change the self-understanding of the elderly'.[12] In this conception, the main role of old age is portrayed as preparation for dying. This can lead to a deprivation of meaning linked to ageing, especially for those who experience an extended state of infirmity and longevity. The idea that decrepitude in ageing forces the individualistic Westerner into patterns of inter-dependence, that makes one more receptive to grace as a potential outcome (rather than a given) and, therefore, further consideration should be given to the variables that lead to this graceful state.

In a similar way, Lars Tornstan contrasts normative cultural understandings with a theologically informed conception of ageing. He promotes the idea of 'gerotranscendence', which is 'a shift in meta-perspective, from a materialistic and pragmatic view of the world to a

---

11 Schlitt, *Theology and the Experience of God*, 149.
12 Christiansen, *A Catholic Perspective*, 445.

more cosmic and transcendent one'.[13] He presents the idea of spiritual thickness, where ageing is not simply a time of loss and diminution, but becomes a time of spiritual enlargement and fulfillment. This process is girded by a set of spiritual resources—*thickness*—that allows the individual to confront the final stages of life. This theory of gerotranscendence has been popular in the ageing literature and encourages a positive understanding that counters the many negative conceptions present.

Another positive understanding of ageing is evident in Lucien Richard's *Toward a Theology of Aging*, which proposes a social theology for the liberation of ageing persons. Liberation from ageism, he says, is comparable to racism and sexism, in that it involves a process of systematic stereotyping that permeates an individual and society's understanding of and relating to the elderly. This is vital and is a theology of ageing that stands in opposition to a culture based on domination and mastery, with the argument that humanity should be understood on the basis of self-emptying and inter-dependence or kenosis. The idea of kenosis is derived from Philippians 2:7, and the Greek word κενόω meaning 'to empty'. This type of theology is focused on the cross, which provides a basis for authentic optimism and hope, even for the aged person.

In *A Theology for the Older, Female HIV-Infected Body*, Christina Landman also argues from a liberation perspective. She demonstrates the case of HIV-infected widows who have been rejected by society provides an example to assist the reconsideration of ageing from a feminist viewpoint that takes embodiment seriously. For her, the physical body is embodied as a site of resistance and enjoyment, the symbolic body is the site of relationship and beauty, the political body is the site of energy, and the spiritual body can be viewed as the site of recreation and resurrection. Landman challenges us to view the body as a way of relating to God that is not determined by illness, social stigmatisation or religious prejudice. In the era of #metoo and #churchtoo, this is a valuable reminder that there is a clear gendered element to the experience of ageing that is not adequately considered in the literature.

---

13 Tornstam, *Gerotranscendence*, 144.

Raymond Studzinski provides a lived perspective in *A Practical Monastic Theology of Ageing*, wherein ageing is imagined as an unwanted guest who requires us to do things differently and find new ways to serve. This approach argues for an emphasis on hospitality first to the self, which necessitates the virtue of humility calling us to a truthful recognition before God as we deal with the 'shame' of ageing. He draws attention to the fact that 'successful ageing', a common theme in the ageing literature, implies that old people should be healthy, sexually active, engaged, productive and self-reliant. In other words, the old should be young, and this negates the lessons that ageing alone can teach. This reminds us that any theology of ageing must stay focused on the particular challenges and opportunities that ageing presents, as opposed to developing general ideas that are only tangentially linked to ageing.

Finally, Lawrence Lenoir offers a reflective piece titled *Graceful Ageing: A Reflection*, which contrasts his father's negative experience of ageing with that of his mother's, and with his own journey into old age. He argues graceful ageing requires an emotional stability that is fundamentally predicated on the ability to love and forgive. The opposite to love and forgiveness are 'emotional forts', which reflect cognitive distortions and a lack of meaning. This is as much a reflection on his relationship with his father, whose early trauma is portrayed as interfering in their relationship, and who the author is trying not to emulate as it is a piece about ageing.

There are also a number of articles that propose a pastoral theology of ageing, which tend to address primarily the question of how to deal with the old people in our faith communities. This is an important consideration that raises some of the practical issues in meeting the needs of the elderly beyond immediate family members. However, in these articles, the theology is often secondary and not well developed and, therefore, they will not be covered here.

Implications

I have so far provided a brief overview of some of the territory that has been covered within the literature on theologies of ageing. It is worth noting ageing is not a homogenous experience. It is informed through a lifetime of work or unemployment; children, grandchildren and family or none; success; failure; illness; and health. There are so many trajectories life can take that the idea of ageing as a unitary experience is quite problematic. Furthermore, these affects are cumulative and often exacerbated over many years, and, in turn, can magnify the original difference. This is reflected in the literature and should be seen as an opportunity enabling us to consider the complexity and breadth of the experience of ageing. It reflects the wider field of gerontology, which also includes a diverse number of disciplines including psychology, sociology, biology, anthropology and others. It is also a caution not to essentialise the experience or meaning of ageing, because in doing so some people would inevitably be excluded.

There are clear gaps in the literature related to theologies of ageing, just as there are multiple ways of approaching theology leading to a plethora of assumptions, perspectives, and theological lenses. Therefore, it is unsurprising that developing a singular theology of ageing is difficult—and perhaps impossible. However, the nature and experience of ageing, along with the growing proportion of people who are older within society more broadly and who are part of our faith communities, are deserving of consideration and theological attention. In this endeavour, three ideas should be kept at the forefront.

First, it must be about ageing. A number of the theologies of ageing read like a general theology, with ageing tacked on as an afterthought. William Hendrick's notes in the introduction of *A Theology for Aging* that childhood and old age are the bookends of life. He had written a theology of childhood, and this was his theology of ageing. This text read like a general protestant theological discourse, with occasional references to issues that an aged person may be dealing with. There was nothing specific to the experience of ageing, the challenges and benefits.

Unfortunately, this approach is not exceptional. Many pieces that claim to be theologies of ageing do not relate specifically to the ageing process or experience. This is not to suggest ageing is such a distinct process and time that it has no correlations with other stages of life. I argue here, however, that if you are going to write on ageing, it needs to engage with a number of the specific concerns of ageing (e.g., physical, mental and emotional decline, reduced capacity for social involvement, potential increases in spirituality and wisdom, and dealing with the loss of loved ones). How to deal with those approaching death is another area that has not been systematically dealt with in terms of theologies of ageing—although, it has been covered within the areas of ethics and pastoral care. There are likely other issues of ageing that would also benefit from theological consideration that have not been approached within research. These ideas can only be revealed when we undertake the work of listening to people who are actually experiencing old age.

Within the literature, there has been very little research conducted on healthy aged members of faith communities. Much of the research on ageing focuses on individuals who are in aged care, or are the beneficiary of specific aged-related interventions. This is understandable given they present a 'captive' population for research, so to speak. However, this focus limits our understanding of the vast majority of people who are ageing in place. It may also subtly encourage a focus on the losses and difficulties of ageing, rather than the experience of satisfaction and growth. Given this, there is potential for writing and research on topics such as celebrating age as a rite of passage, theologies of retirement and the movement out of full-time paid work for both men and women, and relationships with children, grandchildren and perhaps even great grandchildren. Choosing to focus on older people within our communities and listening to their experiences reminds us to see the older people filling the pews as valid and valued members of the community.

Second, a theology of ageing must be theological. This may sound like a tautology; however, a number of works have 'theology' and 'ageing' in the title but are little more than personal reflections. This is not to suggest reflection is not useful or beneficial. It also does not imply reflection cannot or should not provide a suitable basis for a theology of ageing. However, a good theology must go beyond our individual experiences. Ideally, it will link into the wider Christian discourses and consider how our understanding of ageing impacts our theological thinking, and how the theological imagination relates to our perception of ageing.

An example of this is how a Christological perspective on ageing may wrestle with the fact that the incarnated Christ was crucified in his early thirties, long before the impact of ageing would have been felt within his body. Therefore, there is a need to consider how his words, actions and example may be applicable to those in the second half of life. Another tangent that could be explored is an ecclesiological consideration of ageing. How does the church view its ageing members, particularly in a time when they are the majority attenders? How does this fit with church traditions? Has the role of ageing within congregations changed historically, or are we living in such a time that it should change? There is also work to be done exploring the idea of intergenerationality and how older people interact with, support, engage and live in relationship with others of different age groups for the benefit of all. This would be a particularly interesting discussion in contexts such as *Messy Church*, where grandparents and grandchildren come together in new forms of worship. Furthermore, this raises questions regarding the role of grandparents within the church— biological, familial, and adopted as family in Christ. These ideas are the tip of the iceberg in terms of the potential to develop understandings of ageing within the theological tradition.

It should be noted a number of the articles mentioned here do engage theologically with ageing. Principally, these contain Tracy's consideration of eschatological elements of ageing and Landman's engagement with embodiment and Christian community. These two articles demonstrate an ability to hold theological insights and frameworks in tension with the benefits and difficulties of ageing, from both an individual and a community perspective. They provide an excellent start; however, they are brief articles, which necessarily limits the discussion. And here we come to the last point: it is time for some extended thinking on these topics.

There are very few texts that develop a book or thesis length theology of ageing. As noted, there are a few that deal with biblical perspectives on ageing, and some older texts that have general theologies with a smattering of ageing. There are also books on spirituality and ageing or ageing and pastoral care; however, there are very few books that specifically endeavour to develop a theology of ageing. This represents a substantial gap in the literature that should be addressed.

A New Testament theology of ageing or development of a Pauline perspective on ageing would be valuable given that most of the biblical theologies of ageing focus mainly on Old Testament examples. The case of widows and the way they are an exemplar for ageing women is a possibility for further consideration. Alternately, a theology of ageing may engage with the ideas of soteriology, biblical anthropology and other areas of systematic theological discourse to explore how these may interact with the lived experience of ageing.

There is the possibility of considering how the ideas of continuity and change can be parsed through the lens of ageing. The metaphor of life as a journey may also be a rich source of material: What does it mean to reach the destination? What is the destination? And how does it affect the journey not knowing when we will get there or any details about what we will find when we get there?

Is there a place for a theological consideration of memory and ageing? If we lose our memories, do we lose our humanity? And when we cannot share in communal remembering, what happens to our place in community? This topic has been addressed somewhat in the literature on dementia and spirituality, but there does not seem to be anything with a specific theological focus. These are just a few of the possibilities.

In my doctoral thesis, I am writing on the intersection between shame and ageing for women. I am taking a gendered approach to ageing as I know that women are more likely to live longer and be in ill health for an extended period before they die. They are also increasingly more likely to be living in poverty at the end of their life. The negative experience of ageing for women is also exacerbated by constructions of what it means to be female, which are tied up in youth, beauty and having children. This can lead to a sense of invisibility and uselessness that is often seen as shameful for older women.

When I have mentioned the topic of my thesis to some older women, they gleefully inform me that, in their old age, they have less shame than ever before. I am genuinely pleased for them and acknowledge old age can be a time when the shackles of social demands are thrown off. This also would be an interesting area for further investigation. However, I also know shame is a very difficult topic to talk about, one that is often hidden, and I wonder, given time to explore further, whether I would find there are untold stories of shame and what it means to be an old woman.

My research also makes me aware there should be research looking at the shame of old men. I suspect this has a different quality to female shame, especially given constructions of masculinity that are rooted in ideas of physical strength. This is also an area where further investigation could be conducted.

In this way, theologies of ageing may reflect the interdisciplinary breadth of gerontology and consider psychological, biological, sociological and cultural forms of ageing. The literature to date has mostly focused on Western understandings that ignore intersections of race, culture, sexuality and gender identity.

Conclusion

There is a wide range of literature that takes a theological approach to ageing, from biblical theologies through to pastoral considerations. However, most of the work is superficial in content and understanding. Therefore, there is an opportunity to develop our understandings of ageing from a range of theological lenses. This may assist those who are facing the concerns and difficulties of old age to value their own experience and to also be valued by the wider faith community. There is much more to be said on this topic, and we invite those working in this area to continue dialogue with the Human Ageing Project as we seek to answer some of the questions raised throughout this chapter.

Bibliography

Ajayi, J. A. A.	*Biblical Theology of Gerassapience* (New York: Lang Peter Publishing Inc., 2010).
Christiansen, D.	'A Catholic Perspective', in Kimble, M., McFadden, S., Ellor, J., Seeber, J. (eds.), *Aging, Spirituality, and Religion: A Handbook* (Minneapolis: Augsberg Fortress Publishers, 2003), 444–59.

Dahlstrom, E. C.   'Toward a Theology of Aging', *The Covenant Quarterly* 37, no. 1 (1979): 3–15.

Dulin, R. Z.   *A Crown of Glory: A Biblical View of Aging* (New Jersey: Paulist Press, 1988).

Gray, R. M., and Moberg, D. O.   *The Church and the Older Person* (Grand Rapids: William. B. Eerdmans Publishing Company, 1977).

Harris, J. G.   *Biblical Perspectives on Aging: God and the Elderly* (Abingdon-on-Thames: Routledge, 2013).

Hendricks, W. L.   *A Theology for Aging* (Nashville: Broadman Press, 1986).

Knox, I. S.   *Older People and the Church* (Edinburgh: T & T Clark, 2002).

Landman, C.   'A Theology for the Older, Female HIV-Infected Body', *Exchange* 37, no. 1 (2008), 52–67.

Lenoir, L.   'Graceful Aging: A Reflection', *New Theology Review* 23, no. 4 (2010), 21–29.

Minois, G.   *History of Old Age* (Cambridge: Polity Press, 1989).

Painter, J.   'Outward Decay and Inward Renewal: A Biblical Perspective on Aging and the Image of God', *Journal of Religious Gerontology* 12, no. 3–4 (2001, 2001), 43–55.

Richard, L.   'Toward a Theology of Aging', *Science et Esprit* 34, no. 3 (1982), 269–87.

Schlitt, D. M.   *Theology and the Experience of God*. (American Liberal Religious Thought, 8; (New York: P. Lang, 2001), 149.

Stockhausen, C. K.   'Paul's Theology of Aging', *The Bible Today* 30 (1992), 341–46.

Studzinski, R.   'A Practical Monastic Theology of Aging', *Benedictines* 61, no. 1 (2008), 6–21

Thane, P.   *The Long History of Old Age* (London: Thames & Hudson, 2007).

Tornstam, L.   'Gerotranscendence: The Contemplative Dimension of Aging', *Journal of Aging Studies* 11, no. 2 (1997), 143–154.

Tracy, D. W.   'Eschatological Perspectives on Aging', *Pastoral Psychology* 24, no. 229 (1975, 1975), 119–34.

CHAPTER 6

Karl Barth on the dignity and crown of suffering: Reimagining the fourth age for discipleship

Chris Swann

Abstract

This chapter explores some of the more unpleasant realities of ageing, dwelling in particular on the ways the so-called fourth ag is imagined as a period of dramatically diminished agency or even non-agency—and the effects of this on the way the preceding third age of active retirement is imagined. In this context, the chapter undertakes a retrieval of a distinction Karl Barth draws between the dignity and crown of suffering in the context of his late doctrine of sanctification (in Church Dogmatics IV/2 §66). After vindicating Barth's treatment of suffering against its critics, it proposes some important coordinates for its constructive appropriation of the dignity-crown distinction in reimagining the fourth age in terms of discipleship.

Confronting the Reality of Ageing

A voice called me in. I pulled back the curtain to the private room—if you could call it that. It was more of a cubicle in the corner of the hospital's geriatric ward. A chaplain had been requested. I was it. The woman on the bed inside staggered upright. She looked like a skeleton with gaunt, jaundiced skin draped over it. The room did not smell sanitary.

I was still attempting to compose myself so I could offer to pray with her when her adult children walked in with a nurse. As it turns out, it was the children who had requested a chaplain. They wanted to talk with me. Their mother was at the end of her life. As they shared, I learned the woman's daughter was saddened by the loss of dignity—and capacity—her mother was being subjected to. What her mother was enduring hardly seemed like life to her. In contrast, the woman's son longed for his mother to continue living. He was terrified on his mother's behalf of the unknown. Surely something—even this—was better than nothing.

I relate this story not to claim any particular insight or even that this situation was unique. It was particular. But it was also thoroughly ordinary. As ordinary as the end of life can be in our late-modern, medicalised Western context. We can prolong life—almost indefinitely in some cases—but we struggle to know how to begin answering questions regarding what makes a life really worth living. We may feel we know it when we see it. Nevertheless, debate about it always seems to arouse strong and visceral reactions, rapidly devolving into sharp divisions between camps that view each other with mutual incomprehension. Rarer still is clarifying disagreement let alone constructive progress.

It could be argued that, in an important sense, the astringency of contemporary debates around end of life issues—particularly where these touch on what scholars have begun to describe as the fourth age, that period of life beyond the bounds of active retirement—simply manifests the negativity and lack of coherence of the category of the fourth age itself. In fact, this is what Gilleard and Higgs contend.[1] They argue the fourth age is a social imaginary that functions as a dumping ground for all that we attempt to exclude from the preceding third age, which we are so busy rehabilitating and extending—whether medically or existentially—that anything that lies beyond it is rendered intrinsically repulsive. As they note, 'the commodification of the

---

1   Gilleard and Higgs, 'Aging without Agency'.

body, the development of anti-aging strategies, and the increasing differentiation of mass consumer society all illustrate how later life has been transformed as a field of agency and choice'.[2] Later life is now the arena of active (if not deferred) retirement and endless cruises or 'grey nomad' adventures, rather than a period of decline and preparation for death. Insofar as this narrow vision of flourishing captures our imagination about the third age, whatever comes after it is evacuated of positive meaning and content, becoming its inverse mirror image. As Gilleard and Higgs put it, the fourth age has become 'a kind of social or cultural "black hole" that exercises a powerful gravitational pull on the surrounding field of aging'.[3] The consumeristic and ageist distortions of the third age they catalogue are but one consequence of this negative gravitational effect.

The theological ethicist Oliver O'Donovan draws attention to the sphere of intergenerational communication as another place in which the negative gravitational effect of the fourth age may be witnessed. The distorting and pathological consequences of the fourth age imaginary in this sphere cluster around the reciprocal emotional themes of fear (on the part of the young) and bitterness and resentment (on the part of the old). O'Donovan observes that, with regard to the generational divide, 'when fear prevails on the one side and bitterness on the other, the relation between the generations can become a struggle for mastery, each trying to suppress the memory of human temporality the other's presence brings to mind'.[4] The extent of this distortion is particularly evident in contrast to the positive possibility of fruitful and healthy intergenerational relationships. As he describes:

> Each generation represents to the other a truth of its own human being: the truth of human generations who were here in the world before us, and of human generations who will be here in the world after us. The tone of the relation is [...] a wonder open to the appreciation of those who are simply different and not in competition. For the old it is an opportunity

---

2 Gilleard and Higgs, 'Aging without Agency', 121.
3 Gilleard and Higgs, 'Aging without Agency', 121–122.
4 O'Donovan, *Entering into Rest*, 216.

to recall their youth; for the young an opportunity to expand their horizons. Yet this exchange of gifts is accomplished in the relation of the two, not by mutual imitation but simply by enjoying the other's presence. To imitate is to be ridiculous, assuming the pompous dignity of years with inappropriate haste or aping the dress or speech of youth when it is no longer becoming, like an unseemly parody. Youth and age are mutually accessible in correspondence, not in assimilation.[5]

In his lyrical and poignant (possibly autobiographical) reflection, O'Donovan goes on to offer insight on the unique temptations older people face and enumerates various ways in which the tug towards competition and assimilation (rather than appreciation and correspondence) may make itself felt. These temptations do not only have physical aspects, such as those that often accompany the challenges and limitations of ageing bodies, where 'once cheerful, we may find ourselves often depressed; once outward-looking, we may become self-preoccupied'.[6] They also have social and cognitive as well as more 'spiritual' aspects.[7] In one way or another, each of them thematises the sense of threat at or grief over a loss of agency.

Socially and cognitively, for example, the world as one generation learns to inhabit and appreciate it is replaced by the world inhabited and appreciated quite differently by succeeding generations. Agency in world-making—or making oneself at home in the social world and reshaping it in the process—transfers from one generation to the next. And, as it does so, the older generation typically resists, resents and eventually laments this. 'The old are quite naturally perplexed at how the young arrange their business, at the compromises they make and the compromises they refuse to make'.[8] While perfectly understandable and appropriate in its place, the typical result of this is bewilderment, if not bitterness. Rather than a gift, the world-making activity of the

---

5   O'Donovan, *Entering into Rest*, 218.
6   O'Donovan, *Entering into Rest*, 219.
7   Interestingly, each of the aspects O'Donovan examines could be mapped more or less neatly onto the various chapters of Nussbaum and Levmore's *Aging Thoughtfully*.
8   O'Donovan, *Entering into Rest*, 220.

young is experienced as a threat. This occurs at the same time as when the old becomes ill-fitting, occasioning loss and grief—'our cultural clothing was not tailored to outlast us'.[9] Likewise, there is a 'spiritual' aspect to the temptations of ageing, which O'Donovan describes in terms of 'the burden of past experiences returning to haunt us'. Specifically, he highlights the way the experiences of youth can return 'in free radicals of [...] memory that react with casual stimuli to produce chance deposits of shame and grief'. One outcome of this is a loss of objectivity about one's own past agency such that 'we do not see youth's strengths, only its inexperience and inadequacy'.[10]

Of course, each of the distortions and temptations that accompany the diminution of agency with age may afflict people in the third as well as the fourth ages; yet, their total effect is differential. When it comes to the third age, they tend to contribute to a sense that agency is something to be wrested back—cosmetically, medically and existentially—from the encroachment of death. The threatening rise of the next generation is just one particularly potent avatar of this intuition. However, even as they feed and give shape to the third age as an era of reasserted agency, the combined effect of these distortions and temptations is to further exacerbate the immense and horrifying gravity of the fourth age as an imagined realm of lost (or, at least, severely diminished) agency. Gilleard and Higgs suggest that to cross the boundary of the fourth age is to pass 'beyond the social world, beyond both its comforts and its contradictions'.[11] Not only agency but reflexivity and even relationality vanish in the way the fourth age is imagined and portrayed. Furthermore, they note, 'for observers, influenced in varying degrees by the commodification of their life world, the fourth age offers no opportunity to create a status or articulate a lifestyle; nor is there reason to trust that previous agentic choices will ever be honored or acted upon'.[12] In a very real sense, then, the fourth age comes to refract the 'long dying' that Michael Banner argues now characterises the end of life in the late modern West. According to Banner, neither

---

9   O'Donovan, *Entering into Rest*, 221.
10 O'Donovan, *Entering into Rest*, 221.
11 Gilleard and Higgs, 'Aging without Agency', 125.
12 Gilleard and Higgs, 'Aging without Agency', 125–126.

the hospice nor euthanasia—the two culturally-dominant forms of 'the imagining and scripting of death'—have the traction they once did here.[13] In the past, the end of life may have typically 'announced itself as imminent, or [...] as so many months away'.[14] But now a protracted process of 'dwindling' has taken its place, and death is perpetually deferred via medical and other interventions—in hope and imagination, if not in reality. When agency is gradually eroded and diminished like it is in the contemporary imagination of ageing, the 'choice' between different ways of approaching the end of life becomes a vanishing point.

Against the backdrop of the vicissitudes of agency in contemporary ageing, the issue I will address in the remainder of this chapter stands out as particularly pressing. The issue is, how can we reimagine the fourth age as more than simply a zone of non-agency and abjection, a shadowy place 'where our greatest fears reside but which can only be addressed by allusion and metaphor' rather than directly and constructively?[15] What resources does Christian theology offer for conceptualising—and then actually embracing—flourishing at the end of life? These are grand questions, to be sure. And I do not expect to make more than a modest contribution. Nevertheless, I contend there are some important resources to be found in the way one particular Christian theologian—Karl Barth—brings suffering within the ambit of discipleship at a key point in his magisterial Church Dogmatics. Specifically, I consider his treatment of suffering in the context of his late doctrine of sanctification in CD IV/2 §66. The way I identify and mobilise these resources as I do this is twofold. First, I clarify Barth's approach to suffering in this context. In particular, I defend it against the charge some critics have made that Barth draws suffering and discipleship dangerously close together. I do this by highlighting the distinction he makes here between the 'dignity' and the 'crown' of suffering. Second, having clarified Barth's discipleship-shaped approach to suffering, I indicate some constructive uses to which this distinction

---

13 Banner, *The Ethics of Everyday Life*, 114.
14 Banner, *The Ethics of Everyday Life*, 118.
15 Gilleard and Higgs, 'Aging without Agency', 126.

between 'dignity' and 'crown' may be put in relation to the issue of the fourth age. That is, I indicate how I think it could have helped me on that hospital ward. Specifically, I believe it could have enabled me to reimagine that woman's experience—which manifested a number of aspects of the fourth age—as a matter of positive discipleship.

Karl Barth on the Dignity and Crown of Suffering

To begin, I need to clarify Barth's approach to suffering, especially as he treats it at the conclusion of CD IV/2 §66 under the heading 'The Dignity of the Cross'. Barth's reflection on suffering here falls within the ambit of his revision of the doctrine of sanctification. Significantly, it brings non-agency into the sphere of discipleship, which for Barth is a fundamentally active thing, where Christ's sovereign agency in calling and directing is brought into conjunction with the creaturely, human agency of Christians in hearing, responding, and following after him:

> 'Follow me' is the substance of the call in the power of which Jesus makes men his saints [...] The lifting up of themselves for which He gives them freedom is not a movement which is formless, or to which they themselves have to give the necessary form. It takes place in a definite form and direction. Similarly, their looking to Jesus as their Lord is not an idle gaping. It is a vision which stimulates those to whom it is given to a definite action. The call issued by Jesus is a call to discipleship.[16]

Consequently, Barth's vision of discipleship embodies what might be called a 'practical compatibilism', treating God's agency and activity in Christ as compatible with ours (rather than swallowing up, competing with or somehow existing in paradox with it).[17] Unlike some

---

16 Barth, *CD IV/2 66.3*, 533.
17 Katherine Songderegger has recently written eloquently of the straightforward compatibilism evident in the biblical narratives. See Sonderegger, *Systematic Theology: Volume 1*, 77–85. What I have in mind advances on this by turning this theoretical descriptor into a practical matter of stance and expectation in Christian discipleship.

other construals of Christian discipleship, Barth's account resists the valorisation of human agency. Human agency is crucial to discipleship as Barth envisages it, but it is relative and secondary rather than being absolute and primary. Christian disciples are acted upon before they engage in any activity of their own; yet, this passivity is not the last word on their agency, declaring it finished before it has even begun. Rather, it is constitutive of their agency, summoning and setting in motion their properly creaturely and, indeed, human moral activity as liberated by God's sovereign acting in Christ. In this way, suffering is not only admissible (if heroically chosen or embraced by the disciple); it is foundational to discipleship. This coincides with O'Donovan's assertion that even though 'we experience suffering as [...] the frustration and termination of our agency', it is a theme that rightly finds a home within 'the concern of ethics for life and action'.[18]

Some critics have argued this construal of discipleship leads Barth to identify suffering too closely with the glory of following Jesus. One such critic is Alexander Massmann, whose full-scale analysis of Barth's theological ethics is published as *Citizenship in Heaven and on Earth*. According to Massmann, the way Barth treats suffering primes his approach for abuse against those who might be coerced—directly or structurally—into positions where they 'must' accept suffering and victimhood. However, Massmann's hesitation first emerges with respect to a much earlier moment in Barth's project. He points out Barth thematises cruciformity (conformity to the sufferings of Christ) when he lays the foundations for his ethics of reconciliation in CD IV/1. Massmann rightly notes 'humiliation and exaltation coincide' for Christ in Barth's examination of his reconciling work through the lens of the 'journey of the Son of God into the far country' in CD IV/1 §59—a treatment that famously views Christ's incarnate self-emptying not in terms of the setting aside or concealment of his divinity, but as the full expression of it. Massmann astutely observes that, for Barth, 'Jesus Christ is true to his divine majesty precisely in the lowliness of his suffering'.[19]

---

18 O'Donovan, *Entering into Rest*, 202.
19 Massmann, *Citizenship in Heaven and on Earth*, 342.

Massmann goes on to suggest this 'coincidence' between humiliation and exaltation, suffering and glory, applies in Barth's thinking not only to Christ, but also to those who follow after him. He detects in this the introduction of a dangerous imbalance into Barth's vision of human flourishing.[20] Specifically, he remarks on Barth's apparent tendency to privilege unilateral and hierarchical power relations among people, deriving from the way terms such as 'submission', 'subordination' and 'obedience' feature so prominently in the account of Christ's identity and activity in §59. In the context of Barth's treatment of male–female relations, in particular, he develops an ill-advised and one-sided analogy with the Son's unilateral 'obedience' to the Father. Massmann is not the only critic to remark on the lopsidedness of Barth's discussion here. For example, Paul S. Fiddes wonders what has become of the essential 'alongside' Barth had earlier insisted on in the relationship between men and women such that 'reciprocity takes "absolute precedence" over any difference in order between male and female'.[21] One might also wonder what has become of the New Testaments suggestion that the socially—and culturally-configured power differential between men and women is to be an occasion for service and self-sacrifice rather than an immutable hierarchy and privilege to be insisted upon? So pronounced and troubling is the imbalance in Barth's thinking that it invites reflection on possible links between this and his troubled and troubling relationships with the women in his life.[22]

Barth's inclusion of suffering within the purview of sanctification and discipleship may be further problematised because, while it appears to render potentially meaningful our experiences of suffering (including the suffering associated with the fourth age), it simultaneously opens the door to abuse. It is easy to imagine how abuse may follow from identifying discipleship with suffering, whether that suffering is directly inflicted or the result of more diffuse structural factors (as the

---

20 Massmann, *Citizenship in Heaven and on Earth*, 359–368.
21 Fiddes, 'The Status of Woman in the Thought of Karl Barth', 153.
22 See Tietz, 'Karl Barth and Charlotte von Kirschbaum', 86–111. Caution must also be exercised here. Even the details that have recently emerged to light do not entirely obviate the fact that as Susan Selinger observes, 'one must be careful not to think one can know' the precise nature of their relationship. See Selinger, *Charlotte Von Kirschbaum and Karl Barth*, 13.

suffering that frequently accompanies ageing and disability typically is in societies that display 'normate bias').[23] To begin, claims that God wills such experiences for the disciple's good may be left unqualified. This, in turn, could be twisted into a supposed theological rationale for subjecting oneself to such experiences or remaining subject to them as a matter of faithful discipleship, thus facilitating oppression. Indeed, even if the idiom of 'oppression' and 'liberation' were to be applied to such situations, that does not automatically exclude such a distortion. The Croatian-American theological ethicist Miroslav Volf points out some troubling ambiguities around this conceptual pair, the very first of which is 'the paradoxical and pernicious tendency of the language of victimisation to undermine the operation of human agency and disempower victims' particularly by 'imprison[ing] them within narratives of their own victimisation'.[24] Even an insistence that discipleship means freedom from and resistance to all imprisoning and idolatrous claims could therefore foreseeably be twisted to suggest all suffering is good—without qualification—and should therefore be accepted and embraced without question by a disciple.

Further complicating these potential problems that are more or less intrinsic to Barth's discipleship-shaped approach to suffering, extrinsic factors in the current cultural context demand it be vigorously interrogated. We are in the midst of wide-ranging and necessary public conversations regarding the way the powerful have not only stacked the social deck in their favour, but also freely played their hands against the powerless, across a range of social sectors—in the church and other previously-trusted social institutions, in relation to women as well as indigenous people and minorities, in the finance industry, and significantly in aged care. Compounding this, our instinctive (albeit, culturally-conditioned) revulsion at the loss of agency that marks our

---

23 Pentecostal theologian Amos Yong describes 'normate bias' in terms of 'the unexamined prejudices that non-disabled people have toward disability and toward people who have them'. He goes on to observe: 'These assumptions function normatively so that the inferior status of people with disabilities is inscribed into our consciousness'. The result is that 'non-disabled people take their experiences of the world as normal, thereby marginalising and excluding the experiences of people with disabilities as not normal'. Yong, *The Bible, Disability and the Church*, 10–11.
24 Volf, *Exclusion and Embrace*, 103.

shared imagination of the fourth age plays into a valorisation of agency in the ever-expanding third age. Consequently, any move to stress the dignity of enduring the sufferings associated with ageing falls under suspicion. It is suspicious insofar as it implicitly suggests that resistance to the encroachment of death may not be an unqualified good to be endorsed. Such a suggestion may be seen as tantamount to advocating an abandonment of agency, demanding the acceptance of victim status and leading inexorably to the objectification of older people. Indeed, it may be seen (understandably) as a precursor to subjecting those who are ageing to enforced institutionalisation or worse.

In light of such criticisms and suspicions, we should pay attention to a crucial distinction Barth makes in his treatment of suffering in §66.6—namely, the distinction between the 'dignity' and the 'crown' of any suffering Christian disciples may experience. Barth is explicit about this distinction:

> The crown and the dignity which comes to the disciple in discipleship are two distinct things. The crown of life, which the disciple is promised that he will receive at the hand of the King (Rev. 2:10), is the goal of the way which he may go here and now as the bearer of this dignity.[25]

Note that Barth is careful to both distinguish and relate 'dignity' and 'crown' here, generating a dynamism that makes this distinction particularly promising and fruitful. They are two distinct things. Barth is careful to underline this. The crown is not something present in this life, which is marked with sufferings of various sorts. Rather, it is the goal of the way '[we] may go here and now'. Dignity, however, is something the disciple may bear in the present. Barth goes on to speak more fully of this 'dignity' a few pages later:

> Between Christ and the Christian, His cross and ours, it is a matter of similarity in great dissimilarity. There is, of course, a great and strong and obvious similarity. It is because of this that we can speak of the dignity of the cross. Christians are

---

25   Barth, *CD IV/2*, 600.

> distinguished and honoured by the fact that the fellowship with Jesus into which He Himself has received them finds final expression in the fact that their human and Christian life is marked like a tree for felling.[26]

Apart from furnishing an evocative image for the Christian life—as that 'marked like a tree for felling'—Barth here makes it clear the dignity of suffering as we follow after Christ is something that characterises Christian suffering somewhat unexpectedly; it is a similarity in the midst of 'great dissimilarity'. In this way, the dignity is related to the crown. It precedes and anticipates the crown as a marker of the fact that the disciple treads the road towards that goal. Fellowship with Jesus—a fellowship Barth envisages as taking the fundamental shape of discipleship, with Christ calling and leading and his disciples listening and following—is the common factor. However, this fellowship is manifested differentially: as dignity in the present and crown in the future. The crown that awaits us is our final exaltation to the joy of unhindered fellowship with God. This is a final gift from the risen King. And, our anticipation of this future exaltation bestows dignity on our suffering here and now. As we await the crown, the suffering Christians endure dignifies us as Christ's disciples. It is, so to speak, his signature. Therefore, our cruciformity in suffering speaks of how we are acted upon by Christ, who lays claim to us and makes us his own.

Three important factors in the context in which Barth deploys this dynamic distinction between the dignity and crown of suffering further illuminate it:

1. Within the broad framework of CD IV/2, Barth develops his discipleship-shaped vision of sanctification and suffering under the heading 'The Exaltation of the Son of Man'. He views the work of reconciliation through the lens of the kingly, royal 'office' of Christ, interpreting his nature as the true, representative human being (the Son of Man) in terms of his 'state' of exaltation (as the one lifted up to humanity's proper covenant partnership with God) and vice versa. This complements the perspective adopted in IV/1,

---

26 Barth, *CD IV/2*, 605.

interlocking with it in a dynamic pattern of reinforcement, qualification, and completion. In IV/1, Barth employs the priestly lens to view Christ's divine nature (as the Eternal Son) in terms of his 'state' of humiliation (on his 'journey into the far country'), and vice versa. One effect of the way these perspectives interlock is to cause an informed reader to ask how the vision of discipleship developed in IV/2 relates with the insistence on cruciformity in IV/1. The distinction between dignity and crown provides an important part of the answer to this larger question.

2. Zooming in on §66, it must be noted this account of suffering appears in the midst of Barth's radical reinterpretation of Calvin on sanctification as simultaneous with justification. One significant aspect of this revision is the way sanctification is personalised, such that the living, present Lord Jesus Christ is installed as its active centre. The programmatic subsection for this part of the Church Dogmatics is §66.2, which is entitled, 'The Holy One and the Saints' (Der Heilige und die Heiligen). Barth's is a Christology of sanctification, rather than a theology more generically. One result of this, I suggest, is that sanctification is given a distinctive shape as discipleship, for the living Lord Jesus Christ at its heart calls those he has chosen to follow after him. Being Christ-centred is dynamic rather than static; it is about hearing and responding to Christ's call as his disciples. Furthermore, what Christ calls his disciples to is freedom. Mirroring his own freedom, a freedom to which his call primarily attests in the Gospels, Christ's call to his disciples to leave their livelihoods, families, and familiar patterns—to die to themselves in other words (actively surrendering their agency)—is actually a call to freedom. This is because it means joining Christ in resisting the tyranny and idolatry of the good things we wrongly invest with ultimate significance (e.g., family, tribe, possessions, and even religion).[27]

3. §66.6, Barth completes his presentation of sanctification by highlighting the 'correspondence' (Entsprechung) disciples have with

---

27 John Webster's examination of this theme in the Gospels is masterful and deeply indebted to Barth. See Webster, 'Discipleship and Calling'.

their master in taking up their cross and suffering like him. This is evident in the way Barth emphasises the dignity that may be found in suffering on the path of discipleship is 'a matter of [the] similarity in great dissimilarity' between them and Christ. Barth parses this similarity in the midst of great dissimilarity using the language of correspondence, which he develops here in terms governed by the image of disciple and master. The way correspondence provides the explanatory context for his distinction between dignity and crown is even clearer in the sentences immediately preceding his introduction of this distinction:

> The exaltation accomplished in His crucifixion and therefore in the suffering of that rejection is His and not that of His disciples or the world above which He was exalted as the Lord in His death. To His exaltation there *corresponds* that of His elect and called, the elevation which now comes to Christians and is promised to all men, their awakening from the mortal sleep of the slothfulness of sin. And we have seen already that this upraising of man has its basis and thrust in Him, in His exaltation to the right hand of the Father as effected in His death; that it becomes and is a fact wholly and utterly in virtue of this exaltation. Yet their elevation is not identical with His exaltation. It is only thanks to His exaltation, and in the strength of it, that it takes place at all.[28]

In the exaltation—and, therefore, the suffering—of the cross, master and disciple are united but not identical or interchangeable. As Barth immediately adds, 'the relationship between the two is irreversible'. The master's suffering is the cause and occasion of the disciple's, but no suggestion of parity of interchangeability is allowed to creep in. Barth is uncompromising at this point: the Christian's cross-bearing does not re-enact Christ's. In fact, the correspondence

---

28 Barth, *CD IV/2*, 600 (emphasis added).

between the two is explicitly construed in terms of the relationship and difference between disciples and their master:

> If their elevation consists ultimately in the fact that they have to take up and carry their cross, this is not a re-enactment of His crucifixion. It takes place in *correspondence* to it; with the similarity proper to a disciple following his Master; but not in any sense in likeness, let alone identity.[29]

The standard English translation unfortunately obscures the point here. Upholding the genuine 'similarity' (Ähnlichkeit) Christians display to Christ in bearing their cross, Barth draws on the logic of discipleship to insist this cross-bearing is 'not in equality (Gleichheit), let alone identity (Identität)' with Christ's. It is any suggestion of equality or interchangeability rather than likeness or similarity that Barth wants to guard against. The master and disciple are decidedly unequal—and necessarily so. But their likeness and similarity are precisely the point. Disciples follow after the master and come to resemble him in doing so. According to Barth, Christian suffering has its basis and origin in Christ's. It corresponds to it in a way governed by the logic of discipleship. In establishing this, Barth effectively defines the important but elusive notion of correspondence in the terms supplied by the image, concept, and reality of discipleship. Christian correspondence with Christ is a matter of following after him, not repeating or otherwise rising to the level of ontological equality or identity with him.

What these contextual factors mean for the distinction between 'dignity' and 'crown' is that, where Barth insists the suffering of Christ is identical with his glorification (his 'lifting up' in the terms of John's Gospel)—the perspective that Massmann rightly detects as dominant in IV/1—the matter is significantly different with Christian disciples. Unlike Christ, the suffering experienced by disciples is not the same as their exaltation. It corresponds to his suffering to be sure. Yet this correspondence is a matter of similarity within very great difference. Indeed, Christ's suffering and the suffering Christians experience is *not* equivalent in significance or in nature. Christ, Barth argues,

---

29 Barth, *CD IV/2*, 600 (emphasis added).

suffered uniquely what we deserved. Barth's presentation is explicitly and unashamedly substitutionary at this point, leaning heavily on 'the pattern of exchange' one Barth scholar has observed in his view of the atonement.[30] Even so far from legitimating violence and 'baptising suffering' so that it becomes an unqualified good, this emphasis on Christ's substitutionary suffering as one with his glory actually functions in the first instance to displace our suffering. Our suffering cannot be like Christ's suffering in this essential sense. His glorious suffering is unique and unrepeatable. It is the suffering of the master whose disciples never outstrip or supersede him. Our suffering is that of disciples, following after our master. It is the aftershock of an earthquake that has altered the landscape forever.

Functionally, Barth's distinction between the dignity and crown of Christian suffering—and the discipleship-shaped vision of the Christian life it attests—plays a significant role in the dynamic and dialectical treatment of the conjunction between suffering and discipleship he goes on to develop. This in turn enables Barth's vision of suffering as essential to discipleship to sidestep the charges that may be laid against it, without thereby valorising human agency and playing into the cultural denigration of the fourth age. In particular, this distinction relentlessly places Jesus at the centre of Christian suffering just as Barth does more generally with discipleship. Moreover, it makes him the active and dynamic centre of our suffering, refusing either to grant it (or its absence) a positive meaning in itself or to deny the meaning it might acquire in being received as a gift from Christ. For the disciple, suffering has no meaning in itself. Nevertheless, it can become meaningful in relation to the master. Speaking of the way in which the cross determines the 'life-movement of the Christian' such that it is 'crossed through' as it is swept up in the movement of the exaltation of humanity in Christ, Barth contends:

> The cross involves hardship, anguish, grief, pain, and finally death. But those who are set in this movement willingly undertake to bear this because it is essential to this movement

---

30 McMaken, 'Election and the Pattern of Exchange in Karl Barth's Doctrine of the Atonement'.

that it should finally, i.e., in its basis and goal, be crossed through in this way. We are necessarily outside the movement if we will not take up and bear our cross; if we try to escape the tolerantia crucis (Calvin).[31]

Although striking a note of willingness, and, thereby, granting the reality, integrity and significance of our agency in undertaking to bear suffering, Barth situates this within a prior and determining 'passivity'. We only willingly bear our suffering insofar as we are 'set in this movement' by an agency and activity not our own—that is, insofar as we are acted upon. Being acted upon like this is a necessity for Christian disciples. Indeed, 'we are necessarily outside the movement if we will not take up and bear our cross'. However willingly disciples may embrace our sufferings, we have no choice but to do so if we claim to be Christ's disciples. Because discipleship entails taking up and bearing our cross, Christian suffering must fall within the scope of the activity characteristic of discipleship. Indeed, the activity of self-denial that lies near the heart of discipleship involves a decisive break with oneself that is so radical that it is nothing short of a death. And the extent to which this death is more than metaphorical comes into focus here in §66.6.

Having insisted that discipleship and suffering belong together, Barth immediately counters two potential misunderstandings. On one side—in terms of the suffering entailed by the cross—Barth declares that 'it is not a matter merely of hardship, pain and death in themselves and in general'.[32] Suffering is not automatically 'baptised' by being included within a vision of active, willing discipleship—far from it. Suffering has no positive significance in itself. Accordingly, Barth emphasises it is simply ordinary self-care to avoid and seek to ward off suffering. This ordinary and perfectly valid impulse is underpinned by the intuition that suffering forms no part of God's original and ultimate intention for creation; rather, it opposes it:

> In themselves and as such, pain, suffering and death are a questioning, a destruction and finally a negation of human

---

31 Barth, *CD IV/2*, 602.
32 Barth, *CD IV/2*, 602.

life. The Christian especially cannot try to transform and glorify them. He cannot find any pleasure in them. He cannot desire or seek them. For he sees and honours and loves in life a gift of God. And he is responsible for its preservation.[33]

This echoes his framing of the ethics of creation in CD III/4 as a matter of preserving and promoting life. Barth argues Christians 'cannot be [...] lover[s] of death'. To love death would amount to a paganisation of Christianity. At the same time, unlike non-Christians who affirm life in itself—thereby idolising it—Christians affirm it as a good gift of God: 'it is for [them] more than a matter of life'. As the gift of God, Christians gratefully receive and love life in obedience to God's will in Jesus Christ—that is, Christians affirm life as part of their discipleship. Viewing suffering through the lens of discipleship, therefore, safeguards the Christian affirmation of life: 'Because he does not love his life in itself and as such, he cannot love its negation and therefore pain, anguish and death as such'.[34]

Barth argues the Christian affirmation of life is anchored in the recognition that it is a gift from God to be cherished and preserved as God wills. Because of this, however, Barth also insists that Christians can affirm the negation of life in death and in the tremors that warn of its coming. Christians can do this because the negation of life may proceed from God. Even death may be a gift. The disciple recognises the lordship of Jesus not only in life, but also in death. Belonging to Jesus and doing his will, therefore, becomes 'that which is more than dying in the dying of Christians':

> To be the Lord's includes this alternative of dying. The Christian knows better than others—than those who for different reasons have lost their zest for life and long for its end and dissolution—what he is doing when he says Yes to the negation of life, to pain and suffering and death. He says Yes to these because his sanctification in fellowship with Jesus Christ, in His discipleship, in the conversion initiated

---

33 Barth, *CD IV/2*, 602.
34 Barth, *CD IV/2*, 602.

by Him, in the doing of good works, ultimately includes the fact that he has to see and feel and experience the limit of his existence.[35]

In other words, Christ's sanctifying call to discipleship—and this alone—can bestow positive meaning on suffering. Suffering is not something Christians should seek or wish for in itself, but something that they 'will not negate but affirm [...] just as elsewhere and right up to this frontier [they] will not negate but affirm life'.[36] Suffering and its absence are both to be received by disciples as gifts from the gracious hand of Christ.

Barth immediately moves to confront another potential misunderstanding of suffering by refusing to grant primacy to the disciple's moral agency and activity. While it may be true for every disciple that 'to save his life he must surrender and lose it', Barth maintains this does not mean the disciple will 'seek or induce this loss'.[37] Discipleship does not entail a death wish. Although Barth insists that the loss of life discipleship demands 'will come to [the Christian]',[38] disciples are first of all passive in being acted upon in losing our lives. Nevertheless, this being-acted-upon constitutes and calls forth our agency. It does this in not negating but affirming the suffering we receive, like our life, as a gift from Christ's hand. Suffering must not lead disciples to reverse this conception. Such a reversal occurs when we imagine our activity is primary and our suffering heroically chosen for ourselves. When this happens, discipleship becomes an inverted parody of itself, as Christ's summons to take up the cross is twisted to serve a perverse desire for death and a drive to experience persecution.

In fending off these misunderstandings, Barth guards against either emptying out or romanticising suffering. Barth refuses to empty of significance the suffering Christians incur on the path of discipleship. The reality of our correspondence with Christ in suffering prevents us from imagining it is somehow swallowed up by Christ's suffering

---

35 Barth, *CD IV/2*, 602.
36 Barth, *CD IV/2*, 603.
37 Barth, *CD IV/2*, 603.
38 Barth, *CD IV/2*, 603.

or otherwise stripped of value by it. Equally, Barth does not romanticise Christian suffering by giving it more weight than it can bear. Commenting on Calvin's treatment of cross-bearing, Barth underlines the filial confidence with which Christians may embrace suffering:

> The Christian does not take up his cross, and yield to God, because it is quite futile to resist One who is so superior in strength. If we obey God only because we must, our secret thoughts are all of disobedience and evasion, and we refrain from these only because they are impossible. The Christian yields in recognition of the righteousness and wisdom of divine providence which rules his life. He obeys a living, not a dead, command. He knows that resistance or impatience is wrong. He understands that it is for his salvation that God lays his cross on him. He thus accepts it [...] not with his natural bitterness, but in thankful and cheerful praise of God.[39]

Barth goes on to suggest Calvin's picture would have been completed if Christ had been explicitly brought in as its basis. Jesus is the first and foundational reason for our confidence that God loves and is favourably disposed towards us. Our suffering is a matter of concrete fellowship between Christ and us. It speaks to us of that fellowship with Christ and the welcome in God's family it entails. Such is the deep dignity Christ's cross bestows on our suffering.

All the same, Barth maintains the suffering of Christians on the path of discipleship only receives this dignity indirectly. Disciples enjoy our fellowship with Christ—and the access to and inclusion in God's family it entails—on the basis of his suffering and obedience, not our own:

> As Christians take up and bear their cross, they do not suffer, of course, with the direct and original and pure obedience which for all its bitterness it was natural and self-evident for the Son of God who was also the Son of Man to render to His Father. Their obedience will never be more than the work of the freedom which they are given. It will always be subsequent.

---

39 Barth, *CD IV/2*, 604.

> It will always be so stained by all kinds of disobedience that if in the mercy of God it were not invested with the character of obedience it would hardly deserve to be called obedience. Nor is their suffering even the tiniest of contributions to the reconciliation of the world with God. On the contrary, it rests on the fact that this has been perfectly accomplished, not by them but by God Himself in Christ, so that it does not need to be augmented by their suffering or by any lesser Calvaries.[40]

In putting it like this, Barth excludes any possibility of over-investing our suffering with meaning by underscoring the graced nature of the disciple's obedience and suffering. In particular, he resists romanticising suffering itself and the position of victim as such. While suffering does genuinely victimise and oppress human life—as a demonic force opposed to God's purposes—there are no 'pure' victims in Barth's terms. Even when Christians face rejection as Christ did, as disciples following our master, Barth insists there remain significant differences. Not only do we not face God's rejection as Christ did, we 'will never be quite innocent in [our] suffering' either.[41] Nor will we ever 'suffer merely through the corruption and wickedness of others, or through the undeserved decrees and buffetings of fate or the cosmic purpose'. Without surrendering to the paganisation of suffering he has already identified as so difficult to resist if life is affirmed simply for its own sake, Barth maintains that for Christians 'there is always a very definite (if sometimes disguised) connection between the sufferings which befall them and their own participation in the transgression and guilt in which all men are continually implicated'.[42]

It is worth noting Christian suffering derives both its significance and its liminal status from the grace of Christ, and specifically from his work on the cross, which both originates and mitigates it. Barth's affirmation of universal guilt and deservingness, even on the part of Christians who suffer unjustly, therefore functions less to 'blame the victim' than it does to underline how our suffering is overshadowed by

---

40 Barth, *CD IV/2*, 604.
41 Barth, *CD IV/2*, 605.
42 Barth, *CD IV/2*, 605.

Christ's—and will one day be overcome by it. Ultimately, this humanises suffering rather than either demonising or deifying it. Suffering for the disciple becomes an occasion for grace to elicit our active human response. From one angle, this humanisation of suffering appears to diminish the significance of our suffering as we take up their cross: 'In the life of Christians it is not just a matter of themselves and the fulfilment of their sanctification, but [...] of something far greater than themselves—of the glory and Word and work of God, compared with which they and all that they may become can never be more than dust and ashes'.[43] From another angle, however, this is exactly what lends our lives and suffering genuine significance—the thoroughly human significance of witnessing to Christ, his singular holiness, and its future universal revelation:

> This is the limit which is set for the Christian especially, and as a sign of which he comes to bear his cross, not in identity but in similarity with the cross of Jesus. [The Christian's] cross points to fulness and truth of that which he expects, and to which he hastens, as one who is sanctified in Jesus Christ. It points to God Himself, to His will for the world, to the future revelation of His majesty, to the glory in which his Lord already lives and reigns.[44]

The sufferings of Christians are assimilated by Barth to the logic of discipleship. This is how we correspond to Christ in following after our master, actively receiving our suffering as meaningful because we see it as a gift from the one whose suffering was identical with his exaltation.

It has been necessary to interrogate Barth's thinking regarding suffering as closely as we have done for two reasons. The first reason is to vindicate it against the charges critics such as Massmann level against it. As we have seen, Barth is very careful to avoid making a straightforward transfer from Christ's sufferings to those of Christians. The Christians' dignity in suffering is not identical with their crown. There is a gap between Christ and his disciples here. Furthermore, Barth presents the

---

43 Barth, *CD IV/2*, 605–606.
44 Barth, *CD IV/2*, 606.

cruciformity of discipleship in §66.6 in a way bound together with the penultimacy of the suffering and endurance discipleship entails. The ultimate goal and eschatological form of the sanctifying work of Christ in human life is not suffering, not even suffering by bearing the cross. As much as it may dignify disciples to follow their master in suffering while doing so, God's ultimate intention is not for Christians to suffer. Suffering has no positive value in itself. To think that it does, Barth argues, is nihilism. Rather, God's ultimate intention for disciples of Christ is to share in the eschatological crown and triumph of Christ, liberated from all negative effects (and even the memory) of suffering. The second reason it has been necessary to interrogate Barth's thinking regarding suffering in this context is to prepare for its constructive appropriation as a resource for reimagining the fourth age in terms of discipleship. It is to this work of reimagining we now turn by establishing some important overarching coordinates for it.

Dignity and Crown in the Hospital Ward

Turning in conclusion to the constructive aspect of this retrieval of Barth's distinction between the dignity and the crown of suffering, how can it be mobilised as a resource for reimagining the place of suffering (including the sufferings of growing older) as part of discipleship rather than antithetical to it? Barth's affirmation that suffering may bear a particular dignity for Christians is set in dynamic counterpoint to his larger emphasis on Christ's liberation and humanisation of his disciples. It may carry risks to affirm we are victims of inescapable suffering, and that there is a dignity to suffering on the path of Christian discipleship (even to the point of receiving our sufferings as a gift from the risen Jesus). Yet it is indispensable. Furthermore, it can be a profitable resource when it is set within a framework emphasising that suffering is not God's ultimate intention, and that even its dignity will be eclipsed by the glorious crown that awaits those who endure.

In relation to the nexus of theological and pastoral questions around ageing, in particular, Barth's approach may bear fruit by inviting us not simply to write off those whose agency is impaired (which will presumably be all of us, if we live long enough). As John Swinton compellingly argues in the overlapping case of the severely disabled, even to mainly consider how such people could be 'included' in the life of the church falls short. Rather, as bearers of the dignity of being disciples of the crucified Lord, we must ask how we can welcome and mobilise the gifts older sisters and brothers are and can bring as we strive to help them embrace their calling in new circumstances.[45] Those of us who are subjected to the deprivation of age are never simply victims, as much as we may rightly long for liberation from the negative consequences of ageing (if not from ageing itself) and eagerly anticipate the day when all pain and every tear will be wiped away. Even those in the fourth age who travel the path of discipleship with us are gifts to us—and we to them—for our mutual sanctification. Conversely, those whose capacities, whether physical or mental (or both), are diminished by age may appear as sufferers and victims to be pitied, especially to those of us happily exempt from such experiences for the moment. However, while together with them we may rightly hope for the crown one day, for the overcoming of suffering and for the glorious day on which they know as they are known, we must remember even now they bear a special dignity as Christ's disciples. They have gifts to give—if only we can overcome our own insecurity and arrogance to welcome them.

Ultimately, Barth's emphasis on the exaltation of Christ and the corresponding dignity of discipleship bars the way to dehumanising any who suffer or are victims, including those in the fourth age. For example, on that hospital ward, in the midst of the wretchedness and all-too-human pain with which I began, it summons us to resist treating that dying woman as any less worthy of time and attention than anyone else. While obviously diminished and increasingly lacking in agency, her suffering—and that of her family members—remains open to expressing the dignity of the claim Jesus exerts. Especially for those who tread the path of discipleship, following after their master, by grace every step can refract the light of eternity. This is the source of our dignity. At the same time, the Christian hope is that the all-surpassing light of eternity will eventually swallow up the darkness of

---

45 Swinton, *Becoming Friends of Time*, chapter 5.

suffering, ushering in the inexpressible experience of full and direct fellowship with the living God. With this hope burning in our hearts, those who expect and begin to experience (indirectly) the restoration of our humanity as we correspond to Christ in discipleship are increasingly armed to resist anything that would corrode or corrupt it—in ourselves and in others. This includes both the attempt to deny dignity or the possibility of discipleship to those in the fourth age (perhaps for the sake of valorised human agency for those in the third) and to deny the reality of ageing (particularly its painful aspects) by ignoring the changes it brings to bodies, relationships, minds and memories.

Bibliography

Banner, M. *The Ethics of Everyday Life: Moral Theology, Social Anthropology and the Imagination of the Human* (Oxford: OUP, 2014).

Barth, K. *The Church Dogmatics: Volume IV, The Doctrine of Reconciliation (Part 2)*. Translated by Geoffrey W. Bromiley. (Edinburgh: T&T Clark, 1958).

Fiddes, P. S. 'The Status of Woman in the Thought of Karl Barth', in Janet M. Soskice (ed.), *After Eve: Women, Theology, and the Christian Tradition* (London: Marshall Pickering, 1990), 138–55.

Gilleard, C., and Higgs, P. 'Aging without Agency: Theorizing the Fourth Age', *Aging and Mental Health* 14, no. 2 (2010)' 121–8.

Massmann, A. *Citizenship in Heaven and On Earth: Karl Barth's Ethics* (Minneapolis: Fortress, 2015).

McMaken, W. T. 'Election and the Pattern of Exchange in Karl Barth's Doctrine of the Atonement', *Journal of Reformed Theology* 3 (2009), 202–18.

Nussbaum, M. C., and Levmore, S. *Aging Thoughtfully: Conversations about Retirement, Romance, Wrinkles and Regret* (Oxford: OUP, 2017).

O'Donovan, O.	*Entering into Rest: Volume 3, Ethics as Theology* (Grand Rapids: Eerdmans, 2017).
Selinger, S.	*Charlotte von Kirschbaum and Karl Barth: A Study in Biography and the History of Theology* (University Park: Pennsylvania State University Press, 1998).
Sonderegger, K.	*Systematic Theology: Volume 1, The Doctrine of God* (Minneapolis: Fortress, 2015).
Swinton, J.	*Becoming Friends of Time: Disability, Timefullness and Gentle Discipleship* (Waco: Baylor University Press, 2016).
Tietz, C.	'Karl Barth and Charlotte von Kirschbaum', *Theology Today* 74, no. 2 (2017), 86–111.
Volf, M.	*Exclusion and Embrace: A Theological Exploration of Identity, Otherness and Reconciliation* (Nashville: Abingdon, 1996).
Webster, J.	'Discipleship and Calling', *Scottish Bulletin of Evangelical Theology* 23, no. 3 (2005), 133–47.
Yong, A.	*The Bible, Disability and the Church: A New Vision of the People of God* (Grand Rapids: Eerdmans, 2011).

PART 3

Holistic & Spiritual Care for the Ageing

CHAPTER 7

The hidden story: What might be missing in a life review?

Bruce Stevens

Abstract

Life review has been an influential approach to finding personal meaning and has been applied in therapy. This chapter explores the possible beginning of a life review in the concept of a hidden story. Various theories with a learning component such as implicit learning, tacit knowledge, the cognitive unconscious, Bourdieu's *habitus* and attachment theory are approached. This may help us to reach beyond the barrier to explore our first story–the hidden story. It is possible what has been learned can be discovered through a range of therapeutic techniques that have been explored in psychoanalysis and, later, depth therapies. Some suggestions are included in an appendix. The hidden story can then be incorporated into a more comprehensive life review. And on this basis, we can effectively re-author ourselves into a new life story.

Introduction

'The child is father to the man'[1]

There is great potential in conducting a life review. 'Pieces of a puzzle' can come together in order to see the bigger picture. But what if not all the pieces are available? Could there be a story from the first years of life? In this chapter, I argue our first story comes from the period of what has been called 'infantile amnesia' and is based on early learning. The hidden story, if it can be told, could be foundational to developing a sense of our storied self.

Life Review

Robert Butler, a psychiatrist, developed the idea of 'life review'.[2] This task becomes more urgent as we mature and age. He saw it as a normal part of life brought about by the realisation of ageing and eventually death. This 'looking back' helps to gain a sense of meaning. Indeed, in this way, life review can be integrative and therapeutic. This benefit has been supported by empirical research.[3] It has been widely recognised a focus on story can assist in a process of recovery.[4] Life review has had a formative influence on later narrative gerontology.[5] I agree with the observation, 'the beauty of a narrative is that it allows us to tie all the changes of our life into a broad comprehensive story'.[6]

If a life review is important, especially as we age, then the question reasonably follows: what are the beginnings of a life story? If I am to suggest an answer, I first need to briefly review some evidence for early learning.

---

1   William Wordsworth
2   Butler, 'Age, Death and Life Review'.
3   Haight, 'An Integrated Review of Reminiscence'.
4   Gass, 'Narrative Knowledge and Health Care of the Elderly'.
5   De Medeiros, 'Suffering and Old Age: Repairing Threats to Self in Old Age'; De Mendeiros, *Narrative Gerontology*.
6   Pennebaker and Segal, 'Forming a Story: The Health Benefits of a Narrative', 1250.

Origins

What has been characterised as 'infantile amnesia' is an important phase in a child's development. Freud used the term 'amnesia' to describe the first few years of life.[7] It is almost a universal experience that we have few memories of these years.[8] Potentially, this presents us with a difficulty when we think about the beginnings of a life review.

The idea of infantile amnesia rests on a notion of memory; however, this raises difficulties. It can be found in almost every undergraduate textbook in psychology that memory has at least three steps: input, storage and retrieval—only then can something be remembered. However, there is a more straightforward mechanism in learning. We learn from birth but how does this happen?

No child is a 'blank slate'—not even at birth. There have been proposals regarding what may be learned in the womb. Consider the example of a pregnant mother in a war zone, whose anxiety is communicated to her foetus. This child begins with a primal unease, or possibly an impact if the experience of birth is difficult. Psychoanalyst Otto Rank, in his controversial *The Trauma of Birth*, argued birth is experienced as a psychological trauma by the new infant.[9] There has been quite extensive research on how infants learn in their first year of life.[10]

I briefly review here some theories with a focus on early learning and indicate some basis in research. Implicit learning is familiar to undergraduate psychology students and has a long history in academic research. Arthur Reber introduced the term in his 1965 master's thesis. His extensive research is conveyed in his book, *Implicit Learning and Tacit Knowledge*. The definition he offered was 'implicit learning is the acquisition of knowledge that takes place largely independently of consciousness attempts to learn and largely in the absence of explicit knowledge about what was acquired'.[11] He also maintained the primacy of implicit learning, making the point that 'it is actually more

---

7   Freud, 'Screen Memories'.
8   Callaghan, Li and Richardson, 'The Elusive Engram: What Can Infantile Amnesia Tell us About Memory?'.
9   Rank, *The Trauma of Birth*.
10 Bower, *The Rational Infant: Learning in Infancy*.
11 Reber, *Implicit Learning and Tacit Knowledge*, 5.

surprising that any function is conscious than unconscious'.[12] Studies in implicit learning have included artificial grammar learning, sequence learning and probability learning. There are thousands of published studies.[13] Generally, the idea is to show that a participant in an experiment has gained relevant information without being able to verbalise that knowledge.

Michael Polanyi[14] described tacit knowledge as knowing beyond words to express: 'We can know more than we can tell'.[15] Tacit knowledge might be said to be the result of implicit learning. Facial recognition is an example, but there are many others. The idea of tacit knowledge has stimulated considerable research.

John Kihlstrom, from the perspective of cognitive science, has noted a great deal of information processing takes place outside of working memory. He reviewed research in various areas including automatic processes, subliminal perception, implicit memory, and hypnotic alterations to underline the importance of this in cognitive science generally. He concluded there are (within the domain of procedural knowledge) a number of complex processes that are inaccessible to introspection. There is a role for actively linking because 'without such linkages, certain aspects of mental life are dissociated from awareness and are not accompanied by the experience of consciousness'.[16]

The French scholar Pierre Bourdieu proposed an influential social theory.[17] Power is culturally created and constantly re-legitimised through an interplay of agency and structure. He developed the concept of *habitus*, his term for socialised norms or tendencies guiding behaviour and thinking that includes tastes, predispositions and thought patterns. For Bourdieu, *habitus* is an internalised product of environmental conditions encountered through life. This determines our anticipations (often small) of the kind of world we will encounter at each moment, as we are predisposed to a future that preserves

12 Reber, *Implicit Learning and Tacit Knowledge*, 10.
13 Seger, 'Implicit Learning'.
14 Polanyi, *Personal Knowledge*.
15 Polanyi, *The Tacit Dimension*, 4.
16 Kihlstrom, 'The Cognitive Unconscious', 1451.
17 Bourdieu, *Distinction*, 4.

the correlations we have experienced in the past. *Habitus* is not simply cognitive; indeed, it is possible to 'think with the body' and to 'know without concepts'.[18] In other words, all this becomes 'second nature'. A learning model is implied with Bourdieu's 'transposable dispositions'.[19] The result is 'master patterns' of behaviour and, therefore, 'what they do has more meaning than they know'.[20] While such patterns do not carry value or virtue, these habituated patterns can be intentionally formed.

This brief review is not comprehensive. However, what is clear is that much of our first learning is non-cognitive—it is important but not easily expressed in language and, therefore, not readily available for life review. How do we move from 'something' learned to its inclusion in a life story?

Attachment Research

Attachment theory provides a good example of early social learning.[21] Patterns of attachment are an emotional process determined in the first year and clearly evident by 18 months. If a child's needs are met, the belief forms that people are dependable. If not, attachment is anxious in different ways. The following patterns have been identified:

> *A style is avoidant.* The basic assumption seems to be the following: 'Better rely on your own strengths than to need somebody'.
>
> *B style is secure.* There is enough relational stability to rely on others or to be autonomous in a flexible way.
>
> *C style is ambivalent.* The core belief could be the following: 'You have to stay close to people but you can never fully trust them'.
>
> *D style is mixed (disorganised).* This is a confused style of

---

18 Bourdieu, *Distinction*, 470–475.
19 Bourdieu, *The Logic of Practice,* 52–53.
20 Bourdieu, *Outline of a Theory of Practice,* 79.
21 Colin, *Human Attachment.*

attachment with little internal consistency. It is often evident in survivors of childhood trauma and severe neglect. Mood and behaviour often change in an unpredictable way.

Attachment patterns are considered to be foundational to later relationships: someone anxiously attached as a two-year-old is likely to have anxious relationships at 30 or 40. Patricia Crittendon demonstrated the lifelong influence of early attachment patterns on later relationships.[22]

I have mentioned attachment theory in passing, but it is important to my argument. This early social learning, understood in terms of patterns of attachment, can be articulated as an attachment story. Barbara[23] was able to do this when she stated:

> I can see that my attachment to my father was anxious. He was unreliable and I could not count on him reliably meeting my emotional needs. In adolescence, I became more withdrawn. I just had a somewhat 'formal' relationship with him. I would routinely report my academic progress, of which he would approve or not. But I was fortunate with my mother, she was there for me. I knew my needs would be met and that gave me confidence to form emotionally healthy relationships. I can now see that when I began to date, I tended to be attracted to emotionally withholding males, just like my father. I managed to see the pattern and I had some counselling which helped me to identify relationships which might be more healthy.

Arguably, however, this early learning may apply to more than attachment patterns and be extended to attitudes and behaviour, as follows:

> Robbie had a disturbed childhood. His father was a violent alcoholic; his mother was submissive, ineffectual, and a perpetual victim of the father's drunken rages. Robbie was slow

---

22 Crittendon, 'A Dynamic-Maturational Approach to Continuity and Change in Patterns of Attachment'.
23 Barbara, and later Robbie, Brad and Sally are not real people. They are created from my experience of many patients in therapy and used for illustration only. Clinical data has some validity.

to learn to speak, well after two years old, but he had learned much about how families work. Of course, nearly all of this unconscious learning was dysfunctional.

I do not think that it is overly speculative to assert Robbie has learned about male and female roles, power dynamics, and how only males get their 'needs met'. He has learned this by the example of his parents. Unless Robbie later questions or challenges this, it will be natural for him to relate this to later romantic partners in a similar way.

It is easy to see some of the content of Robbie's early learning. How does this form a hidden story? Let us imagine a possible future:

> Robbie is now 28 years old and he has been left by his partner, Tracey. Robbie saw a drug and alcohol counsellor saying, "I need to do something, I am desperately missing Levi, my son. I didn't realise how much it would hurt. I deserve all this, but I used to hit Tracey when I was high on coke. Now Family Services won't let me see Levi without supervision. My life is a mess".

It is rare for someone in Robbie's situation to have the insight to tell his hidden story, but it is possible. I now speculate on how this may come about through a process of discovery aided by therapy:

> Robbie was able to reflect on his six months in counselling. He said, "I can now see how I got things wrong. I saw what my dad did to my mother, so I wrongly believed that being lazy and violent was the 'manly' way to act. What was important was what I wanted [...] when I wanted it. I was stronger physically, so somehow it was right for me to get my way. I knew my mother was unhappy and I can now see it made Tracey so miserable she left me. She was frightened for Levi, so she took him and insisted on him being protected. I must now take responsibility and live differently. Maybe if I am lucky, I might get a second chance".

Robbie has begun to be aware of his hidden story. He simply imitated his father's substance abuse and domestic violence. This continued his father's entitled story of male dominance, but through therapy aspects of what was once Robbie's hidden story have become conscious, which he has now begun to question and no longer simply act out. This provided the chance for a different life story.

Clearly there is something inarticulate—but important—that various thinkers have tried to conceptualise. I have argued it is best thought of as early learning when important things are learned without being conscious of the process. This provides the 'building blocks' for what we can understand as the hidden story. While this hidden story is usually unrecognised, it belongs in a fuller life review since it is absolutely foundational to the evolving life story.

The Storied Self

Telling a story is the way we structure human experience; indeed, consciousness is basically temporal[24] and a narrative provides the structure of meaning.[25] Narrative competence has been defined by Rita Charon as a 'set of skills required to recognise, absorb, interpret and be moved by the stories one hears and reads'.[26] This competence requires a combination of textual skills (identifying the story's structure, adopting its multiple perspectives, recognising metaphors and allusions), creative skills (imagining many interpretations, building curiosity, inventing multiple endings) and affective skills (tolerating uncertainty as a story unfolds, entering the story's mood).[27] This narrative competence can also be understood as a reflective capacity. As Randall and McKim observe, this is a narrative-in-the-making that 'we are composing and comprehending from within: narrative of which we are simultaneously author and narrator, character and reader'.[28] This leads to an understanding of what might be called *the storied self*.

We are also multi-storied—each story contributing depth to a more

---

24 Crites, 'The Narrative Quality of Experience'.
25 Nussbaum, 'Narrative Emotions'.
26 Charon, 'Narrative and Medicine'.
27 Charon, 'Narrative and Medicine', 862.
28 Randall and Kim, *Reading our Lives*, 6.

nuanced, yet integrated and comprehensive life story. The first story is the hidden story before language. I have written elsewhere about the deep story, which includes the lazy story, the trauma story, the messy story, the body story, the problem story and the dark story.[29] The spiritual dimension is acknowledged in the God story. Each, like facets on a cut diamond, can enhance a life review.

Conclusion

Our earliest experiences in life are foundational, but generally unavailable because of what has been called 'infantile amnesia'. I have argued the first years are a period in which learning takes place. It is possible that what has been learned can be discovered through a range of therapeutic techniques that have been explored in psychoanalysis and, later, depth therapies (I include some suggestions below in Appendix A). Once aspects of this early learning are identified, it can be understood in terms of narrative. Our hidden story becomes possible, then, with an appreciation of its influence in shaping a more comprehensive life story. On this basis, we can effectively re-author ourselves into a new life story.

Appendix A: Some Practical Suggestions

This task of finding the hidden story is exciting and has broad implications. As Frederick Buechner observed, 'the voyage into the self is long and dark and full of peril, but I believe it is a voyage that all of us will have to make before we are through. Either we climb down into the abyss willingly with our eyes open, or we risk falling into it with our eyes closed'.[30]

How do we explore this realm of early learning? Coherence therapy has a focus on the discovery of emotional learning.[31] Coherence

---

29 Stevens, 'Deep Story'.
30 Buechner, *The Hungering Dark*, 23.
31 Ecker, Ticic and Hulley, *Unlocking the Emotional Brain*.

therapy has developed a number of useful ways to discover emotional learning, including sentence completion. These techniques are helpful in developing the hidden story.

I make some suggestions here from my experience as a clinical psychologist. While these techniques do not have an 'evidence base', they are useful in practice:

a) *Sentence completion.* This is potentially most useful exercise. Usually there is a stem that a person completes. How would you respond to the following sentence stem: 'the most important thing I learned as a child was_____?' A colleague of mine did this and he ended the sentence with, 'you are on your own, kid'. I tried this sentence completion and was surprised by my response: 'It is hard to be noticed'. Both of us found the exercise stimulated our thoughts about a possible hidden story narrative, though admittedly probably included some measure of speculation.

b) *The step-back technique.* A life can be shaped by a hidden story. The theme is 'out-of-awareness'. We can discover this hidden story through an important principle: cause and effect. All behaviour makes sense, at least emotionally, and this provides a clue. First, we observe.

I illustrate here with a clinical anecdote. Brad was tired of losing money through gambling. He knew he had a problem behaviour but felt unable to change it.

His behaviour appeared irrational. He had gambled for years and always lost in the end: 'only bookies always win'. Sometimes he had a big win on a race, perhaps enjoying a big day, but eventually 'I end up broke, losing important relationships, even my children refuse to talk to me'.

Brad did not lack insight. There was no profit in gambling. He always lost. He had seen it impoverish every aspect of his life. It did not make rational sense.

The next step follows. Brad may ask what led to his problem behaviour being emotionally 'logical'?

He remembered his mother always made him feel special and she would say things like, 'the normal rules don't apply to you. You were born lucky'. She maintained, 'you have the Midas touch'. He considered how his mother's messages may have contributed to his attitude towards gambling. While he remembered her messages, the insight was in the link to his attitude to believing he could benefit from gambling. In some measure, he was performing a life story. It was consistent with what his mother saw as his destiny, even though she was long dead.

In Brad's case the behaviour, seemingly irrational, could be understood as consistent with a hidden story about being 'born lucky'. This was dysfunctional, of course. Notice how it is possible for a hidden story to emerge as the dominant story in a life. Therapeutically, if anything were to change, it would have to be challenged.

c) *Adult-child dialogue.* This is a journal exercise. It can help to bring a child's perspective to life review. This technique is useful in regaining an early perspective, which can possibly highlight themes in the hidden story.

To do this, you should think about a time you felt upset as a child.

Now, *picture* yourself as a child feeling upset. What age are you? Do you see your child-self as sad or anxious or angry? What would you say as an adult to yourself as a child? (Try not to be critical or judgemental. If you find yourself doing that, stop the exercise and come back to it later when you can be compassionate to your child-self). Write a few sentences of positive things you would like to say (use simple words that a child might understand).

Next, *respond* as the child. What would you as a child say back? How does the child see things? What has the child learned about life? How do you expect your life to work out?

Reply as the adult.

Continue as the child. Ask your child how he or she sees life.

And back and forth until you feel you have arrived at a better understanding of how you saw life as a child. This provides a significant early perspective on your story.

Sally did an adult-child dialogue in her journal. She talked with herself as a sad nine-year-old, rejected by the 'popular group' at primary school. She found she felt inferior because of her hand-me-down clothes from older sisters in her large family. She realised through the back-and-forth dialogue she had always spent vast amounts on brand clothes and accessories: 'I believed that if I presented well, I would be acceptable to important people. I think that this has been a guiding principle in my life. But I can also see that I have been driven about my appearance and it has been a constant source of anxiety as well'. In this way, Sally became more aware of possible themes in her hidden story and began to question the cost of living it out.

I have found the discovery of a hidden story is an important part of therapy. This can reveal the cause of symptom formation and deeply engrained patterns of dysfunctional behaviour. Often an insight in a clinical session can lead to profound life changes. While this may be considered anecdotal, it is a common experience of mental health professionals and pastoral carers. This may well fit into life review therapy. However, beyond any clinical utility such insights can add to a life review and provide further depth to a sense of identity.

Acknowledgement

The research mentioned in this chapter was funded by the Wicking Trust.

Bibliography

Bourdieu, P.   *Distinction: A Social Critique of the Judgement of Taste.* Translated by Richard Nice. (London: Routledge, 1984).

Bourdieu, P.   *Outline of a Theory of Practice.* Translated by R. Nice. (Cambridge: Cambridge University Press, 1977).

Bourdieu, P.   *The Logic of Practice.* Translated by R. Nice. (Stanford: Stanford University Press, 1990).

Bower, T. G. R.   *The Rational Infant: Learning in Infancy.* (New York: W. H. Freeman and Co, 1989).

Buechner, F.   *The Hungering Dark* (San Francisco, CA: Harper and Row, 1969).

Butler, R. N.   'Age, Death and Life Review', *Psychiatry* 26, (1963), 65–76.

Callaghan, B. L., Li, S., and Richardson, R.   'The Elusive Engram: What Can Infantile Amnesia Tell us About Memory?', *Trends in Neuroscience* 37, no. 1 (2014), 47–53.

Charon, R.   'Narrative and Medicine', *New England Journal of Medicine* 350 (2004), 862–864.

Colin, V.   *Human Attachment* (New Jersey: McGraw-Hill, 1996).

Crites, S.   'The Narrative Quality of Experience', *Journal of the American Academy of Religion* 39, no. 3 (1971), 291–311.

Crittendon, P. M.   'A Dynamic-Maturational Approach to Continuity and Change in Patterns of Attachment', in Patricia Crittenden and Angelika Claussen (Eds.), *The Organization of Attachment Relationships: Maturation, Culture and Context* (Cambridge: Cambridge University Press, 2000), 343–357.

De Medeiros, K.   'Suffering and Old Age: Repairing Threats to Self in Old Age', *Journal of Aging Studies* 23 (2009), 97–102.

De Medeiros, K.   *Narrative Gerontology: In Research and Practice* (New York: Springer, 2014).

Ecker, B., Ticic, R., and Hulley, L.   *Unlocking the Emotional Brain: Eliminating Symptoms at Their Roots Using Memory Reconsolidation* (New York: Routledge, 2013).

Freud, S.   'Screen Memories', in James Strachey (Trans.) *The Standard Edition of the Complete Psychological Works of Sigmund Freud* (London: Hogarth Press, 2001), 299–322.

Gass, D.   'Narrative Knowledge and Health Care of the Elderly', in Gary Kenyon, Phillip Clark, P., and Brian de Vries, (Eds.), *Narrative Gerontology: Theory, Research and Practice* (New York: Springer Publishing Co., 2001), 215–236.

Haight, B. K.   'An Integrated Review of Reminiscence', in J. D. Webster and B. K. Haight (Eds.), *The Art and Science of Reminiscing: Theory, Research, Methods and Applications* (Washington, DC: Taylor and Francis, 1995), 1–22.

Kihlstrom, J. F.   'The Cognitive Unconscious', *Science* 237, no. 482 (1987), 1445–1452.

Nussbaum, M.   'Narrative Emotions: Beckett's Genealogy of Love', in S. Hauerwas and L. G. Jones (Eds.), *Why Narrative? Readings in Narrative Theology* (Grand Rapids, Michigan: W. B. Eerdmans Publishing Co., 1989), 216–248.

Pennebaker, J. and Segal, J. 'Forming a Story: The Health Benefits of a Narrative', *Journal of Clinical Psychology* 55, no. 10 (1999), 1243–1254.

Polanyi, M.   *Personal Knowledge* (London: Routledge and Kegan Paul, 1958).

Polanyi, M.   *The Tacit Dimension* (London: Routledge & Kegan Paul Ltd, 1967).

Randall, W., and McKim, A.   *Reading our Lives: The Poetics of Growing Old* (New York: Oxford University Press, 2008).

Rank, O.   *The Trauma of Birth* (New York: Kegan, Paul, Trench and Co., 1924/1929).

Reber, A. S.   *Implicit Learning and Tacit Knowledge: An Essay in the Cognitive Unconscious* (New York: Oxford University Press, 1993).

Seger, C. A.   'Implicit Learning', *Psychological Bulletin* 115, no. 2 (1994), 163–196.

Stevens, B.   'Deep Story: A Way forward in Narrative Gerontology?' *Journal of Aging and Geriatric Medicine* 1, no. 3 (2017), 1-2.

CHAPTER 8

Theological, pastoral and clinical insights into human flourishing at the end of life: Music and meaning in dementia and de-medicalising palliative care

Kirsty Beilharz

Abstract

Supporting people in the context of dementia and palliative care has highlighted contemporary Western society's disregard for dying well and flourishing until the end of life. Cultural aversion to meaningful conversations regarding death has generated social stigma and silence on the subject of natural death, and especially its spiritual significance as the final stage of human growth, when a person prepares spiritually for restoration, healing, bodily resurrection, and ultimate reunion with God in the perfected reality He promises. Our fiercely autonomous, financially secure and technological Enlightenment milieu advocates the control of timing, location and conditions of death (e.g., through euthanasia and cultural defiance of natural ageing and disease progression).

Society has lost touch with the physical, psychosocial and spiritual experience of dying well. Palliative care has commonly been relinquished to professionals and institutions, which disconnects an individual from the opportunity for prayer, reflection, reconciliation of relationships, pastoral support and intercession, seeking forgiveness, and sometimes causes resistance to conscious, comfortable passing. This chapter considers the stages of death, facilitation of interaction with friends and relatives, communion with God, and acknowledgement of the individual as a community responsibility (i.e., ways that meaning, dignity and growth can nurture the process of human flourishing until its spiritual conclusion).

Introduction

Whilst ageing and death are integral and natural parts of life, words such as 'palliative care' and 'dementia' predominantly conger up fear, aversion, silence and images of loss of independence, capacity and dignity. It seems that, even amongst Christian populations, who have eternal hope and appreciation for the ephemerality of materiality, human life, and eschatological conviction of reunion with Christ in his fullness and with a new heaven and earth—all seemingly positive attributes of passing—we nonetheless become uncomfortable with difficult conversations about morbidity or diminished autonomy and finitude.

This chapter looks unashamedly at the end of life, with a particular focus on dementia and palliative care, drawing from experiences of research experiments undertaken at HammondCare (a non-denominational Christian sub-acute hospital and nursing-home, aged care provider) and a study at St. Vincent's Health Network across five hospitals in New South Wales, Australia. This research focuses on the positive ways of caring for people, especially from a spiritual perspective, but also taking into account the mental and physical aspects of health which contribute to well-being.

The notion of flourishing until the last breath adopts the eudemonic concept of holistic well-being, satiety, comfort, and not merely superficial 'happiness' but spiritual joy and maturity which stems from authentic personhood, connection with the Transcendent, and cadence in the spiritual quest for harmony, which is not contingent on physicality or materiality. Rather, spiritual well-being grows from acquiescence and peace, a sense of meaning and purpose in a life well lived, in meaningful relationships and fulfilment of humanness.

Included in the investigation of calming and comforting therapeutic practices is the use of music in palliative care and dementia to overcome isolation, pain and to bring connection and serenity, to facilitate spiritual reflection, relief from physical symptoms and mental anguish, and abatement of behaviours related to distress in those conditions. The purpose in reflecting on this time of life is to normalise death and deterioration; to demonstrate there can be ways of achieving contentment and belonging, even if those methods diverge from the methods which brought accomplishment and satisfaction earlier in life; and, finally, to dissipate some of the fears associated with death by speaking openly and honestly about expectations.

Some of the fears for the person nearing the end of life and for onlookers are fears of helplessness and inevitability, as well as fear of the unfamiliar. In a society accustomed to control, loss of it is threatening. For many, the death of a loved one or decline due to dementia, may be their first close encounter with death, and the first instance of being the principal carer and learning the new pastoral and caring skills required. This chapter suggests the end of life is an important stage in *spiritual development,* the final stage of maturation, and one in which family members and carers can make a difference. Furthermore, it highlights flourishing is related to dignity until death and respectful interactions and good treatment are ethical responsibilities as each person is bestowed with worth because they are made in the image of God *(imago Dei)* and human value does not come from anything humanly 'achieved' but purely through God's generous grace.

The attention to the theological foundation for end-of-life care and protecting personhood is motivated by several factors. First, swept up in the anxiety of the moment and the clinical environment, it is easy for clinicians and even attending family members to lose sight of the longitudinal picture of a person's character, important values, spiritual well-being, relationships and wishes. Second, we are in a period of social policy in which 'human rights' and availability of 'freedoms' have usurped the potency of human life with the availability of euthanasia or voluntary assisted dying and 'outsourced' dementia care, aged care, and palliative care to medical and nursing professionals, removing the 'average person' from the realities, mysteries, and knowledge of death and serious illness. Third, at the same time as significant advances in medicine are producing superlative treatments for some medical conditions and some cancers, in Australia as in much of the world, there is nonetheless a significant disparity in the availability and affordability of services and treatments. These treatments range from expensive gene-therapies, targeted chemotherapies and immunotherapies, to stem-cell manipulation and replacement therapies, and different styles of hospital and hospice care are available. In some cases, home-packaged care barely keeps up with patients' needs. Australia is extremely fortunate to have a public health system available to all, but the availability of services is by no means equal for all and there are many who are also unaware of services available due to regional and remote location, language and poverty barriers, social exclusion, and a range of other reasons. Added to these social attributes, the variety of cultural thinking on topics of care and death, family authority and decision-making capacities, cultural traditions, religious beliefs, legal entitlements, and inequity of hospital services all make for impaired navigation in a time of stress.

Background

Approximately 30 per cent of Australians over the age of 85 have dementia (which is approximately 425,000 Australians in 2020). Dementia has become the second-leading cause of death in Australia (and the primary cause of death for women). Dementia affects the social fabric economically and emotionally, costing more than $15 billion per annum, with the greatest emotional burden being borne by families and relationships. As we approach 2050, the nature of the Australian population is ageing and inverting, with an increasing proportion of people elderly and not working. Aged care and specialist high-care provision meeting the needs of people living with dementia is often very costly, requiring a 'bond' or deposit which usually takes the place of the family home to allow for adequate care. For couples, if each person has different care needs, there is no guarantee they will be able to cohabit in communal care homes.

In palliative care at HammondCare Greenwich, more than 90 per cent of sub-acute hospital admissions for symptom management and end-of-life care were for people with cancer or cancer-related symptoms, and the majority were also elderly. At St. Vincent's Hospital (Darlinghurst), the large majority of acute intensive care and long-stay patient admissions were people over 75 years of age. In some wards (e.g., oncology, rehabilitation, palliative care, cardiac and orthopedic), the average age was above 70 years. Compounding medical needs, people from disadvantaged backgrounds and low socio-economic backgrounds including the elderly, people living alone, Indigenous people, people with complex medical needs (e.g., multiple chronic conditions), people with drug and alcohol dependency, homeless people, and people with mental health issues constituted a large and very vulnerable subset of the hospital population. Because this vulnerable group often had few social and family connections, they easily became spiritually vulnerable too, without communities of support, positivity, and spiritual resources (i.e., strengths or spiritual 'strategies' at their disposal) to cope with and adjust to change, such as life-changing illness.

It seems timely to revisit the primary purpose and interdisciplinary delivery of care as people live longer and increasingly contend with age-related illness, isolation, and yet simultaneously assert preference for independent living and 'ageing in place' (i.e., living and dying at home). This is also particularly pertinent at a time when Australia has a government model of consumer-driven choice in aged care. The latter is advantageous in the sense that people assessed to be eligible can receive services and care in their home, maintaining independence for a longer time; however, the resources available can also fall short of safety needs or the 'consumer' (recipient) can make choices which are not necessarily the wisest or most essential (e.g., choosing companionship, outings, and meals over wound-dressing, falls prevention interventions, and personal hygiene services).

This chapter draws on studies conducted at HammondCare facilities. The first uses music engagement in dementia care; the second evaluates the impact of music on psycho-social, physical, and spiritual dimensions of wellness amongst people receiving palliative care services; and the third uses participatory arts groups in the general ageing population. A final study assessed the patient perspective on the role of spiritual care in hospital treatment across five St. Vincent's Hospital sites in terms of whether a patient felt it was important to their holistic care. The survey also probed which spiritual or religious language most resonated with the increasingly secular Australian population, such as synonyms for meaning, purpose and peace, and who people wanted to relate to and trust their spiritual well-being.

This research is particularly interested in ways interdisciplinary and integrative care can attend to the psychological, spiritual, and social needs of people, which are not addressed by the medical model of care. The terminology 'medical model of care' refers to the common practice of interpreting symptoms and pragmatic treatment in hospitals hinging on medical training, which includes training to look at a person holistically and empathetically, but which, with deficits of time and staffing, can easily become symptom management and pathology-focused. Consequently, this loses sight of individuality, personhood, what is important to the patient—their feelings and relationships—and, in less desirable situations, can lead to the patient feeling objectified and pathologised, part of a process in which everything focuses on disease and treatment, and in which people can be marginalised if they have impairments or lack proficiency in speaking English.

What is Flourishing at the End of Life? A Theological Perspective

The quality with which we deliver dementia care and palliative care has the potential to provide choice, control, and life flourishing. Done well, good quality care alleviates the desperation, suffering and lack of control which drive people to explore euthanasia.

A theology grounded in the selfless, boundless love of the Gospel, and the intrinsic worth of humans created in God's image (rather than the zeitgeist's ephemeral, materialistic measure of productivity), underpins the provision of life care and life quality throughout every stage of life, irrespective of an individual's physical or cognitive frailty.

What does the Bible tell us about ageing, human worth, controlling destiny, God's love in old age, sickness or frailty?

- In God's scale of time, life is transient, ephemeral, fleeting and its end time is uncertain.
- God created people: all humans are creatures of His work in whatever form, ability, disability, wellness, illness, and changing conditions throughout life.
- Death is a normal part of life and illness; suffering and death are unavoidable truths in the Fallen world. Each stage and phase of life is ordained *by God*.
- There is hope because there will be a resurrection of the body, and the New Kingdom is a restoration of the perfection of all creation.
- Humans are made in God's image and are therefore bestowed with intrinsic meaningfulness and worth, irrespective of one's own opinion or the opinion of others, social judgment or social measures of value.

God does not wish cruelty and suffering upon people despite the inherent suffering in our Fallen world: He wants the best for us. From the Biblical perspective, God wanting the best for us does not, however, include humans deciding the time and manner of death (such as euthanasia, physician-assisted suicide, or voluntary assisted dying).

This means it is both appropriate to responsibly ameliorate suffering and it is not normal or appropriate to expect a life free from suffering or pain. Some Christians believe in suffering we are united with Christ, and only through suffering can we spiritually grow. Certainly, notions that optimism regarding how post-surgery will be dignified and painless or that medical science can completely cure problems of deterioration, injury or ageing, seem to be widely popular, yet unrealistic misunderstandings. Frequently, people believe pain relief should be absolutely effective, or their repaired injury should replicate its former condition and, consequently, considerable frustration, dissatisfaction and mental anguish result from these idealistic expectations.

- *God's faithfulness.* God's faithfulness rather than our forgetfulness, 'Drawn from a theological understanding of God as three persons—Father, Son and Holy Spirit—"person-centred care"

invites us into relationships of mutuality and reciprocity not dependent on words'.[1]
- Apostle Paul tells us no illness, hardship, or distress—physical or spiritual—can separate us from God (Rom. 8:31–39). Karl Barth explains God seeks us more than we seek God and, therefore, our personhood does not depend on us. God knows us.

How does the Bible influence how we should care for people in need?

Frequently in the Old Testament, we are instructed to show kindness and hospitality to strangers, 'widows' (i.e., people without family support), and the poor and disadvantaged. Care modelled after the good Samaritan knows no boundaries, and is impartial to ethnic background, trauma aversion, or the ability to reciprocate good will or not. For the Samaritan, like the priest who crossed the road to avoid helping the injured stranger, it was taboo, 'unclean', and degrading to help a victimised stranger covered in blood, yet the Samaritan not only helped the nearly-dead stranger but left provision for his care after he had done all that he could, with no expectation of reward or repayment (see Figure 1). The Samaritan gave selflessly and unconditionally, just as Jesus did in his healing ministry and hospitality. Jesus' ministry shows us healing can be both physical and spiritual.

---

1   Hudson, 'God's Faithfulness and Dementia: Christian Theology', 50.

INSIGHTS INTO HUMAN FLOURISHING AT THE END OF LIFE 195

Figure 1. *The Good Samaritan* (c.1612–1615). **Painting by Pieter Lastman; Amsterdam 1583–1633. (Image: Wikimedia Commons Public Domain).**

How does theology inform dementia care? In the story of Job, beset by misery, misfortune, torturous sores and despair, we can learn from his friends how *not* to care. In isolation, and emotional, physical and spiritual pain, people need someone who will listen, and listen patiently, refraining from criticism, argument or advice. Job's friends started out supportively, simply being present, but soon they began to taunt him by offering advice and questioning Job's spiritual integrity. A person with dementia does not need intervention or argument; rather, they need merely companionship, belonging, acceptance, and inclusion.

Where is *personhood* in dementia? Medical diagnosis describes physiological markers and stages as well as psychological and behavioural symptoms of dementia, such as cognitive losses, trouble solving problems, forgetting, becoming lost; sensory deficits such as changes in spatial, visual and auditory perception; a non-chronological sense of time, events and people; deteriorating spatial orientation; observable changes in the brain size, ventricles (i.e., spaces seen on a brain scan); the effect on speech and communication; and emotional disinhibition due to changes in the fronto-temporal lobe of the brain (i.e., physiological pathologies and psychological symptoms). Medicine cannot tell us about spiritual needs and personhood, sense of identity, sustaining stories and self when outward recognition is disintegrating. It is the responsibility of the Church to look after its people and create inclusion, belonging, community, and to maintain stories and familiarity for people at its margins and people who need help. According to John Swinton,[2] dementia is a theological disease: it has also been called a disease of selfhood,[3] which Donna Cohen describes in her book as 'the loss of self'.[4] Furthermore, Tom Kitwood argues the negative way of treating people with dementia accelerates decline and isolation.[5] This observation seems especially poignant in light of the recent Australian Federal Government Royal Commission into Aged Care Quality and Safety which revealed shockingly inhumane instances of elder abuse—emotional and physical abuse, and neglect—and cases of isolation provoking behavioural and psychological symptoms of dementia (BPSD), inadequate hygiene linked to infection, chemical restraints ('medications' sedating residents, subduing and suppressing mobility and emotions) and inadequate medical attention for injuries.

John Swinton says of personhood and the tendency to dehumanise older people: 'In the eyes of many, the individual is perceived as 'dead and gone' somehow, it is assumed that the person who used to be there has been destroyed by the ravages of the disease process. What is left behind is nothing more than a shell of the person that used to be'[6]—typical of the functionalist discussion put forward by Singer and Locke. The problem with the functionalist approach is that the *real* person is defined by their ability to function at a cognitive level, which is determined quantitatively and functionally: 'Dementia is assumed

---

2 Swinton, *Dementia: Living in the Memories of God*.
3 Keck, *Forgetting Whose We Are: Alzheimer's Disease and the Love of God*.
4 Cohen, *The Loss of Self*.
5 Kitwood, *Dementia Reconsidered: The Person Comes First*.
6 Swinton, 'Forgetting Whose We Are,' 44.

to "de-soul" the person.[7] When this occurs, it becomes easy to begin to disregard people with dementia and shut them away (psychologically or physically). Hence, we urgently need to rethink the narrative of dementia as the person-in-relation not the person-in-pathology. The Scottish philosopher, John MacMurray, advanced this theory in opposition to Descartes' *cogito ergo sum*. The same rationale of God-bestowed value (i.e., not dependent on cognitive function) applies to all circumstances of cognitive impairment, learning disabilities, congenital defects and brain injury. In his book *From Bedlam to Shalom*, John Swinton argued for a relational conception of the human being based on Trinitarian theology.[8] He makes a case for human relationality to be viewed as analogous with Divine relationality (i.e., selflessly giving and loving).

A person with dementia experiences many losses—for example, termination of employment, leaving their home, hobbies, pets, loss of independence, friends, communities and societies, skills, loss of the ability to drive, sometimes separation from spouse in care facilities, loss of sensory acuity, and (progressively) loss of dignity. At first, the person with dementia is cognisant and grieving, which is marked by withdrawal from friends and stigma—parallel to the losses experienced by a person with mental illness—or is sometimes even compounded by depression and anxiety. We can develop skills and willingness in the Church to support pastors and carers in this practical theology of caring, listening and inclusion.[9] It requires we learn to listen and communicate in different ways, to allow more time, and to be sensitive to behavioural and bodily cues because speech is often one of the first areas affected by dementia. It is an all too common misunderstanding that, because a person can no longer talk and express themselves conventionally, they no longer have feelings or the will to convey them. This frustration is often linked to the 'behaviours' which concern carers and family, borne out of the struggle to indicate pain or emotion without speech. We can learn not to judge people according to cognitive

---

7   Swinton, 'Forgetting Whose We Are', 44.
8   Swinton, *From Bedlam to Shalom*.
9   Liveability, 'Dementia Friendly Churches'.

capacity because it is our relationship with God which gives humans value; God sits outside of time—and non-chronological thinking or slow thinking is not the only valid way of thinking. We see in Jesus Christ's discipleship he offered kindness and healing to people with all kinds of degrading conditions, such as blindness, leprosy, demon possession, chronic bleeding, and lameness.

People with severe dementia who are withdrawn and assumed to be unable to communicate for the majority of their lives may change when drawn into participating in spiritual practices. Deep, early memories, repetition, ritual, set to music can draw out expression, not to mention the mysterious workings of the Holy Spirit. In his essay *The Gesture of a Truthful Story*, Stanley Hauerwas writes, 'religious education is the training in those gestures through which we learn the story of God and God's will for our lives'.[10] We appreciate the Holy Spirit can work in ways beyond human understanding, and trawl the depths of the heart and soul. In 2 Corinthians 3:2–4, Paul says:

> This "letter" is written not with pen and ink, but with the Spirit of the living God. It is carved not on tablets of stone, but on human hearts. We are confident of all this because of our great trust in God through Christ.

Discipleship is authored by Jesus and written on human hearts.

Thomas Fuchs explains that, 'bodily learning means to forget what we have learned or done explicitly, and to let it sink into implicit, unconscious knowing [...] We might also say: What we have forgotten, has become what we are'.[11] Apostle Paul argues, 'the weaker members of the body are indispensable' (1 Cor. 12:22). The Church should be the exemplar of inclusiveness and compassion towards people on the periphery of social esteem. In Isaiah 46:4, The Lord promises he will carry, sustain and rescue us even when our hair is grey with age because He made us.

---

10 Hauerwas, 'The Gesture of a Truthful Story', 78.
11 Fuchs, 'The Memory of the Body', 3.

What is Dying Well?

What does it mean to die well? This question sometimes elicits nervous laughter until we realise many of us have not given it much thought. The person in palliative care has the advantage that death may be thought about and, to some extent, planned. More seriously, common responses include a desire for reconciliation, restored relationships with significant people and with God; to have loved ones and family present; to die with dignity; and, sometimes, to leave a legacy. If we find ourselves in the role of carer for someone nearing death, some of these wishes can be supported. This may include summoning important people, arranging to set relationships right or restore communication, ensuring loved ones are contacted, offering the reassurance which reduces agitation and anxiety, ensuring the person feels safe and comfortable (which may mean in the hands of expert care), and prepared according to their wishes (e.g., with rituals, clothing, in the desired environment, with the people or things that evoke tranquillity).

Dying is Spiritual

In death, material and physical securities are stripped away: 'For Charles [Wesley] the resignation of things, people in death, the will, were means through which an attitude of resignation towards God of his whole being was formed'.[12] Payne, like Charles Wesley, asserts the ultimacy and vulnerability of death avails a unique opportunity for spiritual growth, the final stage of formation: '[In] the end-experience of death [... it] may be that the greatest spiritual growth occurs as one struggles with physical losses and dying'.[13]

According to Lunn:

> The spiritual experience of resignation to God in death, which was so significant for the Wesleys, not only for those dying but also through their deathbed testimonies to faith for those left behind, is also one we have largely lost. In our culture

---

12 Lunn describes a vulnerability and surrender to God's power and mercy, unique to encroaching death. Lunn, 'Becoming Truly Human', 18,
13 Payne, 'Spiritual Maturity and Meaning-Filled Relationships', 37.

death is clinical; the dying are frequently sedated against pain, but also at the cost of any significant spiritual experience at the point of death.[14]

For Lunn, we can see sedation and unconscious death represents a problem, a betrayal, an opportunity deprived. Ethicist, Dr. Megan Best, also says dying is an important time of spiritual growth. It is a precious spiritual time for prayerfulness, reconciliation, acquiescence, acceptance, peace, reflection and meditation, and forgiveness. It is a time which needs few or no words; instead, simply being, or presence. Importantly, the experience will be a lasting memory for those present.

A number have written about the importance of the experience. Charles Wesley understands sanctification as growth into maturity as a human being, and resignation to God based on deep trust in God.[15] Erik Erikson on psychosocial development articulates stages of life and alternate responses: at [the stage of] old age this is integrity versus despair. Erikson describes integrity as 'a sense of coherence and wholeness' and the strength of wisdom. James Fowler's 'stages of faith' suggest the final years are concerned with 'transformation of present reality in the direction of a transcendent actuality'. Elizabeth MacKinlay explains that, in approaching death, we are 'withdrawing from former social roles [...] Within the Christian tradition, this 'stripping away' is a 'sacramental process' of emptying that leads to God'.[16]

As Jesus teaches in Matthew 25: 34–40, we show our love for God and Christ-likeness, when we give to and love strangers, with unconditional compassion and provision for people we are not bound to, and from whom we expect no reciprocity.

Thanatology is the science of dying and music thanatology is a tradition which has been practiced overseas, especially using the harp. For example, the *Chalice of Repose* pastoral music project, established by Therese Schroeder-Sheker, was created to recognise the presciently embodied, yet spiritual nature of dying calmly.

---

14 Lunn, 'Becoming Truly Human', 16-17.
15 Lunn, 'Becoming Truly Human', 1, 4 & 16.
16 MacKinlay, *The Spiritual Dimension of Ageing*, 33.

Suffering

Suffering is an existential problem which is influenced by cultural, physical, circumstantial and psychological factors. For example, compare the pregnant woman's labour and the pain experienced by a woman with cancer. They may have the same degree of pain, yet they may experience different suffering due to factors such as hope, expectation, outcome, duration of pain, and meaning attributed to the pain. Diagnosis of life-threatening disease is a common trigger for the so-called 'existential slap' (i.e., the need to adjust one's life story).

Milton Hay identifies characteristics associated with spiritual suffering, including pain, which is constant and chronic; insomnia; withdrawal or isolation from a spiritual support system; conflict with family members, friends or support staff; anxiety, fear, and mistrust of loved ones, friends, physicians, and hospice staff; anger; depression; guilt, low self-worth, and comments about self-loathing; hopelessness or a feeling of failure with life; lack of a sense of humour; unforgiveness; despair; and fear or dread.[17]

Many of these characteristics correlate with the stages of death and dying in *The Tibetan Book of the Living and Dead*. Spirituality often involves the search for meaning in a spectrum from centrality of Divine presence at one end and the secular concept of the inner life, personal belief and focus on the self at the other end.

Needs in end-of-life care include the social (e.g., isolation, loneliness, and boredom), emotional (e.g., depression, anxiety, anger, fear, and frustration), cognitive (e.g., neurological impairments, disorientation, and confusion), physical (e.g., pain, and shortness of breath), and spiritual (e.g., a lack of spiritual connection, and the need for spiritually-based rituals).

The Problem of Dying Well

Death is often not well prepared for. We live in a time of the Advanced Care Plan (ACP) or Advanced Care Directive (ACD), but many

---

17 Hay, 'Building Spiritual Assessment Tools'.

people have not filled out their ACP, specifying medical particulars such as 'not for resuscitation' or withholding life-prolonging treatments in the case of a medical emergency. Furthermore, in its current status, depending on the state or territory of residence, ACD's are not legally binding or cannot be expedited by a guardian. In many instances, the ACP is primarily used to determine medical processes but fewer people provide detailed wishes regarding spiritual, ritual, musical and other aspects of dying which would help them feel peaceful.

Even with best planning, death is often a time of anxiety and distress for families and friends, sometimes divisive and disputed. Some people will die alone or isolated from familiar surroundings or people, or in a hospital setting very different from the idealised scenario. For the most part, people do not know what to expect. In *On Death and Dying*, Elizabeth Kübler-Ross describes, for example, stages of denial, anger, acquiescence, and peace in a sequence of stages which some, but not all, people experience and sometimes in unexpected progression. For Durkin, 'death is a disruptive event, not only for the individual who dies but for the larger social enterprise as well'.[18] As Pine notes, the 'beliefs and practices of the members of a society toward dying and death are largely dependent upon that society's social organization'.[19] In our individualist Western society in which identity is tied to capacity and work for many people, in which little is understood of the physiological process of dying and death is a relatively infrequent and unfamiliar experience, the toll is great, the rituals are thin, and community involvement can be quite limited and unsupportive for the bereaved, as compared with third-world countries where whole communities are involved in multi-day rituals and the sight of the dying and dead is a quotidian reality. The West has lost some of its spiritual resources for processing death due to the clinical sanitisation and outsourcing of death to professional Third Parties.

Most people do not know what to expect. Death can be 'good'—calm, accepting, with minimal or medically-controlled pain—but it can also be noisy, distressing, and agitated ('terminal agitation'), with

---

18 Durkin, 'Death, Dying, and the Dead in Popular Culture', 47.
19 Pine, 'Social Organization and Death', 149.

physical changes, such as the person's pallor, facial tension, increased pain, irregular heart rate, feeling cold, upper respiratory gurgles (the 'death rattle') and laboured breathing due to difficulty swallowing (a struggle which is painful to watch), intrusive monitoring equipment, hallucinations, confusion or delirium, all of which are anything but tranquil and spiritual.

In the past, various cultures held texts describing the states of dying, mystical and liturgical practices to focus spiritual experience, preparation for the afterlife, and the beginning of wisdom. These include the Egyptian Book of the Dead, *Manifestation of Light;* the Tibetan Book of the Dead, *Bardo Thödol;* the Mesoamerican Maya Book of the Dead (C15th *Codex Borgia)* and other Mesoamerican Toltec and Aztec material; and, finally, the European Christian medieval eschatological material known as *Ars morendi,* or The Art of Dying (see Figure 2).

The *Ars morendi* (the Christian Book of the Dead) or the Art of Dying dates from the end of the Middle Ages, existing in many forms in Europe (i.e., Austria, Germany, Italy and France). There was intense interest in death during this period, perhaps due to the frequent outbreaks of pestilence, famine, war, disease epidemics and childhood disease which prevented people from reaching adulthood. Funeral rituals were a part of regular life. Furthermore, 'mass burials, burning of cadavers, public executions, even the immolations of heretics and alleged witches and Satanists were conducted on a large scale. According to some estimates, the victims of the Holy Inquisition alone exceeded three million'.[20] The Elder's C16th painting by Pieter Breugel, *The Triumph of Death*, depicts skeleton armies marching through a landscape of death and destruction (see Figure 3).

---

20 Grof, *Books of the Dead*, 58.

Figure 2. Illustrations from the Mesoamerican Maya Book of the Dead (C15th *Codex Borgia);* the Tibetan Book of the Dead, *Bardo Thödol;* and the medieval European Christian *Ars morendi, The Art of Dying.* (Images: Wikimedia Commons in the Public Domain).

Figure 3. Pieter Bruegel — *The Triumph of Death* (Image: Wikimedia Commons in the Public Domain).

A Culture of Denial

In comparison, it could be said we live in a culture of denial, or death aversion. The normalisation and desensitisation of criminal violence and death in pop culture (e.g., TV, movies, novels, graphic novels, and video games) ironically come at the cost of genuine familiarity, empathy and sacredness. Whether through pop culture, commercials selling exaggerated anti-ageing treatments, or cosmetic surgery, we are constantly peddled a lie of immortality. With greater scientific advances, society wants to believe that, with longevity, comes health. In reality, both dementia and cancer are 'age-related' illnesses—specifically, whilst cancer can affect people of any age, its prevalence due to malfunctioning cell-replication processes increases with age and, whilst there is increasing incidence of early-onset dementia, for the most part, it afflicts people over 70 years of age.

Heavy metal music (and its variants such as Death Metal) and rap are inextricably tied to death imagery and language, including bands such as Megadeath, Anthrax, Slayer, and Grim Reaper, and song titles such as 'Suicide Solution', 'Highway to Hell', and 'Psycho Killer', or the Guns N' Roses cover, a song written by notorious killer, Charles Manson. In their expression, all of these appear to idolise, glorify and edify death and violence. The lyrics by rap artists such as Snoop Dogg, Dr. Dre, Eazy-E, Puff Daddy, and Eminem are controversially overflowing with violence, murder, suicide and devaluation of humanity: no longer merely a voice of the marginalised, racially peripheralised and discriminated against peoples of minority, colour, poverty and the ghettoes, the affluent rap superstars have retained the language of oppression and morbidity which birthed the genre decades ago. The deathly impact of drug disputes, gangland shootings and rival anti-establishment groups led to the murder of celebrity icons, Tupac Shakur and B.I.G.

According to Durkin, many of the manifestations of death in U.S. popular culture deal with 'the post-self' (i.e., 'the reputation and influence that an individual has after his or her death'[21]), which is especially the case for deceased celebrities and public figures. Shneidman explains this 'relates to fame, reputation, impact, and holding on'.[22] The post-self constitutes a form of symbolic immortality, whereby 'the meaning of a person can continue after he or she has died'.[23] This is a way for the deceased person to exist in the memories of the living, functioning as a symbolic blur of the bifurcation between the living and the dead. In fact, symbolic immortality diminishes the sting of death and denies its full finitude. To be clear, this is denial, not legacy or spiritual formation.

Rethinking Palliative Care

The year 2018 was the centenary anniversary of Dame Cicely Saunders' birth (1918–2015). Saunders was the founder of the Hospice movement and St. Christopher's Hospice in London. In 1967, she

---

21 Durkin, 'Death, Dying, and the Dead in Popular Culture', 3-4.
22 Shneidman, *Death*, 455-460.
23 Bryant, *Handbook of Death and Dying*, 47.

recognised chemotherapeutic treatment was often neither good *nor* life-prolonging, for all its difficult, systemic side effects. She advocated for the beginning of palliative care, which is about de-medicalising and focusing on the spiritual, emotional, and comfort aspects of care for dying people, as well as recognising quality of life is more important than over-medicalised life. Therefore, palliative care is about living well to the very end (and not about death). Saunders' St. Christopher's Hospice in London was remarkable for its beautiful garden, on-site hairdresser, art, music, poetry, and a home-like, dignified and peaceful atmosphere. As Saunders explained:

> You matter because you are you, and you matter to the end of your life. We will do all we can not only to help you die peacefully, but also to live until you die [...] Suffering is only intolerable when nobody cares.[24]

Quality of Life versus Euthanasia

Patients with cancer and depression experience more physical symptoms, have poorer quality of life, and are more likely to have suicidal thoughts or a desire for a hastened death compared with cancer patients who are not depressed.[25] Using the Good Death Inventory (GDI) validated survey, Kinoshita et al. surveyed 2,247 families of cancer patients in Japan in 2008 and 2011.[26] Their data demonstrated that 'being respected as an individual' was of the greatest importance to people, whatever the location of their death. Most people preferred to die at home or in their favourite place over dying in a hospice or palliative care ward. The other qualities of importance to people and their families at the end of life were, in order of priority, the relationship with medical staff, a comfortable environment and relationship with family, life completion, hope and pleasure, physical and psychological

---

24 Richmond, 'Dame Cicely Saunders', 238.
25 Breitbart, et al. 'Depression, Hopelessness, and Desire for Hastened Death in Terminally Ill Patients with Cancer'.
26 Kinoshita, et al. 'Quality of Death and Place of Death'. 357-63.

comfort, independence, and not being a burden to others.

It was also found in Japan by Kinoshita's team that a significant proportion of people with cancer or depression withdrew their hastened death request when pain and mental illness was properly treated. This seems like an obvious observation; however, unmanaged pain and mental illness are often overlooked in requests for life termination and those criteria are treatable in the majority of cases. It also means pain (physical or mental), rather than a short-life prognosis or the range of other reasons above, is a decisive factor in euthanasia requests.

The title of this section alludes to a collection of related terms referring to patient-initiated premature termination of life upon request. At present in Australia, 'voluntary euthanasia' refers to knowingly and directly causing the death of a patient, at the request of the patient. 'Physician assisted suicide/death' is where the person providing the means (e.g., lethal drugs) is a medical practitioner. The administration of pain relief (everyone has a right to effective pain relief) and the withdrawal of burdensome and futile life-prolonging treatment do not constitute euthanasia, despite frequent speech in the media regarding excessive opioid administration to hasten death.

In Australia in 2019, the Victorian State Government legalised Voluntary Assisted Dying with a set of very precise conditions, in which a person with insurmountable suffering and a terminal condition with adequate capacity can request access to a physician-prescribed drug or 'medication', an anaesthetic-like barbiturate which the patient can ingest along with an anti-emetic (anti-vomit medication) and sweetener designed for self-administration, with or without the assistance of a medical professional. The 'voluntary assisted dying' terminology was decided upon after much consultation to destigmatise the process known in other countries as euthanasia or voluntary suicide. It must be emphasised it is a tightly regulated supply protocol with not many people satisfying the eligibility criteria. The current Victorian legislation excludes people without agency, such as people with advanced dementia or cognitive impairment and those unable to palate the comprehensive instructions and screening processes. Furthermore, it is dispensed from a single location. Measures are in place to secure the medication until its consumption to prevent abuse by someone other than the terminally ill patient.

The ethical concerns surrounding euthanasia are perhaps quite obvious, including vulnerability and exploitation of people with diminished capacity who may feel they are a burden, who may feel family or social pressure for a variety of reasons, and who may be exposed to poor pain management or inadequate medical support; however, perhaps one of the most concerning issues is *economic* and not *ethical* per se. Euthanasia is cheap, and good palliative care and hospice services are expensive. The cost of euthanasia is free or minimal compared with a hospital bed in palliative care, or a hospital bed in acute care, which can run to many thousands of dollars per day. This conundrum challenges the objectivity of governments and families.

Research shows euthanasia has risen steadily in countries where it is legalised.[27] Suicide has also risen in countries with legal euthanasia, perhaps suggesting the normalisation of suicide. Physician-assisted suicide statistics remain unchanged. There is a concurrence of requests for euthanasia and perceived patient burden, elder abuse, depression and pain. Several countries are debating whether to legalise assisted suicide, euthanasia, or both. In 2012, more than 5000 patients died after assisted suicide or euthanasia in states where these practices are permitted. Euthanasia and assisted suicide have been legal in the Netherlands and Belgium since 2002; whereas, assisted suicide has been permitted in Switzerland since pre-World War II, in Oregon since 1997, in Montana and Washington since 2009, and in Vermont since 2013. Data from countries which allow both practices show euthanasia occurs significantly more frequently. Does this indicate a preference for handing over responsibility?

Ameliorating individuals of responsibility for ending their own life through physician assistance may be linked to the normalisation and acceptance of termination:

> Since overall incidence rates of hastened death are much higher in [the Netherlands and Belgium] than in regions where only assisted suicide is allowed, the availability of

---

27 'Regional Euthanasia Review Committees Annual Report 2012'.

euthanasia [...] by a physician could lower the psychological threshold for requesting hastened death.[28]

Who Can Make a Difference?

Who, then, can take steps to improve the quality of life to its final stages? This should be addressed by the person dying and their family and friends; people dying in community; pastoral and spiritual care staff; medical and clinical staff, hospitals, and hospices; and people alone or in remote and regional areas.

One practice from my own experience is music thanatology and music for the end of life—performed live as an empathetic vigil responding to the person receiving care—or curated recorded music sensitively provided by carers. In the end stages of life, music can calm, relax, and reduce 'terminal' agitation; it can transform negative emotions such as anger, fear, sadness, aloneness and isolation, or disorientation; and it can distract from pain, and shortness of breath. Music is particularly pertinent during these stages as hearing is the last sense to shut down. Furthermore, music can overcome communication barriers (those due to language, medication, dementia, inability to swallow and talk); it may mask intrusive noises and sounds; and, finally, it creates a spiritual 'space' for reverie, reflection, meditation, prayer, and presence.

Music provides an antidote to hyper-cognition and ageism. People with cognitive impairment need to be released from the responsibility or expectation of reciting liturgy or prayers, and naming requests for forgiveness or meditation. Since we are made in the image of God—equally bestowed worth, and created according to His plan—it is God's imperative to love everyone equally, and to show love by caring for those in need.

For the musician who wants to learn more about specific modes and harmony, meditative music can be informed by Stella Benson's *Healing Modes* and other studies in therapeutic music.[29] These theories include

---

28 'Regional Euthanasia Review Committees Annual Report 2012'.
29 Benson, *The Healer's Way Companion.*

suggestions for beat and metre, entrainment of breath, comforting stable tempo, resonance and peaceful instruments to play at the bedside. The *Chalice of Repose* project in the United States and Europe sends responsive bedside music thanatologists to create an accessible vigil.

Case Studies

The following subsections provide brief overviews of our research studies relating to music and dementia, palliative care, and ageing in the general population.

Study – Impact of Music for People Living with Dementia

Anthony Storr describes engagement with music as 'a condition of heightened alertness, awareness, interest, and excitement; a generally enhanced state of being'.[30] The potential benefits of music for people with dementia include:

- Joy, quality of life
- meaning and purpose
- engagement, stimulation, involvement, participation
- reduced pain
- reduced behaviours
- improved engagement with mealtimes
- reduced stress around bathing
- reduced agitation
- reduced anxiety
- encouraging movement
- spiritual and emotional support
- ameliorated reliance on anti-depressant and anti-psychotic medications that have demonstrated reduced efficacy for people

---

30 Storr, *Music and the Mind*.

- with dementia yet have side-effects and interactions with other medications
- creative and emotional expression not contingent on speech or memory

Music in the form of individualised playlists of person-specific preferred music was supplied on small mobile devices with headphones to approximately 1,000 people in residential nursing homes across NSW and Victoria at HammondCare nursing homes. In addition, people with dementia enjoyed participatory music groups such as chapel services, performances by visiting and volunteer musicians, festive events including music from different cultures, and pianolas with piano rolls; singing to accompany people through care routines; and experimental musical instruments designed by students for people with dementia.

Feedback from residents, carers and family members indicated music overcomes language barriers, reinforces cultural identity and helps remember heritage—especially for those isolated from family. Music can restore enthusiasm and individuality, and it can serve to retell narratives of identity and often rekindle stories and associations from younger days. We observed people remembering words (including hymns), and the psalter when in the context of music. Notable was the joy of participation—more so than passive listening (which has the advantage of individualisation)—in group sing-alongs, where participants tried the tactile, textural, and physically engaging instruments designed by university students for residents with dementia. Drum and vocal ensembles with appropriate vintage songs and familiar lyrics added a different dimension (i.e., a sense of enabling, contributing, accomplishment, camaraderie, belonging, group interaction, and social involvement). Often staff, visitors, family and friends joined in.

Pastoral care staff and chaplains used music to open up interactions, contemplation, or conversations. Family relatives explained music provided relief and respite, entertainment in day-care centres, and the satisfaction of emotional connection (especially if conversation was scarce or absent), ultimately leading to a sense their relative was 'well' and spiritually nourished.

Study – Arts on Prescription Study

Arts on Prescription was a program designed for older people living in the community who were experiencing healthy ageing amongst the general population of older people with a diverse range of health and wellness needs. Predicated on a United Kingdom program, piloting the idea of General Practitioner's prescribing a course of participatory arts (the form chosen by the individual) to counteract loneliness, depression, social isolation, lack of transport; and harness positivity, zest for learning new skills, showing accomplishments in public – which are factors that influence physiological health and mental health.[31] The range of activities which were undertaken in this program included painting, ceramics, photography, a drumming group, music ensemble (band) and printmaking.

It was evident in the research mental health and spiritual well-being both have an influence on physical health and pain perception. We observed statistically significant improvement upon use of the Warwick-Edinburgh Mental Well-being Scale (WEMWBS), as well as a statistically significant increase in the level of self-reported creativity and frequency of creative activities.

Qualitative findings indicated the program provided the following:

- Challenging artistic activities which created a sense of purpose and direction;
- enabled personal growth and achievement; and
- empowered participants in a setting which fostered the development of meaningful relationships with others.

The results showed *Arts on Prescription* has a positive impact on the mental well-being of older people with diverse health and wellness needs and the *Arts on Prescription* model can assist in a holistic approach to meeting the health and wellness needs of older people. There is a growing body of evidence supporting the role of the arts in

---

31 Rigby, 'Selling Social Inclusion through the Arts', 25-28.

the enhancement of health and well-being.[32] Such 'prescription' is one way in which the activity is validated.

Scandinavian research suggests *Arts on Prescription* may also assist participants' ability to cope with long-standing pain.[33] Some art forms, such as movement and dance, naturally require physical activity. All artists were instructed to encourage physical activity where possible, to stand at an easel, or to walk outside to find objects. Satisfaction came from rediscovering curiosity, learning new skills, and developing a sense of accomplishment. Final works and performances were displayed in an open exhibition and concert, which were attended by family and friends.

Conclusion

It is hoped this overview of death, dying and dementia challenges the notion that loss of identity, dignity and spiritual well-being are inevitable consequences in palliative and dementia care. Revisiting the roots of humanity and God's love for us provides the key to compassionate and impartial care for others. The *imago Dei* (God creating humans in His own image for His purposes) is the basis for a sense of human worth which is not related to capacity and ability, productivity or physical or mental agility, nor to materiality and health, but to a sense of meaning which comes from peaceful relationships with God and with significant people. Value is to be found in belonging, acceptance and a realistic understanding of human finitude.

Just as the Bible grapples with the raw and challenging realities of life, it is hoped we may return to an understanding of the potential spiritual significance and final formation of dying, of recognition it is an important time and a time in which flourishing and spiritual communion is possible and valuable. Though pain and suffering are

---

32 Clift, 'Creative Arts as a Public Health Resource'; Clift and Camic, *Oxford Textbook of Creative Arts, Health, and Wellbeing*; Clift, et al. *An Evaluation of Community Singing for with COPD;* Cann, 'Arts and Cultural Activity'; Boyce, et al. 'The Impact of the Arts in Healthcare on Patients and Service Users'.

33 Rydstad, Löfgren and Drakos, *Rapport från ett pilot project*, cited in Stickley and Hui, 'Social Prescribing through Arts on Prescription in a UK City', 580-586.

difficult, and aversion is a natural human response (like discipline), it is possible to embrace its potential. As did literature, art, and communities of former times, we can afford to be more truthful about the experience of death and be present, patient and loving with people approaching their end, ultimately realising it is a privilege to accompany this aspect of the spiritual journey.

The secularising of society has lost its spirituality, sacraments and rituals for coming to terms with ageing and death in a dignified and gathered community context. Given this, there is an urgent need to retrieve the wisdom and sacredness of dying well.

Acknowledgements

The research mentioned in this chapter was conducted under the Human Research Ethics Committee approval of St. Vincent's Hospital Research Office. The research at HammondCare (2014–2018) was generously supported by The Thomas Foundation, HammondCare Foundation, NSW Government Department of Social Services Funding. Additionally, the research at St. Vincent's Hospital (2019) was conducted in collaboration with the University of Notre Dame Institute for Ethics and Society, supported by the St. Vincent's Health Network.

Bibliography

Benson, S. *The Healer's Way Companion: Soothing Music for Those in Pain, Volume I* (Seattle, WA: NewGrail Media, 2003).

Boyce, M., Bungay, H., Munn-Giddings, C. and Wilson, C. 'The Impact of the Arts in Healthcare on Patients and Service Users: A Critical Review', *Health & Social Care in the Community* 26, no. 4 (2018), 458–473.

Cohen, D. *The Loss of Self: A Family Resource for the Care of Alzheimer's Disease and Related Disorders* (New York: Penguin, 1994).

Breitbart, W., Rosenfeld, B., Pessin, H., Kaim, M., Funesti-Esch, J., Galietta, M. et al. 'Depression, Hopelessness, and Desire for Hastened Death in Terminally Ill Patients with Cancer', *The Journal of the American Medical Association* 284, no. 22 (2000), 2907–11.

Bryant, C. D. (ed.) *Handbook of Death and Dying* (London, UK: Sage Publications, 2003).

Cann, P. L. 'Arts and Cultural Activity: A Vital Part of the Health and Care System', *Australasian Journal on Ageing* 36, no. 2 (2017), 89–95.

Clift, S. 'Creative Arts as a Public Health Resource: Moving from Practice-Based Research to Evidence-Based Practice', *Perspectives in Public Health* 132, no. 3 (2012), 120–127.

Clift, S. and Camic, P. M. *Oxford Textbook of Creative Arts, Health, and Wellbeing* (Oxford, UK: Oxford University Press, 2016).

Clift, S., Morrison, I., Skingley, A., Page, S., Coulton, S., Treadwell, P., Vella-Burrows, T., Salisbury, I., Shipton, M. *An Evaluation of Community Singing for People with COPD (Chronic Obstructive Pulmonary Disease) Canterbury Christ Church University* (Canterbury, UK: Sidney De Haan Research Centre for Arts and Health, 2013).

Durkin, K. F. 'Death, Dying, and the Dead in Popular Culture', in Clifton D. Bryant, and Dennis L. Peck (eds.), *Handbook of Death & Dying* (London, UK: Sage Publications Inc., 2007).

Erikson, E. H. *The Life Cycle Completed: A Review* (New York & London: Norton, 1985).

Fowler, J. W. *Stages of Faith: The Psychology of Human Development and the Quest for Meaning* (1st edn; San Francisco: Harper & Row, 1981).

Fuchs, T. *The Memory of the Body*. <http://www.klinikum.uni-heidelberg.de/fileadmin/zpm/psychatrie/ppp2004/manuskript/fuchs.pdf> [accessed 10 September 2018].

Grof, S. *Books of the Dead* (London, UK: Thames & Hudson, 2013).

Hudson, R. E. 'God's Faithfulness and Dementia: Christian Theology', *Context, Journal of Religion, Spirituality & Aging* 28, no. 1–2 (2016), 50–67.

Hauerwas, S.	'The Gesture of a Truthful Story', *Theology Today* 42, no. 2 (1985), 181–185.
Hay, M. W.	'Building Spiritual Assessment Tools', *The American Journal of Hospice and Palliative Care* 25 Sept/Oct (1989).
Keck, D.	*Forgetting Whose We Are: Alzheimer's Disease and the Love of God* (Nashville, TN: Abingdon Press, 1996).
Kinoshita H, Maeda I, Morita T, et al.	'Place of Death and the Differences in Patient Quality of Death and Dying and Caregiver Burden. *Journal of Clinical Oncology* 33 (2015), 357-363.
Kitwood, T.	*Dementia Reconsidered: The Person Comes First* (London, UK: Open University Press, 1997).
Livability	'Dementia Friendly Churches', Last accessed 10 September 2019. https://livability.org.uk/dementia-friendly-churches-guide
Lunn, J.	'Becoming Truly Human: Charles Wesley's Understanding of Sanctification as Human Maturity and its Implications for 21st Century Ministry', Oxford Institute August (2013), 16–17. <https://oimts.files.wordpress.com/2013/09/2013-2-lunn.pdf> [accessed 10 September 2018].
MacKinlay, E.	*The Spiritual Dimension of Ageing* (London, UK: Jessica Kingsley Publishers, 2001).
Payne, B.	'Spiritual Maturity and Meaning-Filled Relationships: A Sociological Perspective', *Journal of Religious Gerontology* 7, no. 1/2 (1990), 25–39.
Pine, V. R.	'Social Organization and Death', *Omega* 3 (1972), 149–53.
'Regional Euthanasia Review Committees Annual Report 2012' (in Dutch).	<http://www.euthanasiecommissie.nl/overdetoetsings-commissies/jaarverslag> [accessed 25 June 2018].
Richmond, C.	'Dame Cicely Saunders', *British Medical Journal* 331, no. 7510 (2005), 238.
Rigby, T.	'Selling Social Inclusion through the Arts', *A Life in the Day* 8, no. 3 (2004), 25–28.

Rydstad, M., Löfgren, M. and Drakos, G. *Rapport från ett pilot projekt: Kultur på recept vid långvarig smärta* (2015). <https://www.mynewsdesk.com/se/kulturforvaltningen/documents/rapport-kultur-paa-recept-vid-laangvarig-smaerta-ett-pi- lotprojekt-45379> [accessed 8 September 2018].

Shneidman, E. *Death: Current Perspectives* (New York: McGraw-Hill Humanities, 1994).

Stickley, T. and Hui, A. 'Social Prescribing through Arts on Prescription in a UK City: Referrers', Perspectives (Part 2)', *Public Health* 126, no. 7 (2012), 580–586.

Storr, A. *Music and the Mind* (London, UK: Ballantine Books, 1993).

Swinton, J. *Dementia: Living in the Memories of God* (Grand Rapids, MI: Eerdmans, 2012).

———, 'Forgetting Whose We Are', *Journal of Religion, Disability & Health* 11, no. 1 (2007), 37–63.

———, *From Bedlam to Shalom: Towards a Practical Theology of Human Nature, Interpersonal Relationships and Mental Health Care* (New York, USA: Peter Lang Inc., International Academic Publishers, 2000).

Willows, D., and Swinton, J. *Spiritual Dimensions of Pastoral Care* (London, UK: Jessica Kingsley Publishers, 2013).

CHAPTER 9

Spiritual care needs in illness, dying and end-of-life choices

Mavis Salt

Abstract

In the twenty-first century, Western society finds itself contending with multiple choices for all of life but often not planning for life itself to end. Despite this non-attention to end-of-life issues, there is now more choice about how and when to end one's life when faced with illness or suffering. As assisted dying is becoming legalised in more countries, medical personnel, families and carers may struggle to cope when someone chooses to follow that path and end their life. Ageing and illness have a physical impact that is uniquely an individual experience. However, recent studies have highlighted a shared universal experience is in fact a spiritual one and there are spiritual tasks to be worked through towards end of life. This chapter does not endeavour to outline an ethical response to assisted dying; rather, it aims to stimulate thinking around suffering and autonomy and the importance of spiritual care.

Spiritual Care Needs in Illness, Dying and End-of-Life Choices

We are living in times of a global ageing population and increasing years of life for many. This also includes those with disabilities; however, despite longer living, each of us must face death at some point.

Technological advancement and treatments are helping sustain longer living, but also set a broader context around dying and death. In the Twenty First Century, the dying process takes far longer, often involving several chronic health conditions.[1] Increasingly, people die when they are old. They are also more likely than their forebears to know they are going to die in the relatively near future. However, we are not taking the opportunity to help people plan to die well. In the last year of life, many experience a disconnected, confusing and distressing array of services, interventions and relationships with health professionals. And many do not get enough palliative care.

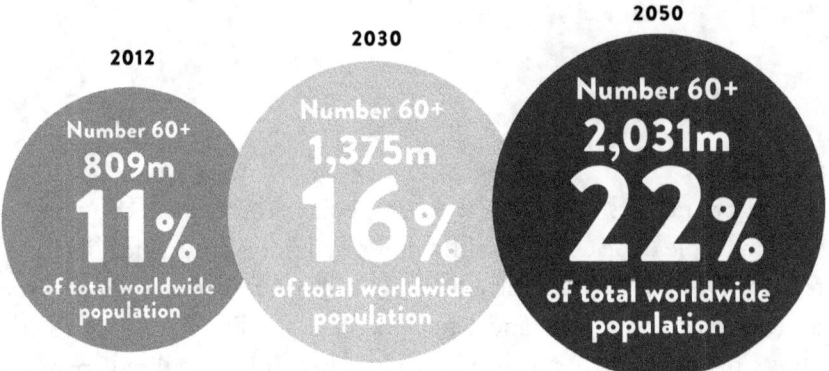

Figure 1: Number and proportion of people aged 60-plus worldwide in 2012, 2030 and 2050[2]

This chapter outlines a context for the church around aspects of the ageing journey, as well as death and dying. Other significant factors are perspectives on autonomy and how a spiritual care response can support addressing existential issues, specifically the importance of preparing for suffering. Suffering impacts all people at some point and can be physical and emotional—importantly, however, it is a spiritual battle when end of life is faced. At the same time, when misinformed or misunderstood attitudes and language are emphasised regarding

---

1   McNamara and Rosenwax, 'The Mismanagement of Dying,' 373–383.
2   Number and proportion of people aged 60-plus worldwide in 2012, 2030 and 2050. UNDESA Population Division, World Population Prospects: The 2010 Revision. Available from http://esa.un.org/unpd/wpp/index.htm

death, dying and disabilities, a negative impact influences whole communities. However, accurate knowledge and preparedness can support the spiritual task. Furthermore, an added context in the Twenty First Century is the legalisation of assisted dying in some countries. Therefore, a potential response is outlined as carers or staff may have people requesting aid in dying and potential risks for vulnerable people, as well as caring for ourselves and scriptural reassurances.

Within populations, there is great diversity of generational age groups, cultural and societal attitudes to ageing, as well as differing expectations and goals for life. There is now a strong culture of individualism and expectation of autonomy, particularly in Western culture. At the same time, there tends to be avoidance towards even thinking about end of life, and certainly death and dying are not talked about easily or planned for, especially so within Western cultures. The avoidance of dealing with prospective death impacts decision-making around illness and dying, and these attitudes also impact the provision of pastoral care within churches. It is a natural human response to fear the unknown and have concerns regarding potential suffering, which may be involved for us individually and with respect to loved ones experiencing the dying process.

Older people, their loved ones and those who would provide pastoral care are dealing with issues that are increasingly complex ethically, emotionally and spiritually due to the impact of longer living with illnesses and ageing. Decisions based on personal value systems can be around, for example, treatment, pain control, organ donation, and requesting assisted death. Although dying is part of the life journey, it often involves suffering, pain, intense aloneness, grief and sometimes hovering for an uncertain time between life and death.[3]

The Figure 2 highlights the impact of institutionalised dying that seems to be the result of not having these important conversations around death and dying.[4] Preference for dying at home not a reality for many older Australians.

---

3   Barbato, *Caring for Living and the Dying*, 7.
4   Broad et al., 'Where Do People Die?' 257–267, cited in Swerissen and Duckett, *Dying Well*, 4.

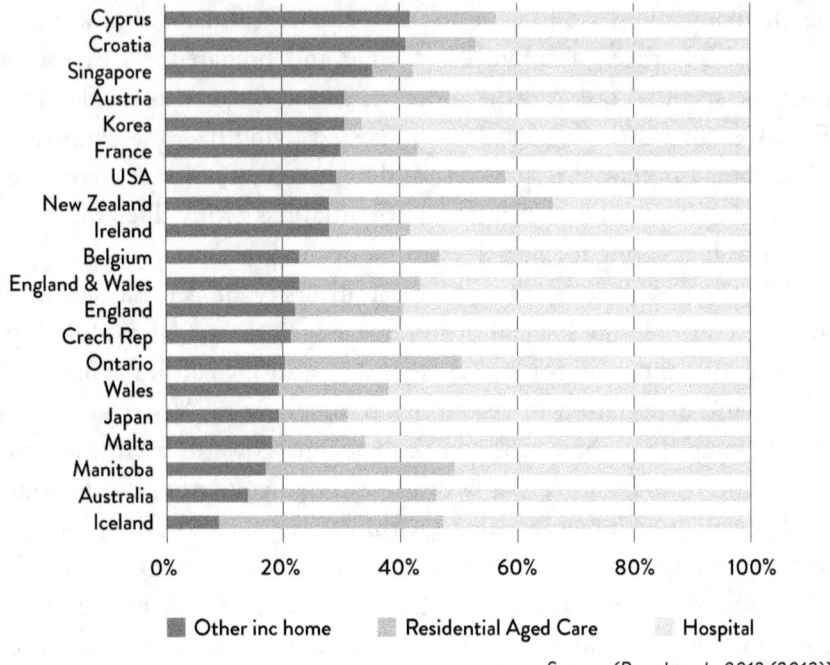

Figure 2: Location of deaths in selected OECD countries; per cent of deaths

Another significant factor impacting decision-making is the Twenty First Century expectation in hospitals by medical professionals, patients and families that all that is medically possible to sustain life must be done. This would seem to be a new ritual, where family members seek assurance they have fulfilled their duties. There are now technological sounds such as heart monitors and other noise, which have replaced the quieter meditative aspects around the dying person within hospitals.[5]

The following statistics regarding dementia, the baby-boomer generation and living longer with disabilities are also important to highlight in conversations around death and dying.

---

5   Gordon, 'Rituals in Death and Dying'.

Dementia Australian Statistics[6]

Dementia is the second leading cause of death of Australians, contributing to 5.4 per cent of all deaths in males and 10.6 per cent of all deaths in females annually. In 2016, dementia became the leading cause of death among Australian females, surpassing heart disease, which has been the leading cause of death for both males and females since the early Twentieth Century. Females account for 64.4 per cent of all dementia-related deaths. Specifically, in 2016, an average of 36 people died daily, where dementia was the underlying cause of death.

In 2018, there was an estimated 425,416 Australians living with dementia:

- 191,367 (45 per cent) males
- 234,049 (55 per cent) females.

Baby Boomers

- The number of older people increase faster than population growth and, consequently, the number of people who die each year in Australia will almost double in the next quarter of a century.
- As the number of people dying each year increases, pressure to improve the quality of dying is also likely to increase.
- In the near future, increased life expectancy and the transition of the baby-boomer generation to older age will see the proportion of older people in the population increase faster than population growth. Those aged over 85 will increase from 2 to 4 per cent of the population.
- People are also living longer with disabilities and may have protracted lengths of time with limited functioning, particularly physical which may be due to comorbidity of disease.

---

6 Dementia Australia, 'Dementia Statistics'.

Disability

Age group	1st	2nd	3rd	4th	5th
75–84	Coronary heart disease (13%)	Dementia (7.7%)	COPD (6.8%)	Stroke (6.1%)	Lung cancer (4.5%)
85–94	Coronary heart disease (17%)	Dementia (15%)	Stroke (8.6%)	COPD (4.9%)	Diabetes (2.7%)
95+	Dementia (21%)	Coronary heart disease (19%)	Stroke (9.2%)	Lower respiratory infections (3.1%)	Falls (2.8%)

■ Infections ■ Cancer ■ Cardiovascular ■ Respiratory ■ Neurological
■ Endocrine ■ Injuries

COPD = chronic obstructive pulmonary disease.
Source: Australian Burden of Disease Study 2011; Table S3.1.1.

Figure 3: Leading Causes of total burden among people aged 75 and over, by age, 2011[7]

For this reason, it is vital a theological and pastoral care response is formulated based on the understanding that when existential spiritual issues are worked through with supportive pastoral care, the physical and emotional experience of dying and death are also supported.[8] A foundational Pastoral theological response that addresses existential spiritual issues can support sustaining meaning, achieving peace throughout ageing, disabilities and coming to the end-of-life stage. Unfortunately, such an intentional response has been lacking generally in the care of older people and training of pastoral carers in the church.[9]

Considerable theological work and reflection is required, particularly within the dying journey, where a separation process between the earthly life and what may lie beyond is part of the process. There may

7 The Australian Institute of Health and Welfare, 'Burden of Disease across the Life Stages', 87.
8 Tomer and Grafton, *Existentialism and Death Attitudes*, 7-37.
9 Gerkin, *An Introduction to Pastoral Care*, 15.

already be a sense of the divine in the one dying; however, the greater need is reassurance as to whether the person is acceptable or in a loving relationship with that divine being.[10]

In Western society particularly, many people still struggle to talk easily and share feelings about their own death and that of the people close to them.[11] In fact, the following euphemism bubble (Figure 4) reflects the variety of words used rather than the terms 'death' or 'died'.[12]

Figure 4

This highlights how important our use of language is and its resultant impact and influence. Additionally, what are realistic expectations around individual perspectives on self-care and autonomy? We need to understand what we are actually saying when we discuss issues regarding ageing, disability, death, and dying, as well as our interpretations of autonomy. A dictionary definition of 'autonomy' is that of self-government and acting or possessing freedom to make independent choices.[13] To a degree, this is acceptable; however, our lives and actions have an impact on others. Newton's third law in physics states that, for every action, there is an equal and opposite reaction with objects, but so too do our lives and choices cause reactions for others.

10 Bregar, *Acquiring Wisdom*, 55.
11 Barbato, *Caring for Living and the Dying*, 4.
12 ABC News, "'Passing Away', 'Kicking the Bucket' and 'Pushing Up Daisies'".
13 *The Australian Pocket Oxford Dictionary*.

The Health Information and Quality Authority in Dublin stress the following points.[14] First, 'personal autonomy is an understanding of human beings as being worthy of respect. This includes respecting a person's dignity, privacy and his or her choices. Respect for autonomy is important in the context of health and social care, as it is central to person-centred care'.

Put this way, it seems this is more a responsibility of those caring rather than a personal battle for an individual. Interestingly, it is also stated that 'autonomy does not always involve total independence. Often, decisions are made based on our relationships with another or with the assistance of others. Respect for autonomy does not mean all choices are facilitated'.[15] Proponents of self-government fail to recognise a healthy, fully-functioning body is required to achieve autonomy, and the medical response to illnesses aims to assist a return to autonomy, which is not always possible or best care.

Contrasting Stories on Autonomy

Harriet was impacted by developing dementia along with depression and was fiercely endeavouring to remain in independent living. She had some home-care visits, but she was often neglecting meals and mixing up medication while relying heavily on friends (who were also aged) to supplement her support needs, often causing them great distress. She was placed in residential aged care, which she bitterly resented and she continued to have a very self-focused viewpoint on her own perceived needs with little understanding of the impact on others.

In contrast, Andrew had, as a younger man, become heavily dependent on alcohol to the point where he was at risk of early death. He made the choice to try and change his life direction, which meant moving into residential care when he was gravely ill. He realised the impact his life choices were having on family as well as himself and, over the final years of his life, chose to focus not only on self-discipline

---

14   Health Information and Quality Authority in Dublin, 'Supporting Peoples Autonomy', 10.
15   Health Information and Quality Authority in Dublin, 'Supporting Peoples Autonomy', 10.

but how to support his community and volunteering to help others.

These stories are not to say one way is right and the other wrong, but they help to illustrate that each individual life and choices can have an impact on others—we can never be totally self-sufficient or fully autonomous.

Along with striving for autonomy and individualism is the belief that everyone has rights which of course is correct in the fair treatment of all people. However, media writers tend to use legal language regarding rights in association with dying and death. What is not stressed is that it is not always possible to make choices that are categorically 'right' morally, which can then cause a dilemma in deciding who may have a greater right than another. Often community opinion or decisions are not based on correct or full information, which can lead to dangerous outcomes, especially around dying and death.[16]

However, we should also consider the influence of news headlines that grab attention with bold statements or headings such as 'right to die', 'self-determination', and 'we want choice about when to die'. Facing death can reveal our values, assumptions, priorities and commitments. There are always differing viewpoints and moral compasses within society and also the church (e.g., the right to choose any action about personal life versus sanctity of life, autonomy versus physician's responsibility, and physician-assisted suicide versus refusal of treatment).

We are now living in an era where assisted dying has been legalised in some countries and is gradually expanding to more countries. How do we provide spiritual and compassionate pastoral care to others in our scope of ministry as well as to ourselves in the face of suffering and loss of meaning or hopelessness?

Today's Challenge Within a New Reality

Life goals in Western societies tend to focus on the first half of life, with emphasis on attaining education, pursuing a career, building material possession, and extending family while living life at a very fast pace.

---

16 Becker, *Ministry with Older Persons*, 130.

This can have the impact of inhibiting the learning of some deeper life lessons, particularly if the goals are not realised. Furthermore, the life journey paradoxically involves loss and gain, which tends to be more so from mid-life onwards.

A valid point raised by Huber is that of 'core identity not being dependent on material possessions, status, relationships, or even own bodies and minds'.[17] Discovering the core involves spiritual work. Nouwen and Gaffney believe there is hard work involved in traversing experiences of loss, grief, pain and suffering.[18] Failure to process the spiritual tasks leads to what Huber interprets as bitterness and stunted spiritual growth of the core self. The longer we live, the more ongoing impact there is of loss (e.g., deteriorating health, decrease in energy levels, limited ability to move around and care for ourselves, loss of loved ones and other relationships through death or relocation, and the loss of memory).

Kathleen Fischer speaks of needing a spirituality of ageing that holds together both the gains and losses of the ageing process.[19] A spiritual perspective on loss reflects that loss is a normal part of life and can lead to personal growth and development. Through ministry with older people, Koepke has found the following:

> Some persons spiritually decline as they grow older, ending in despair as their core beliefs crumble under the weight of age. Others thrive, not because they don't have challenges, but because their spiritual focus reveals other perspectives that are more important and vital for life than the challenges. These people are not defined by the physical, emotional and social perspectives that often are a part of the ageing experience but by the hope, courage and an inner strength that comes from their core beliefs, their 'Essential Spirit'. In order to thrive, the essential spirit is fed and developed.[20]

---

17 Huber, *Aging as Pilgrimage*, 8.
18 Nouwen and Gaffney, *Aging, The Fulfillment of Life*, 45.
19 Fischer, *Autumn Gospel*, 177.
20 Koepke, *The Essential Spirit*.

Spiritual Care: Our Response

Some shared spiritual needs experienced in ageing as well as death and dying can be disempowerment, hopelessness, intense loneliness, and disconnectedness from the church, community and family, all while attempting to process feelings of self-worth, guilt and issues related to forgiveness.[21]

Importantly, to provide effective care, pastoral carers must have faced the reality of their own dying and death, which can also be challenging for those of the Christian faith despite the gospel of hope through resurrection.[22] Therefore, there is both preparatory work involved for the pastoral carer and also the spiritual work required by the dying person that includes dealing with grief, fear, possible depression and the unfinished business of life. The pastoral task is to assist in self-acceptance and forgiveness, which is necessary for a 'good death' despite the quality of life lived previously.[23] Pastoral care language and the images of a shepherd caring for a flock of sheep come from the theological root of God incarnate in the person of Jesus caring for those estranged from God the Father. In laying down his life, Jesus is the good shepherd. He then asks of his church to also care for each other, and discipleship teaching in the New Testament reinforces this aim—that is, 1 Peter 5:2: 'Care for the flock that God has entrusted to you. Watch over it willingly, not grudgingly—not for what you will get out of it, but because you are eager to serve God'.

As people are now living longer, some older people calmly wait for death and prepare well, but there are a number of older people and their family members who are not willing to prepare for their eventual death. However, there is now greater choice available across many areas of life, particularly in terms of medical and surgical treatments, which can have both positive and negative outcomes for all age groups depending on need. It must be emphasised that pastoral care provision to the dying should come from the perspectives of the dying person, their family and other relationships, as well as from the

---

21 Anderson, 'Pastoral Care and the Spiritual Formation of Older Persons', 106.
22 Becker, *Ministry with Older Persons*.
23 Barbato, 'Caring for Living and the Dying', 284.

individual's personal beliefs and value system. Within an ageing context, we understand our spirituality to be that which sustains purpose, gives hope and builds relationship connections, and which may also be expressed through religious practice. We must also be alert to meeting the spiritual needs of those who do not practice religion. In fact, having chaplaincy and spiritual care support in residential care is very important, as expressed by older people themselves in a case study. The following quotes reflect the contrast in spiritual expression: 'I have been supported by the chaplain in maintaining a stronger religious faith, but I think it's also very important having a chaplain for non-churched people, as the spiritual side is important and a big thing when you get old'.[24]

Further quotes from the case study reflect that, 'for me spiritual or spirituality means an awareness of God and that life is boring without spiritual and religious support, as our spirit needs feeding. I have regular devotions and practise the presence of God'. Another older person sees that 'my spirituality or faith has developed more depth in ageing and I really appreciate time with God and my relationships with others'.[25]

It should also be considered that many older people must have questions within longevity. Understanding spiritual needs and supporting the spiritual quest in ageing has the potential to transform a limited viewpoint of the physical earthly life to an eternal perspective and purpose. We all need encouragement to undertake the hard task of spiritual work to support development. Later life can be a time of learning through suffering, gaining spiritual maturity and growing through vulnerability. This is best achieved through the support of meaningful relationships and community.[26] Along with the benefits of spiritual direction is the simple concept of a spiritual support friend, where there is strong connecting and bonding while growing together. We are also reminded of the helpfulness of lament which can assist in the expression of pain, rage, sorrow and grief.[27]

---

24 Salt, *Effectiveness of a Spiritual Care Assessment*, 16.
25 Salt, *Effectiveness of a Spiritual Care Assessment*, 17.
26 Stoneking, 'Modernity: The Social Construction of Aging', 87.
27 Evans, *Is God Still at the Bedside?*, 379.

Within the context of death and dying, Hardwi explains that 'spiritual suffering at the end of life may begin well before one is actively dying. Spiritual care is the core of care for the dying: also that of greater personal choice to himself is not whether he wants CPR or artificial feeding and so on but rather how to face his own death, how to bring his life to a close and how best to help his family go on without him'.[28] It is also now understood that different sources of suffering (if uncontrolled) actually lead to shorter survival as well as impacting quality of life.

Gawande also reiterates this in his experience of medicine, that prolonging life itself is not the only focus requiring support for severely ill and dying people.[29] Other concerns include 'avoiding suffering, strengthening relationships with family and friends, being mentally aware, not being a burden on others and achieving a sense that their life is complete'.

We will all suffer at some point in our lives to varying degrees and, to grow spiritually throughout our lives, we need to build up our resource pool. Paradoxically, the life journey involves loss and gain. Towards this, Huber raised a valid point: 'core identity [is] not being dependent on material possessions, status, relationship and even own bodies and minds'.[30]

Discovering the core involves spiritual work. There is hard work involved in attempts to traverse experiences of loss, grief, pain and suffering. Failure to process the spiritual tasks leads to what Huber interprets as bitterness, and stunted spiritual growth of the core self. The benefit of spiritual work is not only for individuals, but also the greater community. Further perspectives on this, particularly in thinking of the end-of-life stage, are quotes from an older person who found 'the meeting of their spiritual needs actually helped them carry on with life when they were contemplating suicide'. Other older people recognise that 'life can be beautiful and cruel and I am grieving the death of a son as well as my husband, so spiritual support is vital'.

---

28   Hardwig, 'Spiritual Issues at the End of Life', 28–30.
29   Gawande, *Being Mortal*, 155.
30   Huber, *Aging as Pilgrimage*, 8.

Other examples include one woman who took care of her sister's children when her sister died at the age of 32 years and two other women who helped raise grandchildren.[31]

No matter our age, pain (including physical, psychological and spiritual aspects if untreated) heightens the sense of loss of control and having anything of value to contribute to others. It is understandable that pain inhibits enjoyment of life and full engagement in life. When pain is uncontrolled, we may each relate to the following points made by Evans, where 'people stay home which then increases loneliness, loss of meaning builds, there is angst, despair and for older people a feeling of simply growing old and useless'.[32] In particular, spiritual pain comes to the fore when facing death, as impending loss and separation is felt.

It is vital to understand pain has a huge influence on our spirituality and religious beliefs, which can either be strengthened or even relinquished. Additionally, it is relevant that technology not only enhances our living, but can also lengthen our dying. Paradoxically, however, while advancements in technology have helped to prolong and sustain life, such development has generated less regard for those whom the technology supports, such as older people or those with disabilities. There are also perceptions that those with disabilities are 'suffering' and are unable to enjoy a fulfilled life. We live in what Wiebe refers to as 'able-list social conditioning that equates disability with pain, frailty, incapacity and poor quality of life'.[33]

It also seems contradictory that teaching around ageing within the Australian vocational training context talks of empowering older people and those with disabilities, but a major hindrance to this involves external factors that do not keep pace with these ideals. Factors such as ease or difficulty accessing buildings, services, and transport, but also societal attitudes that perceive disability as something that needs to be 'fixed'. Those with disabilities are often not perceived as empowered people who can contribute to society. A further challenge for a person becoming disabled later in life is the able-list perceptions they have absorbed.

---

31 Salt, *Effectiveness of a Spiritual Care Assessment*, 17.
32 Evans, *Is God Still at the Bedside?*, 223.
33 Wiebe, 'Better Dead Than Disabled'.

This can exacerbate loss of meaning and purpose, but also their value as people who can greatly influence choices towards end of life.

Further to these important points is clarity around what supports dignity and well-being. Clear teaching on what comprises dignity is vital, as a perceived lack of dignity can also influence end-of-life choices.

Another perspective on suffering is raised by Fowler when she highlights the following:

> What we in America have done is to attempt to use our medical knowledge and medical power to 'tame the terror and eliminate the darkness', which is suffering, from our lives. We have asked medicine to do something that is not its fundamental purpose. In its care of the body, medicine and technology can dull the sword of disease or pain or even death, but it cannot, itself, either tell us where to 'draw the line' or come to grips with the issue of suffering.[34]

This is a vital point that leads me to wonder whether there is a skewed focus on physical pain to the neglect of addressing other forms of suffering. For example, the experience of ongoing decline, loss, prospective death and beliefs as to whether there is life after death can all contribute to suffering. In this way, it could be a spiritual crisis rather than fear of physical pain that drives the desire for help to die. Additionally, spiritual distress occurs for family members. A commonality we all share would be regret over different aspects of life (e.g., personal choices, relationship breakdown, accumulated grief and loss, issues of guilt and forgiveness). These are all spiritual issues.

In an ever-changing context in many countries, it is now possible to choose how and when to end your life. Euthanasia literally means 'good death', but in our modern understanding, it refers to ending a person's life where an agent other than the person themselves is involved. Active euthanasia is a physician administering a lethal dose of medication to a patient who is the final agent in events leading to the person's death. It is killing by an act of commission. Evans is helpful to this point, suggesting that, instead, the focus can be on euapothenesto,

---

34 Fowler, 'Suffering and Spirituality'.

which refers to good dying and a more helpful moral compass in making decisions.[35]

Passive euthanasia is allowing a person to die or abstaining from treatments to prolong life. In this way, it is omission. It is vital to appreciate it is not dishonourable to accept death as a normal part of life and that choosing to withdraw from receiving life-sustaining treatment (while labelled passive 'euthanasia') is simply allowing the natural outcome of death in a body unable to sustain life.

Suicide is death by one's own hand, as distinct from heroic self-sacrifice, which is giving up one's life for a cause, principle or another person. Physician-assisted suicide is arranging death by mutual agreement between the patient and physician. This can be referred to as 'aid in dying', since patients take the lethal dose themselves. In order to clarify the terms around resulting death, it is important to focus on who acted last. Additionally, treatment options for people include potential to refuse active treatment, withdrawal from treatment, palliative sedation, and reasonable to unreasonable interventions. There is now more potential to negotiate how and when we die.[36]

Responding to Requests

A part of working through a life-limiting illness can be expressing a desire to die but not necessarily acting on that desire. It is also understandable that, if there are many uncontrolled symptoms, life seems untenable when there is a lack of adequate support and relief from symptoms.

At times, people are unaware of how the palliative care team can help and often palliative support is not commenced early enough. Carpenter, as cited in Weir, stresses, 'dying is not just a medical event—it's also a psychological and social experience. Palliative care addresses medical, psychological social and spiritual needs of a person with a serious illness and their care partners'.[37]

---

35 Evans, *Is God Still at the Bedside?*, 61.
36 Evans, *Is God Still at the Bedside?*, 112, 115.
37 Weir, 'How Psychologists Can Bring their Expertise to End-of-Life Care'.

Meador observes that an important foundational step in provision of palliative care is spiritual care which reflects the individual needs of the one dying and also those providing care.[38]

The great pioneer of Palliative Care, Cicely Saunders, stated that, 'you matter because you are you, and you matter to the end of your life. We will do all we can not only to help you die peacefully, but also to live until you die'.[39] This is the challenge within longer living and potential frailty to continue living until death. It is also relevant to point out that studies have revealed pain is not the dominant factor influencing requests for death, but rather clinical depression and hopelessness. Work by Dublin Health[40] and End of Life Essentials Education[41] reiterates and outlines that a diagnosis and treatment of depression is vital. Despite receiving a life-limiting diagnosis, depression is not simply a reaction to the news but an added component for the person that requires treatment. Accordingly, it is important to also treat any mood or anxiety disorder.

While specifically focusing on training for physicians, an online module on *End of Life Essentials* makes the following helpful point, which is relevant for all health professionals.[42] Any request for assistance to die is an invitation for communication and therapeutic intervention. Sitting behind any request is the individual's unique physical, psychological, social and spiritual concerns. The request is also an indication of potential unrelieved suffering. The importance of reflective listening and asking open-ended questions is stressed. In offering spiritual support, it is possible to rekindle hope and look for meaning-making within that situation. Skanse also reiterates this from a chaplaincy perspective, outlining that 'people make choices based on their beliefs.[43] Our job is to help people discover what they truly believe, so they won't regret making the decision and we help them to not feel alone'. A goal for all those in caring roles is to provide

---

38 Meador, 'Spiritual Care at the End of Life'.
39 AZQuotes.com, 'Cicely Saunders Quote'.
40 Health Information and Quality Authority in Dublin, 'Supporting Peoples Autonomy', 10.
41 End of Life Essentials, 'Physician Assisted Suicide'.
42 CareSearch, 'Physician Assisted Suicide'.
43 Skanse, *'Who Decides When to Pull the Plug'*.

clarification around assistance to die, specifically in terms of whether there are any misunderstandings regarding what is involved. Therefore, there is great emotional effort and important consequences involved for family, friends and staff.

Interestingly, actually talking about assisted death does not increase the risk of assisted death being requested and acted on, but may help lessen the risk. Addressing the commonly expressed fears of loss of control, pain and other symptoms, feeling burden to others, lack of dignity, and potential desertion by others can clarify outcomes for people. Some helpful advice is written for nurses but also correlates well for pastoral/spiritual carers. As Fowler recognises:

> Suffering has a cry and that cry is: be. Be with me. Be, not do. Be, even in silence. Just be. Nurses, however, are good at doing, doing, doing, speaking, speaking, and speaking. Here, suffering brings us back to the necessity of relationship. It is in being-with-another and in hearing that person's lament, that the person who suffers comes to totality or completeness. While most laments are phrased in the language of faith, this need not be the case. Laments can be created with no religious content and can be used as a template for the expression of suffering or a mental template for one working with one who suffers, who needs to express their lament.[44]

Other practical suggestions include assisting with recording life stories. The oral telling of our story and assistance writing the narrative can support finding peace. Not only is there a recorded history for family, then, but as Rayburn recognises, 'reflections on where they have been, what they have accomplished and what they have regarded as most meaningful are vital to establishing a sense of what life has been all about and in what way they have contributed to the flow and essence of life'.[45]

To achieve peace towards the end of life, all people, regardless of religious beliefs, have practical matters, family, spiritual and religious

---

44 Fowler, 'Suffering and Spirituality'.
45 Rayburn, 'Clinical and Pastoral Issues', 94.

elements to work through. Attempting to resolve unfinished business is important—that is, opportunities for repentance and forgiveness while working through issues of guilt, sorrow and saying farewells. An important goal for pastoral care is to enhance end of life while also supporting wider family interactions. Rayburn highlights four main points for one dying: having the opportunity to ask for forgiveness, to offer forgiveness, and to express thanks and love, all of which can contribute to healing. A helpful point for those with no religious belief is perhaps focusing on the cosmos and that they may continue as a part of nature.[46]

In particular within a Christian perspective, going over our life story within God's narrative and noting what we understand as God at work throughout our timeline is very meaningful. Experienced hospice staff have found not only the liturgical rituals of worship, prayer and scripture helpful, but also the use of the arts can free up and enable the dying person to express deeper issues. Provision of tools that encourage creativity for painting, sculpting, writing poems and journaling also provides a safe outlet for expressing memories and complex issues. Music is often helpful in different genres, but particularly hymns, chants, requiems and laments can be significant. This can be achieved either through live musicians or music via the Internet. Literature can also be helpful, and looking through photos can stimulate meaningful sharing.[47]

Risks

Wiebe highlights the following points of risk for vulnerable people in choosing to die:

> If anyone is tacitly acknowledged as unworthy, they are at risk, especially when budgeting finances and spending.

---

46 Rayburn, 'Clinical and Pastoral Issues', 107.
47 Evans, *Is God Still at the Bedside?*, 385.

At times, full options of health support are not explored or offered to those with disabilities.

All people have dignity because they are human.[48]

In parts of the United States, assisted death is an option. One personal story involves a young woman not given the chemotherapy option of treatment for her disease by her health fund; however, she was covered for the assisted suicide drug, which cost less financially. In this way, it is understandable that assisted suicide ultimately affects everyone's healthcare if only seen from a beneficial budget perspective rather than more costly treatments. Within the ageing perspective, and particularly in terms of dementia, with greater numbers of people impacted, there is risk in the future of potential decisions to end life. It is understandable that there is danger in making hasty decisions without adequate information and support around illness and dying. It is vital that all representatives from a healthcare team can provide education and support to the family and caregivers as well as the one impacted by illness.

A good death is the correct definition of euthanasia, where the aim is to give people dignity, choice and support to address their physical, personal, social and spiritual needs. The Grattan Institute suggests three specific reforms required within Australia:

- More public discussion regarding the limits of healthcare as death approaches, and what we want for the end of life;
- better planning to ensure our preferences for the end of life are met; and
- services for those dying of chronic illness need to focus less on institutional care and more on people's wishes to die at home and in home-like settings.[49]

The report published in 2014 suggests the voluntary euthanasia debate often clouds this issue. The writers recognise voluntary euthanasia and assisted suicide are rare, even in jurisdictions that permit them. Instead,

---

48 Wiebe, 'Better Dead Than Disabled'.
49 Swerissen and Duckett, 'Dying Well', 2.

this report is about ensuring that when death inevitably comes for each of us, we die comfortably and in surroundings we would choose. We need the courage to promote mature discussions regarding a topic that many dislike but that cannot be avoided.

Self-Care

It is important to understand our own values and responses to end-of-life choices. We need to prepare and continue supporting others who may think and choose different options to us.

When someone chooses to die, both staff and residents in care need opportunities to share how they are feeling and coping, while simultaneously being supported to work through their grief. It is important for everyone impacted to take time to reflect and express how they are feeling. Within residential aged care there are already some good practices regarding grief and loss. However, there may need to be extra focus on different debriefing opportunities and supervision for staff and chaplains in a future where people seek assistance to die.

Finally, we need to recognise suffering is universal and we cannot always prevent or control it. As Fowler explains:

> When I am present for the suffering and lament of another, truly present, I am reminded that suffering is also my lot, even if not right here, right now. As I share in another's suffering and lament I am present to them, I allow the terror and darkness that cannot be controlled to confront me in my own frailty. This presence is a presence in vulnerability-the vulnerability of the shared human condition-that, while it still retains identity boundaries, is open to an ontological change in both persons by virtue of human connectedness.[50]

There are also many scripture reassurances that remind us we are not alone in the complexities of life and as our life journey reaches its end. One passage from Psalm 84:5–8 is particularly helpful here:

---

50 Fowler, 'Suffering and Spirituality'.

> Blessed are those whose strength is in you, who have set their hearts on pilgrimage. As they pass through the Valley of Baca (a place of weeping), they make it a place of springs; the autumn rains also cover it with pools. They go from strength to strength till each appears before God in Zion. Hear my prayer, O Lord God Almighty; listen to me, O God of Jacob.

Furthermore, as Jesus promises in Matthew 11:28–30 of the New Testament: 'Come to me, all you who are weary and burdened and I will give you rest. Take my yoke upon you and learn from me, for I am gentle and humble in heart and you will find rest for your souls. For my yoke is easy and my burden is light'.

In conclusion, Arnold reminds us that 'dying is the final hardest test of courage'.[51]

Additionally, the Apostle Paul, writing from personal experience, encourages us to not lose heart. Our body may waste away, but there is an inward spiritual renewal possible found in 2 Corinthians 4:16–18. The provision of spiritual and pastoral care can assist older people and their families from all cultures and religious expressions facilitate the complexities around ageing, illness, dying and death.

---

51 Arnold, *Rich in Years*, 123.

Bibliography

ABC News. "Passing Away', 'Kicking the Bucket' and 'Pushing Up Daisies': How We Avoid Talking About Death'. Last modified 23 may, 2017. http://www.abc.net.au/news/2017-05-23/why-we-dont-speak-openly-about-death-and-dying/8547824

Anderson, L. 'Pastoral Care and the Spiritual Formation of Older Persons', *Journal of Religion, Spirituality & Aging* 21, no. 1-2 (2008), 104–118.

Arnold, J. C. *Rich in Years: Finding Peace and Purpose in Long Life* (Elsmore, Australia: The Plough Publishing House, 2013).

AZQuotes.com 'Cicely Saunders Quote', Wind and Fly LTD. Accessed January 19, 2019. https://wwwazquotes.com/quote/521987

Barbato, M. *Caring for Living and the Dying* (Adelaide: Griffin Press, Adelaide, 2010).

Becker, A. H. *Ministry with Older Persons* (Minneapolis: Augsburg Publishing House, 1986).

Bregar, J. 'Acquiring Wisdom: A Metaphor for the Theory and Praxis of the End Stages of Life', *Journal of Religion, Spirituality & Aging* 25, no. 1 (2013), 52–64.

Broad, Joanna B et al. 'Where Do People die? An International Comparison of the Percentage of Deaths Occurring in Hospital and Residential Aged Care Settings in 45 Populations, Using Published and Available Statistics', *International Journal of Public Health* vol. 58,2 (2013), 257-67.

Caresearch. 'Physician-Assisted Suicide' (Self-Study Module 14) in *Education in Palliative and End-of-Life care for Oncology: End of Life Essentials: Education for Acute Hospitals*, mm.Learn.org. Accessed Online August 2017

Dementia Australia: 'Statistics', Last modified January, 2020. https://www.dementia.org.au/statistics: (accessed 2017)

Evans, A. R. *Is God Still at the Bedside?* (Grand Rapids, Michigan: Wm. B. Eerdmans Publishing Co., 2011).

Fischer, K. *Autumn Gospel – Women in the Second Half of Life* (Paulist Press, New Jersey, 1995).

Fowler, M.	'Suffering and Spirituality: Nursing and Health Care Ethics: A Legacy and a Vision'. *American Nurse Today* 4, no. 5 (2009).
Gawande, A.	*Being Mortal* (Bevin Way London: Profile Books Ltd., 2014).
Gerkin, C. V.	*An Introduction to Pastoral Care* (Nashville: Abingdon Press, 1997).
Gordon, M.	'Rituals in Death and Dying: Modern Medical Technologies Enter the Fray', *Rambam Maimonides Medical Journal* 6, no. 1 (2015), 1–7.
Hardwig, J.	*Spiritual Issues at the End of Life: A Call for Discussion* (Hastings Center Report 30, no. 2, 2000), 28–30.
Health Information and Quality Authority in Dublin,	'Supporting People's Autonomy: A Guidance Document'. https://www.hiqa.ie/sites/default/files/2017-01/Supporting-Peoples-Autonomy.pdf: Accessed August 2017
Helpage International,	'Ageing in the Twenty-First Century: A Celebration and A Challenge'. www.helpage.org/resources/ageing-in-the-21st-century-a-celebration-and-a-challenge/accessed August 2017
Huber, L. W.	'Aging as Pilgrimage: Spiritual Potentials of Late Life', in M. A. M. S. H. Kimble (Ed.), *Aging, Spirituality, and Religion* Vol. 2 (Minneapolis: Augsburg Fortress, 2003).
Kimble, M. A.	'Beyond the Biomedical Paradigm. Generating a Spiritual Vision of Ageing', *Journal of Religious Gerontology* 12, no. ¾ (2002), 31–41.
Koepke, D. R.	*The Essential Spirit* (Eugene, USA: Wipf and Stock Publishers, 2016).
Meador, K.	'Spiritual Care at the End of Life: 2004', *NC Med Journal*, July/August, Volume 65, Number 4 (2004), 226-228.
McNamara, B., and Rosenwax, L.	'The Mismanagement of Dying', *Health Sociology Review* 16, no. 5 (2007), 373–383.
Mottram, K. P.	*Caring for Those in Crisis* (Grand Rapids: Baker Publishing Group, 2007).

Nouwen, H., and Gaffney, W. *Aging, The Fulfillment of Life* (2nd ed. New York: Bantam Doubleday Dell Publishing Group, Inc., 1990).

Rayburn, C. 'Clinical and Pastoral Issues and Challenges in Working With the Dying and Their Families', *ADULTSPAN* 7, no. 2 (2008), 94–108.

Salt, M. *Effectiveness of a Spiritual Care Assessment and Planning Tool in Residential Aged Care: A Case Study: Master of Arts (Ageing and Pastoral Studies) 2015.*

Skanse, J. 'Who Decides to Pull the Plug', *Plainviews Healthcare Chaplaincy* Vol. 14 No. 12 (2017).

https://plainviews.healthcarechaplaincy.org/articles/Who_Decides_When_to_Pull_the_Plug_and_What_is_the_Chaplains_Responsibility

Stoneking, C. B. 'Modernity: The Social Construction of Aging', in S. Hauerwas, Stoneking, C. B., Meador, K. G., and Cloutier, D. (Eds.), *Growing Old in Christ* (Grand Rapids, Michigan: William. B. Eerdmans Publishing Co., 2003), 63–89.

Swerissen and Duckett. 'Dying Well', *Grattan Institute Report* No. 2014-10, September 2014. https://grattan.edu.au/wp-content/uploads/2014/09/815-dying-well.pdf

The Australian Pocket Oxford Dictionary. Fifth Edition. Oxford University Press, Victoria, Australia, 2005.

Tomer, A. E. and Grafton, T. 'Existentialism and Death Attitudes', in A. Tomer, Eliason, G. T., and Wong, T. P. (Eds.) *Existential and Spiritual Issues in Death Attitudes* (United States of America: Taylor & Francis Group, 2008), 7–37.

Weir, K. 'How Psychologists Can Bring Their Expertise to End-of-Life Care', *American Psychological Association* 48, no. 10 (November 2017).

Wiebe, R. 'Better Dead than Disabled', *Second Thoughts.* https://www.second-thoughts.org/home/files/better-dead-than-disabled.pdf

UNDESA Population Division. 'World Population Prospects: The 2010 Revision'. http://esa.un.org/unpd/wpp/index.htm

PART 4

Ageing in Literature

CHAPTER 10

Two approaches to ageing in antiquity: Comparing Cicero's De Senectute and Paul's intergenerational relationships in Philemon and 1 Timothy

James R. Harrison

Abstract

Although the ages of life are mentioned widely by ancient writers (e.g. Hierocles, Catullus, Horace, Virgil, Perseus, Musonius Rufus, Juvenal, Plutarch, the younger Pliny), the only treatise devoted exclusively to ageing in antiquity is Cicero's *De Senectute* ('On Old Age'). Written before May 11, 44 BC (Cicero, *Ad. Att.* 14.21), Cicero probably commenced the work in 45 BC. The treatise presents an imaginary conversation between three Roman statesmen, each of whom was alive at the time of its composition: namely, Marcus Porcius Cato (soldier and orator), Publius Scipio Africanus Minor (soldier and patron), and Gaius Laelius (soldier and orator). At the outset, Cicero asserts that the average Roman would have viewed ageing with considerable anxiety due to four reasons (Cicero, *Sen.* 15): (1) ageing results in withdrawal from active pursuits; (2) it creates weakness in the body (3); it restricts bodily pleasures; and (4) it leads inevitably to death. In response, Cicero constructs what might be called a 'psychology' of ageing. First, Cicero argues that intellectual gains can still be made notwithstanding the loss of pleasure. Second, old age is shaped positively by one's character as opposed to old age determining one's character, with the proximity of death providing even more opportunities for character development. Third, he consigns 'dotage' to a weakness of mind as opposed to a characteristic of old men. Thus virtue, if assiduously pursued throughout life, insulates one against the privations of old age, a thesis which Cicero vigorously demonstrates by elite examples from the Graeco-Roman world. With this ideological backdrop established, the chapter then compares Cicero's understanding of ageing with Paul's intergenerational construct of relationships in the Body of Christ (1 Timothy 5). What contribution did each approach make to the Western intellectual tradition and praxis regarding ageing?

Cicero's *De Senectute* in its Roman Context and its Legacy for the Western Intellectual Tradition

This chapter focuses on what is popularly believed to be the sole treatise devoted to ageing in antiquity—namely, Cicero's *De Senectute* ('On Old Age').[1] In preferring a Roman text to the extensive Greek literature on ageing,[2] we are acknowledging the obvious fact that the Roman Empire was the dominant ruling power in the New Testament period. Roman attitudes towards the elderly would have held considerable cultural sway in the provinces,[3] even though there would have been social conventions and attitudes towards the elderly in the Greek

---

1   On Cicero's *De Senectute*, see Chandler, 'Browsing through the Ages', 285–289; Twigg-Porter, 'Cicero, the Classic Gerontologist', 1–4; Minois, *History of Old Age*, 105–112; De Luce, 'Continuity and Change', 335–338; idem, 'Themes and Variations in the *De Senectute*', 361–371; Rodeheaver, 'Psychological Adaptation and Virtue', 353–359; Parkin, *Old Age in the Roman World*, 60–68. For an English commentary on the treatise, see Powell, *Cicero*.
2   On the Greek understanding of old age, see Richardson, *Old Age Among the Greeks*; Chandler, 'Browsing through the Ages', 220–224; Haynes, 'The Supposedly Golden Age for the Aged in Ancient Greece', 93–98; Minois, *History of Old Age*, 43–76; Falkner and De Luce, *Old Age in Greek and Latin Literature*, 1–171; Gilleard, 'Old Age in Ancient Greece', 81–92; Diamandopoulos, 'The Ideas of Plato, Aristotle, Plutarch and Galen on the Elderly', 325–328.
3   On Roman attitudes to the elderly, see Haynes, 'The Supposedly Golden Age for the Aged in Ancient Rome', 26–35; Falkner and De Luce, *Old Age in Greek and Latin Literature*, 171–216; Harlow and Laurence, 'Old Age in Ancient Rome', 22–27; Parkin, *Old Age in the Roman World*; Revell, 'The Roman Life Course', 43–63; Harlow and Laurence, *Growing Up and Growing Old in Ancient Rome*.

East that reflected other venerable indigenous traditions.[4] Therefore, the intergenerational attitudes to the elderly revealed in Philemon and the pastoral epistles of St. Paul (or, in the case of the pastorals, possibly a pseudonymous author) are profitably assessed against Roman attitudes to ageing, if only to highlight important differences in custom towards the aged from the dominant culture at the time. Why did early Christians adopt an intergenerational approach towards the ageing as opposed to what can be learned from the 'great men' of Rome in the case of Cicero or the Stoic wise man in the case of Seneca? What contribution did Paul's emphasis on the Spirit transformation of the young and old (Rom 7:6; 8:11-17; 2 Cor 3:18) and the elite and non-elite in the body of Christ (Rom 13:8b; 1 Cor 1:26-30; 12:22-26), make to the development of the Western intellectual tradition?

Moreover, it should also be noted at the outset there was another treatise on the elderly in antiquity, written by the first-century Greek biographer and popular philosopher, Plutarch (46–120 AD). Plutarch confined his examination of ageing to the issue of *Whether an Old Man Should Engage in Public Affairs*. Both the treatise of Cicero and Plutarch should be seen as complimentary to some degree, even though Plutarch constricts his focus entirely to the activities of distinguished

---

[4] Another approach to understanding the culture of the Greek East would be to evaluate the Ephesian culture of 1 Tim. (1:3), including its age related and intergenerational issues, against the backdrop of ethnographic fieldwork studies of modern Mediterranean cultures. See the insightful discussion of Lafosse, *Age Matters*, 47–71. Alternatively, if we localise the evidence regarding 'widow' (χήρα) and 'elder' (πρεσβυνέτρος) to ancient Ephesus alone, then the Ephesian inscriptions provide equivocal results. No Ephesian inscriptions employs the word χήρα; indeed, the word only appears once in an Ionian context (Smyrna 519). By contrast, upon a search of the Packard Humanities Greek Epigraphy programme, πρεσβυτέρος is used 26 times. πρεσβυτέρος can refer to 'elder boys/men' in contrast to 'younger boys/men' (νεώτερος) in contexts referring to the gymnastic games (I Eph. 690, 1101, 1600.27, 1687, 3142), or the ecclesiastical position of 'elder' in Ephesian Christian inscriptions (I Eph. 543, 1251, 2253b, 4305b, 4316), and, finally, the honorific title of the Elder(s) of the Ephesian Gerousia ('Council'; I Eph. 26, 711, 803, 940, 1393A, 1587; *JOAI* 62 [1993], 114 no. 3, 116–117, no. 8). While elderly men normally held the position of Elder in the Ephesian Gerousia, undoubtedly some younger men of wealth, social status, and elite family extraction would also have gained admission to the Gerousia. These inscriptions illustrate the strong honorific culture pertaining to the recompense of the elderly in antiquity. For a discussion of πρεσβυτέρος in 1 Tim., see Trebilco, *The Early Christians in Ephesus*, 448–457. On the Ephesian Gerousia and 'Elders', see Bailey, *The Gerousia of Ephesus*.

ageing men in the civic arena.⁵ Why, then, did Cicero's treatise (as opposed to Plutarch's) become pivotal for future thinking about ageing in the Western intellectual tradition?

Turning to Cicero's *De Senectute*, the famous Stoic philosopher, statesman, and orator composed his treatise before May 11, 44 BC (Cicero, *Ad. Att.* 14.21), probably commencing his writing in 45 BC. Cicero's treatise presents an imaginary conversation between three Roman statesmen—namely, Marcus Porcius Cato (soldier and orator), Publius Scipio Africanus Minor (soldier and patron), and Gaius Laelius (soldier and orator)—each of whom was alive at the time of its composition. At the outset, Cicero asserts the average Roman would have viewed ageing with considerable anxiety based on four reasons (Cicero, *Sen*. 5.15): ageing means (a) withdrawal from active pursuits, (b) weakness in the body, (c) deprivation of almost all bodily pleasures, and (d) the inevitable arrival of death. Nevertheless, it should be noted Cicero's *De Senectute* has been considered by some scholars to be a deficient source for Roman attitudes towards the ageing. Two significant objections to proceeding with the Ciceronian text as the *sole* representative of the Roman attitude towards ageing need to be aired at this juncture.

First, the originality of Cicero's *De Senectute* has been impugned by scholars. The substance of the critique is that Cicero was no more than an unoriginal epitomiser of Plato, Aristotle, Epicurus and the Stoics.⁶ Haynes sums up the case effectively:

> Cicero's lack of originality, his uncritical devotion to Greek thinking, and his facility in remembering *ad verbum* lengthy texts of Greek writers provide, indeed, sufficient grounds for

---

5   Plutarch highlights the superiority of old men in politically dealing with and advising the assembly (*Mor.* 784c–d, 788c, 789d, 790e, 794d). Cautious and prudent, the old man shows gentleness and moderation by persuading the assembly to his viewpoint, as opposed to, in the case of the young man, 'constantly jumping up on the platform [...] like a cock, crowing in opposition to what is said'. The young man, in contrast to the elder statesman, is constantly aroused by envy (*Mor.* 796a): they promenade in the porticoes, court the mob, arouse factions, and only under compulsion perform public services (*Mor.* 796c).

6   Mohr, 'Cicero: Persons and Positions', 123–132 (at 123). For a strong defence of the substantial contribution that Cicero made philosophically in comparison to other social philosophers and by his adapted presentation of Greek thought for a non-philosophically inculturated Roman audience, see Wood, *Cicero's Social and Political Thought*, 11–12. See also Colish, *The Stoic Tradition from Antiquity*, 72–73.

doubting the validity of Cicero's delineation of old age as being a true reflection of the concepts of old age generally held by the people in ancient Rome.[7]

Two examples of Cicero's dependence on Greek thinkers in the *De Senectute* will suffice.[8] Cicero presents the three speakers discussing the issues relating to old age in a way that is reminiscent of the opening to Plato's *Republic* (*Rep.* 1.328d–329d).[9] Furthermore, the passage on the immortality of the soul in De Senectute (18.86–20.73; 22.81–23.84) draws heavily from Plato's *Phaedo*.[10] However, we must not overstate Cicero's dependence on Plato's teaching. M. L. Colish has written with justification that 'Cicero was not merely reporting or mechanically transmitting the ideas of the Greeks. He evaluated them, criticised them, and re-expressed them in ways that would be comprehensible and appealing to his Roman audience'.[11] Moreover, Cicero departs from his Platonic model, which viewed the loss of sexual proclivity in the aged, in the words of Sophocles, as an 'escape from a savage and tyrannical master' (*Rep.* 1.329c). By contrast, even though Cicero cites the same Sophoclean dictum (*De Senectute* 14.47 [*Rep.* 1.329c]), he nevertheless admits that, 'although old age does not possess these pleasures in abundance, yet it is by no means wanting in them' (*De Senectute* 14.48).[12] As Haynes notes regarding this telling concession,[13] Cicero's divorce from his first wife Terentia after 29 years and his remarriage to his young and wealthy ward, Publilia, underscored that Cicero had continued his sexual activity as an aged man. Finally, Cicero adds his own humorous touches to the portrait of Cato despite the work's

---

7   Haynes, 'Aged in Ancient Rome', 33.
8   Peabody (*Cicero*, De Senectute [Boston: Little, Brown, and Co. 1887], 5) writes: 'In this treatise Cicero doubtless borrowed something from Aristo of Chios, a Stoic, to whose work on Old Age—no longer extant—he refers, and he quotes largely from Xenophon and Plato'. For Aristo, see Cicero, *De Senectute*, 1.3. For Xenophon, see Cicero, *De Senectute*, 22.79. For Plato, see Cicero, *De Senectute*, 5.13, 7.23, 12.41, 21.78. We know of three lost treatises on old age in antiquity: Aristo of Ceos (noted above) Theophrastus of Eresus (Diogenes Laertius 5.43) and Demetrius of Phalerum (Diogenes Laertius 2.13, 5.81, 9.20).
9   Payne, *The Ancient Art of Growing Old*, 110.
10 Payne, *The Ancient Art of Growing Old*, 110.
11 Colish, *The Stoic Tradition*, 72.
12 Haynes, 'Aged in Ancient Rome', 33.
13 Haynes, 'Aged in Ancient Rome', 33.

strong ideological thrust, presenting the statesman as entering into rambling asides on farming, being an expert in the discipline ('Why need I discuss the advantage of manuring, already dealt with in my book on agriculture?'; *De Senectute* 15:53). While the reader may wryly smile at Cato's pomposity in asserting the pleasures of agriculture are 'in the highest degree suited to the life of the wise man' (*De Senectute* 15:51), the deep humanity of Cicero's characterisation of Cato lifts his work from the mundane and prosaic to something more special that illustrates the intellectual flourishing of the elderly at Rome.

Additionally, despite the derivative nature of many of the arguments in *De Senectute*, Cicero's treatise nevertheless remains an important work in the Western intellectual tradition.[14] J. De Luce sums up its significance thus:

> [...] while it would be naive to argue that Cicero simply validates twentieth century gerontological theory, the correspondences between ancient and modern thought are too provocative to ignore. There is the thrill of recognition as readers familiar with current theory turn to Cicero's essay: here we find old age described in terms of the physical, the psychological, the social. Here we find the distinction between disease and old age, between the characteristics of old age and the characteristics of particular people who happen to be old. Here we find strong arguments for preparing for old age in youth, and for the continuity of personality over time.[15]

Cicero's argument that ageing is not a 'narrative of decline', but rather a positive process involving the development of human strengths resonates with the twentieth- and twenty first-century 'life cycles' theories of psychologists such as Erik Erikson,[16] Daniel Levinson,[17] and George

---

14 Caution, nevertheless, is required 'when making claims for the relevance of ancient to modern experience' (De Luce, 'Continuity and Change', 335–338).
15 De Luce, 'Continuity and Change', 335–336.
16 Erikson, *Childhood and Society*; idem, *Identity: Youth and Crisis*; idem, *The Life Cycle Completed*. See also Agronin, 'From Cicero to Cohen', 30–39, here 31–34.
17 Levinson, 'The Mid-Life Transition', 99–112; Levinson, with Darrow, Klein, and Levinson, *Seasons of a Man's Life*, See also Agronin, 'From Cicero to Cohen', 34–36.

Vaillant.[18] Each of these theorists identified various stages of social transition and human development as people moved from adolescence into adulthood. These famous psychological studies have culminated in the recent 2006 monograph of Gene. D. Cohen,[19] a student of Erickson, who identified four developmental stages of human development, which, significantly for our purposes, commenced at middle age, from which strengths such as wisdom and creativity emerged as each of the four phases unfolded well into the twilight years.[20] Notwithstanding its philosophical lack of originality, Cicero's *De Senectute* presaged, to some degree, modern psychological analyses in the discipline of gerontology, contributing richly to the development of the Western intellectual tradition. Rather than presenting old age as a reason for abject resignation in the face of physical and cognitive decline, Cicero opined that ageing was an opportunity for personal growth in virtue and wisdom, bringing to a holistic completion a life well lived.

Second, in confining our investigation to the late republican evidence of Cicero, it could be viably argued we are excluding consideration of the variegated Roman perspectives on ageing available from other republican and imperial writers. A necessarily brief overview of the literary and material evidence is perhaps apposite at this juncture. There are the demeaning references of the satirist Juvenal (Second Century AD) to the ugliness, impotence, and the physical frailty and dementia of old men.[21] The acerbic and vulgar references

---

18 Vaillant, *Aging Well*; Vaillant and Mukamal, 'Successful Aging', 839–847.
19 See also Agronin, 'From Cicero to Cohen', 36–38.
20 *Cohen, The Mature Mind.*
21 Ugliness: Juvenal, *Sat*. 10.188–202 ('voice and body trembling alike, head now quite smooth, a baby's dripping nose [...] weaponless gums', *ll*. 196–200). Impotence: ibid., 10.204–208 ('his stringy little prick lies limp with its enlarged vein and will stay limp though you coax it all night long. Or is there anything else these sickly white-haired genitals can hope for?'). Frailty and dementia: ibid., 10.225–239 ('One is crippled in his shoulder, another in the groin, another in the hip. The loss of both eyes makes this man jealous of one-eyed men [...] But worse than the physical decline is the dementia. It doesn't remember the names of slaves or recognise the face of a friend who dined with him in the previous evening or the children he fathered and raised himself', *ll*. 225–227, 232–236).

of the poet Martial (38/41–103 AD) to ageing women[22] demonstrate how savagely the intersection of ageism and misogyny operated in a Roman context. The Stoic musings of Seneca (4 BC–65 AD) on ageing frequent the philosopher's epistles.[23] Seneca is entirely realistic about the struggles the aged faced. He compares his own 'increasing senility' to a dilapidated building in Rome;[24] when confronted as an old man with shortness of breath, Seneca characterised his experience as 'practising how to die';[25] and, finally, throughout his epistles, Seneca frequently refers to the ultimate physical dissolution of the body.[26] Notwithstanding the gravity of the continuous physical decline of the aged, Seneca highlights how the wise man should daily approach the ultimate threat of death:

> Let us go to our sleep with joy and gladness; let us say: I have lived; the course which Fortune set for me is finished. And if God is pleased to add another day, we should welcome it with glad hearts. That man is happiest, and is secure in his own possession of himself, who can await the morrow without apprehension. When a man has said: 'I have lived!', every morning he arises he receives a bonus.[27]

A letter of the younger Pliny (61–113 AD), the governor of Bithynia, appeals to the positive exemplum of the elderly father, Corellius Rufus, whose impressive life confirms the moral excellence of his dignified ancestors..[28] Additionally, Pliny mentions the highly disciplined reg-

---

22 Martial, *Ep.* 3:93: 'You see as well as owls in the morning, you smell like the husbands of the nanny goats, and your bony cunt would defeat an aged cynic' (*ll.* 10–13). Other imperial poets worth considering for their evidence regarding ageing are Tibullus, Catullus, Horace, Virgil, and Persius. For discussion, see Falkner and De Luce, *Old Age in Greek and Latin Literature*, 171–216 (Horace, Virgil, Ovid); Minois, *History of Old Age*, 96–100 (Tibullus, Horace, Ovid); Parkin, *Old Age in the Roman World*, *passim*.
23 For discussion, see Minois, *History of Old Age*, 101–102; Parkin, *Old Age in the Roman World*, 69–72.
24 Seneca, *Ep.* 12.
25 Seneca, *Ep.* 54.2.
26 Seneca, *Ep.* 26, 30, 54, 55, 65.
27 Seneca, *Ep.* 12.9.
28 Pliny the Younger, *Ep.* 3.3 ('that grave and saintly man your father'). See Kebric, 'Aging in Pliny's Letters', 538–545.

imen characterising the senator Spurrina's well-earned retirement,[29] itself an indelible sign of his moral rectitude.[30] The Roman upper class woman, Ummidia Quadratilla, who died a mentally and physically vigorous 79-year-old, showed her moral character in attempting to prevent her grandson from seeing the desultory performances of local mime troops, as well providing for him in her will.[31] The teaching of the Stoic philosopher Musonius Rufus (25/30–101 AD) on old age is conveniently epitomised, setting out for his students the importance of living according to nature.[32] Nor should we forget the visual evidence of the late republican bust portraits and statues in which 'the gravitas of leaders in their mature, lined, wrinkled, and even scarred, realistic faces' are graphically depicted.[33] Older women, however, are unfavourably stereotyped in Roman literature, with the aged female

---

29 Pliny the Younger, *Ep.* 3.1. Note, too, Pliny's rendering of l. Verginius Rufus in *Ep.* 2.1; 6.10; 9.19. L. Garafalo ('Silent Virtue: Pliny's Verginius Rufus as Imperial Exempla') argues that reframes his mentor's fame for posterity. In Ep. 9.19, Pliny 'defends Verginius' legacy from competing claims of contemporary historiography and new types of memorialisation. In these letters, Pliny portrays Verginius as both particularly traditional and well-attuned to imperial realities'. See https://classicalstudies.org/.../silent-virtue-pliny's-verginius-rufus-imperial-exemplar

30 Harlow and Laurence, *Growing Up and Growing Old*, 124. However, Pliny is very realistic about the decrepitude that the aged faced. See his description of the crippled and deformed Domitius Tullius, a wealthy man, but whose immobility in every limb necessitated having his teeth cleaned by his slaves (Pliny, *Ep.* 8.18).

31 Pliny the Younger, *Ep.* 7.24.

32 Musonius Rufus, XVIII ('What is the Best Viaticum for Old Age?'): '[...] the best viaticum for old age is [...] to live according to nature, doing and thinking what one ought. For so an old man would himself be most cheerful and would win the praise of others'. Tr., Lutz, 'Musonius Rufus, 'The Roman Socrates'', 3–147. Pace, note the emphasis of Cicero (*De Senectute* 2.5) on the role of nature in orchestrating a flourishing conclusion to life for the aged: 'I am wise because I follow Nature as the best of guides and obey her as a god; and since she has fitly planned the other acts of life's drama, it is not likely that she has neglected the final act as if she were a careless playwright'.

33 Harlow and Laurence, 'Old Age in Ancient Rome', Harlow and Laurence (23–24) conclude: 'The essential male attributes of virtue and gravity were depicted in the lines of the mature adult face. These images reflected an ideology that held older men in high esteem and assumed respect and honour to increase as individuals aged. This ideology assumed respect for the older male in society and was underpinned by the institution of paternal power, which gave authority to fathers over their sons and was a defining feature of Roman society'. For a fine example of Roman civic virtue displayed in the statue of an elderly man holding two portrait busts of his middle-aged man ancestors, see Harlow and Laurence, *Growing Up and Growing Old*, 120. Nevertheless, the Romans did occasionally reproduce the graphic Hellenistic statues of old men (Harlow and Laurence, 125). Harlow and Laurence (125) write: 'The body is no longer erect, the veins are clearly shown, and the flesh has lost the tight muscularity of the adult body'.

body being routinely subsumed under the topos of the 'grotesque'.[34]

Finally, the early republican comedies of the Roman playwright Plautus (254–184 BC) present stereotypical portraits of the *senex* ('old man').[35] A. Gosling captures in broad brushstrokes the comic portrait of Plautus' *senes* ('old men'):

> Almost all Plautus' *senes*, whether angry spoil-sports, complaisant parents or lecherous would-be lovers, lack dignity. They are easily duped by their slaves; they are the butt of their slaves' or their neighbours' wit and sarcasm; and they are at the mercy of domineering wives who hold the purse-strings.[36]

By contrast, the later comedies of Terence (195/185–c. 159 BC) mollify Plautus' 'grotesque characterisations' of his characters (i.e., older men, slaves, wives, and courtesans) for 'more subtle delineations' of the same stock figures.[37] In the case of the *senex* in Terence, the playwright does not introduce the farce and crudity of Plautus' amorous old man into his comedies.[38] The credulous and easily deceived father of Plautus shows more shrewdness and native cunning in Terence's comedies, with the playwright crediting to the father genuine psychological insight into his personal situation notwithstanding his flaws.[39]

Why, then, should we consider Cicero's *De Senectute* a superior source of evidence for any investigation into the Roman understanding of ageing? In their depictions of the ageing process, too often the Roman sources discussed above only articulate a narrative of 'decline'

---

34 Harlow and Laurence, 'Old Age in Ancient Rome', 27 write: 'Elderly prostitutes were graphically described by the satirists Horace and Juvenal who make great play on make-up cracked faces which failed to conceal wrinkles, toothless gums seeking kisses, sagging breasts under jewellery that failed to disguise the ugliness of the body and inappropriateness of behaviour—some writers associate the techniques of the disguise of age in the brothel with those of the undertaker presenting a corpse'. See Rosivach, 'Some Older Women in Latin Literature', 107–117.

35 Minois, *History of Old Age*, 92–96. On the *senex* in Roman Comedy, see Duckworth, *Nature of Roman Comedy*, 242–249.

36 Gosling, 'A Rather Unusual Old Man', 53–59, here 55. See also Ryder, 'The *Senex Amator* in Plautus', 181–189.

37 Duckworth, *Nature of Roman Comedy*, 242. See also Estevens, '*Senex* as Spouse in Plautus and Terence', 73–76.

38 Duckworth, *Nature of Roman Comedy*, 246.

39 Duckworth, *Nature of Roman Comedy*, 249.

(Seneca), or idealise the virtuous aged in a static manner (Pliny; the republican busts and statues),[40] or primarily illustrate Stoic philosophical principles (Musonius Rufus). The Roman satirists (Juvenal, Martial) belittle and demean the aged for comic effect; whereas, the comic playwrights (Plautus, Terence) emphasise the 'stinginess, senility, quickness to anger, stupidity, and, especially, lecherousness' of the old man.[41] Undoubtedly, Cato's mature wisdom in old age—a product of a dignified life lived out from the time of his youth and middle age—is similarly idealised in the *De Senectute*, but Cato's portrait is humanised by the comic elements of his pompous confidence in his special area of intellectual expertise. Importantly, however, in this process of humanisation, the intellectual flourishing of the aged is underscored positively in a wider argument for the personal development than takes place in the ageing process. The dignity accorded the aged in the *De Senectute* and the prospect of continued personal growth throughout their twilight years fits well with what we know about the deep respect of the republican and imperial elites for their aged ancestors, the composition of the Roman senate with elderly men,[42] the honour and authority accorded to the *paterfamilias* of Roman houses,[43] and in the college of augurs precedence in debate according to age.[44] This does not mean that Cicero's idealistic impression of old age is without deficit in comparison to other Roman authors. Pliny, for example, was realistic about the sufferings that old age could entail, displaying an

---

40 Caution is required here. While Pliny spoke positively about the productive declining years of the Roman poet Silius Italicus from the Neronian era (Pliny, *Ep.* 3.7), he is nevertheless 'frank to the point of malice'. As Vessey ('Pliny Martial and Silius Italicus', *Hermes* 109–116, here 116) argues, 'although prepared to allow Silius credit where it could not be denied, he bursts the bubble of pretentiousness, laying bare those faults and follies which Martial had either ignored or encouraged'.
41 Haynes, 'Aged in Ancient Rome', 28.
42 De Luce ('Themes and Variations in the *De Senectute*', 362) notes that the Latin word for the 'senate' (*senatus*) derives from *senex* ('old man'). Note the comment of Cicero, *De Senectute* 5.19: 'If these mental qualities were not characteristic of old men, our fathers would not have called their highest deliberative body the 'senate''.
43 See Haynes, 'Aged in Ancient Rome', *passim*. For the blind and aged Appius Claudius as *paterfamilias*, see Cicero, *De Senectute* 11.37: 'He maintained not mere authority, but absolute command over his household; his slaves feared him, his children revered him, all loved him, and the customs and discipline of his forefathers flourished beneath his roof'.
44 Cicero, *De Senectute* 18.64.

'antithetic attitude' towards death, 'looking forward to old age while fearing the ageing process and what it might bring, including a premature death'.[45] As we have seen, however, Cicero's treatise—in contrast to the rest of Roman literature—provided the social impetus for the Western intellectual tradition to develop our modern psychological theories of ageing.

What picture of ageing emerges from Cicero's *De Senectute*? What values does it espouse? What social blind spots regarding the ageing process and the care for the elderly emerge from its presentation?

Cicero's Depiction of Ageing in *De Senectute*

The personal and career circumstances under which Cicero wrote *De Senectute* are clear enough, but the motivations for so doing remain conjectural. Cicero wrote the treatise in early 44 BC, mentioned in Cicero's 11th May letter of the same year to Atticus (*Att.* 14.21.3) and, contemporaneously, in the *De Divinatio* (2.3), completed soon after the Ides of March. J. G. F. Powell rightly observes the treatise was written in the period of Cicero's great philosophical outpouring in 45–44 BC.[46] Certainly, the work reflects the philosophical tenor that must have characterised the previous (now lost) Greek works on old age.[47] But the treatise coincides with a series of telling circumstances in the orator's life: the deeply felt death of his daughter Tullia in February 45 BC (*Att.* 12.15; cf. *ad Fam.* 4.6–4.7); the divorce of his longstanding wife Terentia because of her alleged lack of grief over her daughter's death, and subsequently, his own remarriage (as a *senex*) to his young ward Publilia; and, finally, the increasing unlikelihood of the triumph of the senatorial cause in the face of the unravelling of the

---

45 Kebric, 'Aging in Pliny's Letters', 540. But Cicero concedes the difficulties of old age: *De Senectute* 1.2 ('our common burden of old age [...] the annoyances of old age'); ibid. 2.6 ('the weight of increasing years'); ibid., 3.8 ('old age cannot be a light thing, not even to a wise man'); ibid., 23.85 ('old age is the final scene [...] in life's drama, from which we ought to escape when it grows wearisome, and, certainly when we have had our fill').
46 Powell, *Cicero, Cato Maior* De Senectute, 1.
47 Cicero, *De Senectute* 1.2, 'Philosophy, therefore, can never be praised as much as she deserves, since she enables the man who is obedient to her precepts to pass every season of life free from worry'.

Roman republic under Caesar and his supporters up to his assassination and beyond. Possibly the current vicissitudes of Cicero's life and the prospect of its further decline due to old age called for a strong personal statement of human flourishing on his part. If Cicero was to enjoy the sexual delights of his new wife[48] and muster the personal resilience required to uphold the senatorial cause over and against the contemporary careerists (who were seeking their personal glory rather than the glory of the republic), then Cicero needed to justify his continued claim to be a *paterfamilias* and statesman.[49] Consequently, *De Senectute* is populated with elderly exempla of *virtus* ('virtue', 'manliness') and 'gloria', that is, the senes ('old men') who had made truly great the Roman republic and its empire in its heyday. Thus, as J. De Luce suggests,[50] the work represents a 'life review' on Cicero's part as much as a philosophical treatise and work of social ethics.[51] How, then, does Cicero address the four reasons for Roman anxiety regarding ageing (Cicero, *De Senectute* 15), mentioned above?

At the outset, before Cicero addresses fully the four reasons for Roman anxiety regarding ageing (*De Senectute* 5.15), he previews a central thrust of his argument: how should the aged react to the loss of sensual pleasures and to a decline in celebrity (*De Senectute* 3.7)? According to Cicero, those who bore old age without complaint do so because of the quality of their character as opposed to their circumstances (*De Senectute* 3.7). As a strategy to ensure worthiness of character in the elderly, the virtues must be cultivated at every stage of one's life, not just in the twilight years (*De Senectute* 3.9; 18:65). The incentive for the early cultivation of a morally impeccable life resides in the Roman culture of the memorialisation of virtue: 'it is most delightful to have the consciousness of a life well spent and the memory of many deeds worthily performed' (*De Senectute* 3.9; cf. 6.19). Cicero devotes extensive space to the exemplum of Quintus Fabius Maximus,

---

48 Cicero, *De Senectute* 2:7: 'My contemporaries [...] used to lament [...] because they were denied the sensual pleasures without which they thought life not life at all'.
49 Parkin, *Old Age in the Roman World*, 65–66.
50 Luce, 'Themes and Variations', 367–70.
51 Parkin (*Old Age in the Roman World*, 65) argues that philosophy 'becomes Cicero's refuge in the mid-forties BC' (*De Senectute* 1.1).

the delayer of Hannibal's advance on Rome (*De Senectute* 4.10–5.15), not only outlining the general's *cursus honorum*, but also highlighting how his dignity was tempered with courtesy and his disposition not altered with age (4.10).

First, as far as Roman anxieties regarding old age, Cicero lists a cavalcade of elderly Roman statesmen and generals (the Scipios, Fabricius, Curius, and Corancanius) to demonstrate they did not withdraw from civic activities (*De Senectute* 6.15), as supposed to old men in their dotage. Cicero supports his case with the illustration of the tiller continuously steering his ship (6.17) and the deliberative body of the Roman senate and the elders of the Lacedaemonians (6.10–20). Nor is the memory impaired in the case of the elderly (7.21): the aged representatives from the professions (7.22), the agriculture of Sabine famers (7.24), and the mental agility of the Athenian law-maker Solon and Cato himself (7.26) indicate otherwise. Importantly for our purposes, Cicero notes how the vibrant intellectual culture of the elderly creates an intergenerational culture of sharing and a role modelling of virtue, through the young seeking the company of the old (7:26).[52] Noteworthy, however, is how Cicero maintains social hierarchy here: no mutual modelling of virtue is envisaged between the generations.

Second, as far as the onset of bodily weakness in old age, Cicero counters how the orator's voice gains resonance with age (9.28), the intellectual power of the elderly teachers of liberal arts continues unabated (9.20), and throngs of the young still attend elderly Roman nobles (9.28). To be sure, the 'blessing of strength' should be enjoyed while it is available and not bemoaned when it is lost (10.33). Each of the various stages of life—'the weakness of childhood, the impetuosity of youth, the seriousness of middle life, the maturity of old age' (10.33)—bears some of Nature's fruit, with each crop appropriate to the season. We see here how the Western intellectual tradition, through modern psychological studies in the discipline of gerontology, found in Cicero the precedent for their own investigations of the human psyche. Notwithstanding, Cato makes it clear one must maintain a moderate

---

52 Cicero (*De Senectute* 7:26) writes that 'young men find pleasure in their leaders, by whose precepts they are led into virtue's paths'.

regimen of health so that physical weakness can be kept at bay for as long as possible (11.36). But more than just exercise is required for human flourishing at the end of life. Cato concludes his undiminished vitality as an 84-year-old in the senate and assembly (10.32), as well as in writing the seventh volume of his *Antiquities* and investigating religious and secular law (11.38), stems from his own regular 'intellectual gymnastics' and the 'race-courses of his mind' (11.38).[53]

Third, in regard to the absence of sensual pleasures in old age, Cato admits there are significant sensual pleasures he continues to enjoy as a *senex*—for example, dining with his companions in clubs in honour of Cybele at Rome (13.45); engaging in 'afternoon banquets' (or symposia) where the talk among the banqueters is what really matters (14.46–48); and, finally, the pleasures of agricultural life (15.51–60). However, after quoting Archytas of Tarentum (12.39–41), Cato draws the following conclusion regarding pleasure:

> [...] if reason and wisdom did not enable us to reject pleasure, we should be very grateful to old age for taking away the desire to do what we ought not to do. For carnal pleasure hinders deliberation, is at war with reason, blindfolds the eyes of the mind, so to speak, and has no fellowship with virtue.[54]

But, according to Cato, the accumulation of public honours in old age is a most precious form of 'influence' (*auctoritas*) that far outweighs the seductions of youthful pleasure (17.61). Wrinkles and old age cannot diminish the *auctoritas* that is generated by a life nobly spent and that finds its culmination in old age. The dynamics of this 'influence' and its significance for the aged is elaborated on with great clarity:

> For these very things, that seem light and trivial, are marks of honour—the morning visit, being sought after, being made way for, having people rise at one's approach, being escorted

---

53 Cicero (*De Senectute* 12.38) sums up thus: 'For the man who always lives amid such studies and pursuits of mine is not aware of the stealthy approach of age. Thus employed his age gradually and imperceptibly glides into old age, and succumbs, not to a quick assault, but to a long-continued siege'.
54 Cicero, *De Senectute* 12.42.

to and from the forum, being asked for advice—civilities most scrupulously observed among us and in every other state in proportion as its morals are good.[55]

The importance of what Cicero is saying here about the status, esteem, and priority that accrued for the aged through their *auctoritas* is further illustrated by the famous claim of Augustus regarding his principate from 15 January 27 BC onwards: 'I excelled everyone in influence (auctoritate), but I had no more power (*potestatis*) than others who were my colleagues in each magistracy'.[56] Those aged citizens of Rome who possessed 'influence' (*auctoritas*) could still maintain significant connections with elite circles because of their moral pre-eminence, without necessarily having to rely on their continued formal rank and their accompanying powers, given they would progressively have had to withdraw from the demands of Roman political life for a quieter existence as old age increasingly constricted their activities. Note especially in this regard the comment of the octogenarian Cato about his senatorial prestige, notwithstanding his withdrawal from military life: 'I [...] am unemployed now that I do not go to war, and yet I direct the senate as to what wars should be waged and how' (6.18). The invisible but very real status and pre-eminence the elderly republican elites held for the long term within Roman society by virtue of their widespread esteem is in plain view here. Behind this strong emphasis on *auctoritas*, we also perhaps see Cicero's continued justification of his elite status and pre-eminence, despite the fact that his enemies were gradually circling around him before his eventual murder in 43 BC.

Fourth, regarding the anxiety of the aged about the imminent approach of death, Cato reminds his dialogue partners that life prepares us for death (20:76), coming more pleasantly to the aged than the young (19:71), preparing us, in arguments reminiscent of Plato, for immortality (21:77), serenity and hope (23.84–85).

What social values does Cicero's *De Senectute* espouse? The viewpoint is entirely androcentric, with no women being named in the

---

55 Cicero, *De Senectute* 17.63.
56 *Res Gestae* 34.2.

text, apart from one fleeting reference to a Gallic courtesan (12.42). Furthermore, J. de Luce is correct in saying 'this is an essay about a particular old age which only free, middle to upper middle class Romans could have enjoyed'.[57] Consequently, there is no concern for the socially marginalised or those facing the privations of poverty among the aged, even though Cicero acknowledges the 70-year-old Roman poet, Ennius, suffered the two burdens of poverty and old age (5.14). The elderly exempla provided for imitation by posterity belong to the republican noble elites, who were animated by the quest for ancestral glory and virtue, which was achieved by their prestigious magistracies in the *cursus honorum*, civic benefactions, and military victories on the battle field (e.g., 4.10–13; 5.15; 9.29; 13.43; 14.50; 17.61). But what about those without honour or 'influence' among the aged? What about the anonymous paupers of no significance in Rome who passed away unnoticed, whose bodies the *vespillones* (corpse-bearers) carried off 'like a thousand that the pauper's pyre receives' (Martial, Ep. 8.75)? They are of no concern to Cicero. Moreover, where intergenerational relations and imitation actually took place, it was strictly hierarchical, with the younger men subordinate to their elders for their advancement or favour and the elders gaining kudos as the social superiors. Finally, if formal powers were inadequate or lacking in the case of certain individuals, the aristocracy of esteem promoted by the noble houses still enabled their ageing members to rely on their *auctoritas* for continued social pre-eminence, notwithstanding their advanced years.

With this ideological backdrop established, it remains for us to compare Cicero's understanding of ageing with Paul's intergenerational construct of relationships in the body of Christ (Phil.; 1 Tim. 5). What commonalities and differences in approach are there between Cicero and Paul (or the pseudonymous author of 1 Tim.)? What contribution did each approach make to the Western intellectual tradition and praxis regarding gerontology?

---

57 Luce, 'Themes and Variations', 367.

Paul's Intergenerational Construct of Relationships in the Body of Christ

Paul as πρεσβυτής

We turn to the epistle of Philemon where Paul clearly articulates he is an 'old man', *senex* in the Latin, πρεσβυτής in the Greek (Phil. 9). First, commentators have debated the meaning of πρεσβυτής. The interpretative options are:

- some scholars claim the word means 'aged man,' 'old man';[58]
- other scholars argue the (allegedly) corrupted word πρεσβυτής should be restored as 'ambassador' (πρεσβευτής) or that πρεσβυτής could also mean 'ambassador'; [59]
- others suggest Paul exploits the potential of both words, assuming his audience will hear both resonances there, thereby eliciting a sympathetic hearing by virtue of his old age, while simultaneously commanding apostolic honour respect as Christ's ambassador;[60] and
- finally, some posit Paul's use of the term is entirely rhetorical, representing Paul's own self-positioning in relation to Philemon, employed as an additional means of enforcing his authority over his convert.[61]

The most likely option, the reasons for which we cannot account here, is that Paul is asserting his elderly age, with πρεσβυτής, based on the contemporary lexicographical evidence of Philo (*Op mundi* 105–105). In Philo, πρεσβυτής denotes elderly men from 49–58, as opposed to gerōn, an old man of 59 and beyond.[62] While it may be true that Paul, as a πρεσβυτής, was still healthy and fit, with the result that its meaning in the apostle's case is technically inappropriate, we must not forget Paul is also employing the word as an honorific, indicating his pastoral

---

58 Fitzmyer, *The Letter to Philemon*, 105–106.
59 Barth and Blanke, *The Letter to Philemon*, 321–333.
60 Nordling, *Philemon*, 230.
61 Hock, 'A Support for His Old Age: Paul's Plea on Behalf of Onesimus', 67–81.
62 Arzt-Grabner (*Philemon*, 76–77), setting out the literary and documentary evidence argues that, while the word πρεσβυτής could refer to people over 60, it more commonly referred to people on their 50s.

and apostolic experience as an aged man committed to Christ, as much as his calendrical age.⁶³

Paul's Inversion of Hierarchical Expectations

What then might Paul be saying socially about old age in the epistle to Philemon? What emerges is that Paul's sponsors intergenerational relationships in missional ministry and in-house church relationships, but in ways the outworking of ministry upsets significant traditional social conventions.

First, in returning the 'runaway' slave Onesimos to his master, Paul makes several unusual observations about the status the slave has acquired in his own ministry. In a clever word-play upon the slave's name, Ὀνήσιμος ('beneficial', 'profitable', 'useful'),⁶⁴ the formerly 'useless' slave had become 'useful' to Paul in Christ, now fulfilling the original potential indicated by his name. But more than the realisation of untapped potential is involved here. Intriguing is the reversal of the hierarchical expectations associated with a traditional partnership involving an elderly patron and his younger charge; however, here the 'usefulness' of the younger man to the older man is highlighted, not the reverse. This reverses the traditional dependence of the younger client on the older patron.

This impression of changes in social expectations is also facilitated by the father/son relationship between Paul and Onesimos (Phil. 10: 'my child [...] whose father I have become') and the mutual brotherhood and of Philemon (Phil. 19b) and Onesimos (Phil. 16b: 'a beloved brother'). The slave 'outsider' in the household is no longer a slave but a valued family member (Phil. 15–16). The new 'usefulness' of Onesimos (Phil. 11) to the older apostle and to his master, Philemon, is reinforced by Paul's language of affection for his younger missionary assistant, Onesimos (Phil. 12: 'my very heart'). Onesimos takes

---

63 On the honour of the 'elder' in social relations, see Plutarch (*Moralia* 615f–616b), referring to the role of the father. Conversely, note the how a senator from Xanthus is called πρεσβύτης Ἀσίας ('elder of Asia') as an honorific, with no reference to his actual old age. See Christol and Drew-Bear, 'Un sénateur de Xanthos', 203–206. I am indebted to Prof. Alan Cadwallader for these references.
64 Nordling, *Philemon*, 236.

over the place of his brother-in-Christ, Philemon, in helping his older father-in-Christ, the apostle Paul, while he is in chains at Rome. What is clear in this new intergenerational set of relationships in Christ is their mutuality and the breaking down of traditional hierarchical relationships (slave/master; client/patron; young man/old man).

But further reversals are still to come. Onesimos is to be welcomed at the house of Philemon as the presence of the elderly apostle himself (Phil. 17: 'welcome him as you would welcome me'). Since Paul had requested a guest room in the house of Philemon (Phil. 22), the former slave is now, ironically, Philemon's guest, representing the apostle Paul in advance of his arrival.[65] The former master, Philemon, is now Onesimos' host in his own house at Colossae and, equally, a brother-in-Christ of Philemon. The reversal of hierarchy and the reordering of relationships in the household of Philemon that has occurred because of the conversion of Onesimos is powerful: the elderly Paul is the spiritual *paterfamilias* of both Onesimos and Philemon in the new household of God at Colossae, but the apostle enlists both men as his fellow slaves of Christ in the missionary work of their common heavenly father (cf. 2 Cor 4:5; cf. Mark 10:35–45). While Paul is accorded loving respect as the ageing apostle, the status of his co-workers and sons-in-Christ is upended in paradoxical ways that undermine the traditional hierarchies of antiquity between young and old, slave and freeman, and client and patron.

Intergenerational Relationships in 1 Timothy 5

Turning to the approach to ageing in 1 Timothy 5, it is possible intergenerational conflict within the church at Ephesus had broken out, though such a position, admittedly, rests on a mirror-reading of the text. Paul (or the pseudonymous author of 1 Timothy) had affirmed the conservative age structures of his age, encouraging children to display piety towards parents by caring for them (5:4,8) and by not disrespecting their elders (5:19–20). The reason for such a stance may have been a response to the interloping false teachers in the church

---

65 Koenig, *New Testament Hospitality*, 79.

who had forbidden marriage (4:3), thereby undermining family structures.[66] Consequently, Paul exhorts Timothy to speak to older men and women like fathers and mothers, and age-peers like siblings (5:1–2). Adult children were to care for their widowed mothers and grandmothers (5:4).[67] Old women over sixty were models of virtue (5:9–10), and worthy elders were to receive double honour (5:17). In this wide-ranging response,[68] Paul's vision for the care of the ageing in the church emerges: a fictive kinship that is truly intergenerational.

It is interesting to see how 1 Timothy 5 contrasts to Cicero's *De Senectute*, a text which, as we have seen, was characterised by androcentric, hierarchical and elitist approaches to ageing. Significantly, Paul (or the pseudonymous writer of 1 Timothy 5) begins with widows in need, the Old Testament figure characterised by vulnerability, poverty and dependence on God (5.5; cf. Exod. 22:22–24; Deut. 10:18; 24;17–21; Ps. 68:5; 146:9; Prov. 15:25).[69] Benefaction of those widows who are really in need is the priority (5:3). By contrast, younger widows, who can remarry, should do so in order that the church is not burdened by their care and they are not led astray by sensual pleasures (5:11–15).

Returning to widows genuinely in need, although Paul has highlighted the importance of fictive kinship groups that incorporate all ages in its care, the members of the birth family should take the lead in caring for their own widows (5:3–4, 8, 16a). It is surprising how Paul describes the charity exercised by children and grandchildren with the traditional benefaction parlance of the Graeco-Roman elites: children are urged to repay their parents and grandparents, reflecting the teaching of popular philosophers such as Hierocles on the payback system

---

66 See the well-argued position of LaFosse, *Age Matters*, 186–193. For the suggestion and rejection of the idea that widows were spreading heresy—based upon a heterodox doctrinal understanding of 1 Tim. 5:13 in terms of the widow's speaking in the churches—see Zamfir, *Men and Women in the Household of God*, 181–188.
67 Zamfir (*Men and Women in the Household of God*, 111–112) argues that more than financial aid is involved here, including also the rendering of honour to widows (1 Tim. 5:3), thereby 'touching on the attitude of the church leader towards this somehow prominent group' (ibid., 112).
68 Older men, younger men, younger women: 1 Tim. :5–12. Older men: 5:1, 17–22. Widows over 60: 5:9. Younger widows: 5:11–15.
69 See Thurston, *The Widows*.

(5:4). Paul also employs the verb προνεεῖ (5:9) to denote the care of widows and household members. This verb and its noun (πρόνοια) were traditionally reserved in the honorific inscriptions for the care of cities by elite benefactors through the provision of various benefits.[70] In other words, the terminology for the duties reserved for the wealthy elites has been transferred to the everyday family life of believers. What was the civic virtue reserved for the civic elites has now been transferred to ordinary believers in their family lives, thereby democritising virtue throughout the body of Christ in the process. Androcentric, hierarchical, and elitist approaches towards the care of the elderly have been decisively pinpricked.

Note also how honour and beneficence should be extended towards real widows over 60 without a family: this responsibility is now to be taken up by the wider body of Christ (5:1, 5, 9–10, 16b). Once again, the fictive family, God's household (3:15), extends beneficence to non-blood members. This is an unusual but not entirely unique phenomenon in antiquity. In the Jewish word, the local synagogue is the best approximation of early Christian alms-giving, providing temporary accommodation and food for travellers,[71] while employing paternal and maternal terminology for their synagogue leaders.[72] Correspondingly, in the Graeco-Roman world, the local associations also imitate this phenomenon, allocating to their leaders paternal accolades and, via the imposition of fees or by a benefactor's donation, paying for the funeral costs for members and the food for their association feasts.[73] What is distinctive in a Graeco-Roman context—and, indeed, in a Jewish context, where synagogue benefactors were also occasionally recompensed

---

70 See Harrison, 'Benefaction Ideology and Christian Responsibility for Widows', 106–116.
71 See the famous Theodotos inscription (before 70 AD) found on the lower eastern slope of Ophel, Jerusalem: Runesson, Binder and Olsson, *The Ancient Synagogue from Its Origins to 200 CE*, 52–54.
72 For examples of 'Father' terminology in the honorific inscriptions of the Greco-Roman associations, see Ascough, Harland, and Kloppenborg, *Associations in the Greco-Roman World*, 91, 319, 322. For examples of 'Mother' terminology in the honorific inscriptions of the Greco-Roman associations, see ibid., §322. See also Harland, 'Familial Dimensions of Group Identity (II)', 57–79; Hemelrijk, 'Patronesses and 'Mothers' of Roman *Collegia*', 115–162.
73 For 'Mother' terminology in synagogue inscriptions, see Brooten, *Women Leaders in the Ancient Synagogue*, 57–63. For 'Father' terminology in synagogue inscriptions, see Ascough, Harland, and Kloppenborg, *Associations in the Greco-Roman World*, §§46, 329j/k.

with Graeco-Roman honours[74]—is the motivation of early believers for the exercise of beneficence towards widows by their fictive or blood families: it is pleasing in God's sight and it demonstrates the reality of one's saving faith (5:4b, 8).

Finally, another distinctive element of these intergenerational relationships is the mutuality in relations and the refusal to fall into the trap of ageism. Elders are to be accorded the double honour (5:17), but, at the same time, Paul reminds the young Timothy not to let anyone despise his youth. Instead, he is to convince his critics of his maturity through his godly exemplum and by the development of his gifts (4:11–16; cf. 2 Tim. 1:4). Similarly, blood relatives are to look after their widows while the fictive family of God's household attends to 'real' widows; however, real widows are expected to exercise hospitality, wash the feet of the saints, and help those in trouble by performing good deeds (5:10). There is a spirit-given interconnectedness in the body of Christ here that transcends the categories of age, allowing members to minster selflessly to the needs of others by using their gifts to God's glory, but with the confidence the mutuality of giving experienced in the body of Christ will provide them all with divine recompense as well.

Cicero, Paul, and the Western Intellectual Traditions of Ageing

Which tradition, Cicero or Paul, contributed most to the Western intellectual tradition of gerontology? The question is impossible to answer and is far too polarised in its evaluative intent. Both traditions contributed in differing ways. There is little doubt Cicero anticipated the 'stages of life' model that now proliferates modern psychological literature on ageing. However, Cicero's approach is class-riddled, androcentric, and hierarchical in its approach to ageing and intergenerational relationships.

By contrast, Paul's approach affirms, reconfigures, and undermines hierarchy in a transgenerational community, depending on the context

---

74 For examples, see Brooten, *Women Leaders in the Ancient Synagogue*, 'Appendix' §§3, 6.

of his discussion. Paul's emphasis is more holistic than Cicero's, moving beyond the spiritual needs of the ageing to their physical requirements as well. The giftedness of each person has primacy for every stage of their life, stemming initially from their creation by God as image-bearers and, in the case of believers, reflecting the charismatic ministry of the indwelling spirit. The potential for the ageing to flourish in an intergenerational community, contributing to and being contributed to, ensured that older people (as much as young people) would be empowered and see their capabilities enhanced.

Finally, the abject weakness and dishonour of Christ on the cross at the end of his life helps us to shape our response—personal and institutional—in honouring and caring for the disabled, those with dementia, and the frail in their twilight years. Both traditions, Ciceronian and early Christian, have shaped the discipline of gerontology in the Western intellectual tradition.

Bibliography

Agronin, M. E.   'From Cicero to Cohen: Developmental Theories of Aging, from Antiquity to the Present', *The Gerontologist* 54, no. 1 (2013), 30-39.

Arzt-Grabner, P.   *Philemon (Papyrologische Kommentare zum Neuen Testament 1;* Göttingen: Vandenhoeck & Ruprecht, 2003).

Ascough, R. S., Harland, P. A. and Kloppenborg, J. S.   *Associations in the Greco-Roman World: A Sourcebook* (Waco: Baylor University Press, 2012).

Bailey, C.   *The Gerousia of Ephesus* (Ph.D. dissertation, University of British Columbia, 2006).

Barth, M., and Blanke, H.   *The Letter to Philemon: A New Translation with Notes and Commentary* (Grand Rapids: Eerdmans, 2000).

Brooten, B. J.   *Women Leaders in the Ancient Synagogue* (Atlanta: Scholars Press, 1982).

Chandler, A. R.   'Browsing Through the Ages: Aristotle on Mental Aging', *Journal of Gerontology* 3, no. 2 (1948), 220-224.

_____, 'Browsing Through the Ages: Cicero's Ideal Old Man', *Journal of Gerontology* 3, no. 4 (1948), 285-289.

Cohen, G. D. *The Mature Mind: The Positive Power of the Aging Brain* (New York: Basic Books, 2006).

Colish, M. L. *The Stoic Tradition from Antiquity to the Early Middle Ages. 1: Stoicism in Classical Latin Literature* (Leiden: E. J. Brill, 1990).

Christol, M. and Drew-Bear, T. 'Un sénateur de Xanthos', *Journal des savants* 3 (1991), 195–226.

De Luce, J. 'Continuity and Change: Four Disciplinary Perspectives on Reading Cicero's *De Senectute*, x', *Journal of Aging Studies* 7, no. 4 (1993), 335-338.

_____, 'Themes and Variations in the *De Senectute*', *Journal of Aging Studies* 7, no. 4. (1993), 361-371.

Diamandopoulos, A. 'The Ideas of Plato, Aristotle, Plutarch and Galen on the Elderly', *Journal of Gerontology and Geriatrics* 65 (2017), 325-328.

Duckworth, G. E. *Nature of Roman Comedy: A Study in Popular Entertainment* (Princeton: Princeton University Press, 1952).

Erikson, E. H. *Childhood and Society* (New York: W. W. Norton, 1950).

_____, *Identity: Youth and Crisis* (New York: W. W. Norton, 1968).

_____, *The Life Cycle Completed* (New York: W.W. Norton, 1997 [orig. 1982]).

Estevens, V. A. '*Senex* as Spouse in Plautus and Terence', *The Classical Bulletin* 42 (1996), 73-76.

Falkner, T. M., and De Luce, J. (Eds.). *Old Age in Greek and Latin Literature* (New York: State University of New York Press, 1989).

Fitzmyer, J. A. *The Letter to Philemon: A New Translation with Introduction and Commentary,* (Anchor Bible 43C; New York: Doubleday, 2000).

Gilleard, C. 'Old Age in Ancient Greece: Narratives of Desire, Narratives of Disgust', *Journal of Ageing Studies* 21 (2007), 81-92.

Gosling, A.   'A Rather Unusual Old Man: Hegio in Plautus' *Captivi*', *Acta Classica* 26 (1983), 53-59.

Harland, P. A.   'Familial Dimensions of Group Identity (II): 'Mothers' and 'Fathers' in Associations and Synagogues of the Greek World', *Journal for the Study of Judaism in the Persian, Hellenistic and Roman Period* 38 (2007), 57-79.

Harlow, M. and Laurence, R.   'Old Age in Ancient Rome,' 53, no. 4 *History Today* (2003), 22-27.

———,   *Growing Up and Growing Old in Ancient Rome: A Life Course Approach* (London: Routledge, 2005).

Harrison, J. R.   'Benefaction Ideology and Christian Responsibility for Widows', *New Documents Illustrating Early Christianity* 8 (1997), 106-116.

Haynes, M. S.   'The Supposedly Golden Age for the Aged in Ancient Greece: A Study of Literary Concepts of Old Age', *The Gerontologist* 2 (1962), 93-98.

———,   'The Supposedly Golden Age for the Aged in Ancient Rome (A Study of Literary Concept of Old Age)', *Gerontologist* 3 (1963), 26-35.

Hemelrijk, E.   'Patronesses and 'Mothers' of Roman *Collegia*', *Classical Antiquity* 27 (2008), 115-162.

Hock, R. F.   'A Support for His Old Age: Paul's Plea on Behalf of Onesimus', in L. M. White and O. L. Yarbrough (Eds.), *The Social World of the First Christians* (Minneapolis: Fortress, 1995), 67-81.

Kebric, R. B.   'Aging in Pliny's Letters: A View from the Second Century AD', *The Gerontologist* 13 (1983), 538-545.

Koenig, J.   *New Testament Hospitality: Partnership with Strangers as Promise and Mission* (Philadelphia: Fortress, 1985).

Lafosse, M. T.   'Age Matters: Age, Aging and Intergenerational Relationships, with a Focus on 1 Timothy 5' (Ph.D. dissertation, University of Toronto, 2011).

Levinson, D. J.   'The Mid-Life Transition: A Period in Adult Psychosocial Development', *Psychiatry* 40 (1977), 99-112.

Levinson, D. J. with Darrow, C. N., Klein, E. B. and Levinson, M.   *Seasons of a Man's Life* (New York: Random House, 1978).

Lutz, C. E.   'Musonius Rufus, 'The Roman Socrates'', *Yale Classical Studies* 10 (1947), 3-147

Minois, G.   *History of Old Age: From Antiquity to the Renaissance*, translated by S. H. Tenison (Chicago: University of Chicago Press, 1989).

Mohr, J. W.   'Cicero: Persons and Positions', in C. Edling and J. Rydgren (Eds.) *Sociological Insights of Great Thinkers* (Santa Barbara: Praeger, 2011), 123-32.

Nordling, J. G.   *Philemon* (Concordia Commentary; St Louis: Concordia Publishing House, 2004).

Parkin, T. G.   *Old Age in the Roman World: A Cultural and Social History* (Baltimore and London: John Hopkins Press, 2003).

Payne, T.   *The Ancient Art of Growing Old* (London: Vintage Books, 2015).

Peabody, A. P.   *Cicero, De Senectute* (Boston: Little, Brown, and Co. 1887).

Powell, J. G. F.   *Cicero, Cato Maior* De Senectute (Cambridge: Cambridge University Press, 1988).

Revell, L.   'The Roman Life Course: A View from the Inscriptions', *European Journal of Archaeology* 8, no. 1 (2005), 43-63.

Richardson, B. E.   *Old Age Among the Greeks: The Greek Portrayal of Old Age in Literature, Art, and Inscriptions, with a Study of the Duration of Life among the Ancient Greeks on the Basis of Inscriptional Evidence* (Baltimore: John Hopkins Press, 1933).

Rodeheaver, D.   'Psychological Adaptation and Virtue: Geropsychological Perspectives on Cicero's *De Senectute*', *Journal of Aging Studies* 7, no. 4 (1993), 353-359.

Rosivach, V.   'Some Older Women in Latin Literature', *The Classical World* 88, no. 2 (1994), 107-117.

Runesson, A., Binder, D. D. and Olsson, B.   *The Ancient Synagogue from Its Origins to 200 CE: A Source Book* (Leiden/Boston: Brill, 2008).

Ryder, K. C.   'The *Senex Amator* in Plautus', *Greece and Rome* 31, no. 2 (1984), 181-189.

Thurston, B. B.	*The Widows: A Woman's Ministry in the Early Church* (Philadelphia: Fortress, 1989).
Trebilco, P.	*The Early Christians in Ephesus from Paul to Valentinian* (Tübingen: Mohr Siebeck, 2004).
Twigg-Porter, G.	'Cicero, the Classic Gerontologist', *The Classical Bulletin* 39, no. 1 (1962), 1-4.
Vaillant, G.	*Aging Well* (Boston: Little, Brown and Co., 2002).
Vaillant, G., and Mukamal, K.	'Successful Aging', *The American Journal of Psychiatry* 158 (2001), 839–47.
Vessey, D. W. T. C.	'Pliny Martial and Silius Italicus', *Hermes* 102, no. 1 (1974), 109-16.
Wood, N.	*Cicero's Social and Political Thought* (Berkeley/Los Angeles: University of California, 1988).
Zamfir, K.	*Men and Women in the Household of God: A Contextual Approach to Roles and Ministries in the Pastoral Epistles* (Göttingen: Vandenhoeck&Ruprecht, 2013).

CHAPTER 11

Elders and disciples in Egypt's early monastic literature

Doru Costache

Abstract

This chapter examines the written records of the fourth- and fifth-century monastic wisdom produced in and about the ascetic milieus of Egypt. It focuses on two aspects related to ageing in that literature. First, the perception of Christian discipleship as ongoing growth, which culminates in the wisdom of the 'beautiful elder'. Motivated by this understanding, novices learn from the advanced by observing their behaviour, by listening to their wisdom, and by obeying their advice. Second, the understanding of Christian discipleship in terms of novices attending to the needs of the elders. Thus, the elders represent both role models and objects of care. In this light, discipleship, in desert literature, means learning wisdom from and taking care of the elders.

Introduction

The brave new world, the first world, is full of paradoxes and inconsistencies. One such inconsistency refers to our perception about growing old and about older people. While our society is ageing, we desperately attempt to conceal our age. We even send our elderly away, as though to avoid contagion. These are symptoms of 'ageism', as the trend is currently known. Behind it hides our fear of the last enemy (1 Cor. 15:26): death. Christ freed us of this fear (Heb. 2:14–15), but the vain dream of ageless youth and deathless life surreptitiously led us back to it. In turn, to forget about our debilitating fear, we created the utopia of endless thriving, of bright smiles and other cosmetic adjustments. But we cannot escape the fundamental truth of our existence. As Emil Cioran unsettlingly revealed, 'death is immanent to life' and, therefore, unavoidable.[1] Our utopia cannot but lamentably end. And since the very form of this world will change (see 1 Cor. 7:31; 2 Pet. 3:8–13; 1 John 2:17), we must ask ourselves what truly matters in this life. Against this backdrop, it is our duty to acknowledge the significance of ageing as a profoundly human experience, as the culmination (not the decline) of our earthly sojourn. We are yet to do so.

Following from the above more or less trivial facets of 'ageism', our society ignores matters considered proper to getting older in traditional cultures, such as becoming wiser and better. As Lucian Blaga would have it, to each age, its own. In his words:

> The child laughs:
> 'Playing is my wisdom and my love!'
> The youth sings:
> 'Love is my play and my wisdom!'
> The elderly keeps quiet:
> 'Wisdom is my love and my play!'[2]

There is something of every age in each age, but the way we embody shared human experiences differs from one age to another. As wisdom develops from earlier ages, playfulness and youthfulness remain present in the alchemy of our lives to the end. After all, we can all laugh, sing, and keep quiet. Nevertheless, proper to growing older is above all getting wiser, not sillier (see 1 Cor. 14:20; Eph. 4:11–16). As Paul instructed, 'the elderly [must] be sober, holy, temperate, and sound in faith, in love, and in endurance' (Titus 2:2). By fearing old age, we miss

---

1 Cioran, *On the Heights of Despair*, 24. Translation mine.
2 Blaga, *Three Faces*, in vol. *The Poems of Light*, 51. Translation mine.

all of this, especially the crowning of our lives: wisdom. Consequently, we remain silly until the end. Given modernity's nontraditional—if not antitraditional—outlook, 'ageism' is perfectly understandable. But the context cannot justify it; on the contrary, it just shows that we are culturally conditioned to think shallowly and to behave stupidly.

In what follows, I introduce a very different paradigm from the 'first world' view of ageing, where growing older, part and parcel of one's personal becoming, means glory, not defeat. It is the universe of Egypt's early monastics. For them, the ascetic pursuit was a philosophical way of life, a lifelong experience of wisdom-loving and wisdom-seeking that accompanied the ageing process.[3] In contrast with our attempt to freeze life in snapshots of our younger selves and to avoid development into older selves, the early Egyptian ascetics sought maturity, wisdom, and holiness. They added life, as the saying goes, to their years, not just years to their lives. Fearing death, we interrupt our own development and so regress mentally, psychologically, and physically. But they continued to push themselves throughout their lives, ending up better off—lucid, free and, in many cases, healthier.[4] Growing older and attaining eldership status was their badge of honour, not something to fear and despise. Correlatively, discipleship was to be in the presence of the elders, to learn from and to care for them. This understanding of ageing, I propose, constitutes a mature alternative to the infantilism of our 'ageist' culture.

The cases I discuss here focus on two categories of desert dwellers:

---

3   See for example the philosophical appraisal of the generally Christian and particularly monastic way of life in the early Fifth Century, by Neilos the Ascetic in *Ascetic Discourse*. English version in *The Philokalia*, 1: 200–203. Here, the term 'philosophical' refers to what Hadot calls 'philosophy as a way of life'. See his *Philosophy as a Way of Life* and 'Forms of Life', 483–505. Who mediated the idea of spiritual exercises in a Christian sense, before the emergence of Egyptian monasticism, was the Alexandrian philosopher and theologian, Clement. See Costache, 'Being', 56–64.

4   A typical example is that of Antony, whose ascetic regimen increased his health and vigour instead of diminishing them. See *Life of Antony*, 93. See Crislip, 'Illness and Ascetic Merit', 163–168. That said, sickness was not disparaged; on the contrary, it was considered an opportunity to exercise one's spiritual fortitude. Joseph of Thebes 1; Poemen 29; Syncletica 7, 8. See *The Sayings of the Desert Fathers*. To this version I refer throughout. The name indicates the collection of sayings associated to a monastic figure. The number(s) shows the relevant saying in that collection. Similar views are recorded in the systematic collection. See *The Book of the Elders*. See also Moberg, 'The Use of Illness', 591–599.

the elders themselves and their disciples. Their relationship echoes the rapport between Paul and his own spiritual children (see 1 Cor. 4:15). Both categories illustrate the view of Christian discipleship as ongoing growth in the company of saintly people.[5] Growth culminated in the mature wisdom of the spiritual *abba* ('father'), or *amma* ('mother'), alternatively known as the *kalogeros* (masc.) and the *kalogria* (fem.), meaning 'beautiful elder'. The elders represented both role models and objects of care. The disciples did more than learning from their elders, their spiritual guides; they attended to their needs, especially when sickness and old age weakened them. Monastic discipleship meant learning wisdom from and taking care of the elders.

Concretely, after I introduce early Egyptian monasticism and its literature, I focus on two ageing-related aspects in that literature: the elders' experience and that of their disciples.

Early Egyptian Monasticism and Its Literature

Egyptian monasticism emerged in the first half of the Fourth Century out of a rich spiritual ground. Already in the first Christian century flourished the Therapeutae, Jewish or perhaps Jewish Christian seekers of spiritual healing who, not unlike the Palestinian Essenes, established settlements in remote areas.[6] Philo's account on the Therapeutae describes their philosophical or devotional practices in great detail.[7] Ascetics of both genders renounced property and family, preferring to live in semi-seclusion. Their daily routine consisted in fasting, scriptural reading, meditation, and prayer, all of which they considered cathartic exercises. They congregated only at the end of the week, for worship. Other groups or isolated ascetics emulated this lifestyle, leading to the rise of the fourth-century monastic movement. Equally instrumental were two Christian intellectuals of Alexandria: Clement

---

5 For holy companionship in the Egyptian desert, see Costache, 'Adam's Holiness', 330–333.
6 Essene 'philosophical life' was perceived by Christian monastics as anticipating their own experience. See Neilos, *Ascetic Discourse*, 201.
7 Philo's *On the Contemplative Life* in its entirety explores the way of life of the Therapeutae. See *Philo*, vol. 9; Finn, *Asceticism*, 36–39; Grant, 'Theological Education', 180, 187.

(d. c. 215) and Origen (d. 254), who articulated the philosophical path based on their own spiritual exercises.[8] Clement's views greatly impacted the monastic thinking of Evagrius Ponticus (d. 399),[9] while the spirituality of Origen influenced Antony's (d. 356) and Athanasius' (d. 373).[10] Additionally, Alexandria and other cities hosted houses of virgins, which continued a New Testament tradition (see 1 Cor. 7:25–28,34).[11]

Against this backdrop, fourth-century Egypt witnessed three distinct orientations in monastic life. Semi-eremitic (or *lavra*) asceticism mirrored the experience of the Therapeutae. Such settlements existed in Sketis, Kellia, and Nitria, being spread far apart, roughly at a distance of a whole-day walk between neighbours. Each settlement was home to an elder and less than a handful of disciples. The elder and the disciples prayed, worked, and ate together, but they also reserved times for personal isolation by undertaking desert retreats. They did not have fixed rules, their lifestyle being experimental and personal. The only meal of the day, dinner, was followed by what John Cassian (d. 435) called *conlationes* ('spiritual conferences'), during which the elder and the disciples reflected on theoretical as well as practical topics.[12] Cassian, a disciple of Evagrius, visited several such settlements and interviewed a number of elders.[13] By allowing for both isolation and fellowship, the semi-eremitic form blended two other ways of life: the anchorite (properly eremitic) and the cenobitic one. Paul of Thebes (d. 342) and Antony pioneered the anchorite lifestyle,

---

8   Finn, *Asceticism*, 94–97, 100–112; O'Keefe, 'Origen', 1–12.
9   Bunge, *Despondency*; Casiday, *Reconstructing*; Casiday, *Evagrius Ponticus*; Harmless, *Desert Christians*, 345–259; Ramelli, *Evagrius's* Kephalaia gnostika; Sinkewicz, *Evagrius of Pontus*.
10 Finn, *Asceticism*, 112–117, 122–124; Burton-Christie, 'Athanasius', 13–24; Sinkewicz, *Evagrius of Pontus*, xxi-xxxvii.
11 The 'houses of virgins' were a major concern for Athanasius, who undertook to organise them and set rules for them. Brakke, *Athanasius*, 17–67; Neil, Costache, and Wagner, *Dreams*, 88, 90. Recent studies of feminine asceticism in Egypt brought to the fore new details. Dunn, *The Emergence of Monasticism*, 42–58; Finn, *Asceticism*, 91–94; Wipszycka, *The Second Gift*, 401–437.
12 Wipszycka, *The Second Gift*, 306–314, 374–383, 487–513; Casiday, *Tradition and Theology*, 147–157.
13 Casiday, *Tradition and Theology*, 3–6, 119–122, 126–131, 139–147; Chadwick, *John Cassian*, 13–33; Finn, *Asceticism*, 124–129; Harmless, *Desert Christians*, 373–402; Stewart, *Cassian the Monk*, 7–12, 29–35.

characterised by extended times of utter isolation in remote areas. The exercises they underwent were peculiar to each ascetic, depending on personal strengths and goals,[14] and as with the semi-eremitic life, the anchorite experience did not have rigid rules. At times, the hermits accepted disciples, whom they instructed in asceticism. Such times usually coincided with open days, so to speak, when the elders welcomed visitors. By alternating isolation and fellowship, the eremitic and the semi-eremitic forms largely overlapped. As a rule, however, visitors and even disciples were not a permanent feature of the eremitic experience.[15] Noteworthy is Antony's approach, who alternated utter solitude, the experience of limited companionship, and life in a larger nearby settlement. The latter was located in Pispir, where a monastery still exists. Leader of this settlement—whose rhythms did not differ from the semi-eremitic pathway—was his disciple Ammonas. The third form is the cenobitic one, where the ascetic life unfolded within common monasteries, sometimes hosting hundreds and thousands of monastics. Most monasteries were reserved for men and some for women. They were run by the firm guidance of a leader (abbot) and an intermediary hierarchy (priests, deacons, and experienced elders), whose responsibility was to supervise the compliance of their disciples to rigid written rules. The best example of cenobitic asceticism is the monastic federation founded and led by Pachomius (d. 348) and his successors in Upper Egypt.[16]

The literature generated by the monastics of Egypt themselves—such as Antony, Serapion (d. after 362), Evagrius, and the unknown editors of three collections of sayings—and their disciples—such as Athanasius and John Cassian—is sizeable. These sources primarily refer to the anchorite experience and the *lavra* form of life. To these must be added, however, the literature produced by Pachomius, Shenoute, and their disciples, representing the monasteries. Additionally, the

---

14 Neil, Costache, and Wagner, *Dreams*, 86–93.
15 Dunn, *The Emergence of Monasticism*, 1–24; Brakke, *Athanasius*, 201–265; Stewart, 'Rethinking the History of Monasticism', 4–7, 8–10; Wipszycka, *The Second Gift*, 13–17, 301–305.
16 Brakke, *Athanasius*, 80–129; Dunn, *The Emergence of Monasticism*, 25–34; Finn, *Asceticism*, 132–136; Krawiec, *Shenoute*. Meinardus, *Monks and Monasteries*, 5–7, 33–36, 72–74, 144–145, 156–162; Papaconstantinou, 'Egyptians and "Hellenists"', 15–21; Veilleux, *Pachomian Koinonia*.

narratives of their visitors and admirers, such as Basil of Caesarea (d. 379), Gregory the Theologian (d. 390), Rufinus (d. 410), and Palladius (d. 430). These sources provide us with first-hand knowledge regarding early Egyptian monasticism, making possible for contemporary scholars to reconstruct its features in great detail.[17] Our understanding is enriched by papyrological and archeological evidence.[18]

It is against this backdrop that below I discuss matters pertaining to desert eldership and discipleship, focusing on the early monastic attitude towards ageing. Of the documentary material available, I conduct my enquiry in the aphoristic literature of the *Sayings of the Desert Fathers*. To this I must now turn.

Enter the *Sayings*

Illustrating the semi-eremitic and the anchorite experience of settlements located west of the Nile's delta (Sketis, Kellia, Nitria) and also eastwards (Antony's Inner Mountain), three collections of wisdom sayings and exemplary stories were formed sometime from the end of the Fourth to the Sixth Century. There is no way of identifying with any certainty their compilers and editors.

Before I introduce the three collections, it is noteworthy that they share a common origin: the oral monastic tradition. This tradition was based on eyewitnesses of the elders, especially their immediate disciples and visitors, who treasured their wisdom. In time, stories about the elders' encounters, deeds, and pronouncements came to be communicated between settlements, being used as topics for spiritual reflection. That this was their destination transpires through the recurrent occurrence, in the written form of these aphorisms and anecdotes,

---

17 Burton-Christie, *The Word in the Desert;* Cain, *The Greek Historia Monachorum;* Chryssavgis, *In the Heart of the Desert;* Frank, *The Memory of the Eyes;* Harmless, 'Monasticism', 493–517; Harmless, *Desert Christians;* Herbel, *Sarapion of Thmuis;* Katos, *Palladius of Helenopolis;* Louth, 'The Literature of the Monastic Movement', 373–381; Mayers, *Listen to the Desert;* Rubenson, *The Letters of St. Antony;* Sheridan, 'Mapping', 323–340; Vecoli, 'La Conversion', 17–41; Ware, 'The Way of the Ascetics', 3–15; Wipszycka, *The Second Gift*, 27–260.
18 Brooks Hedstrom, 'Archaeology', 156–159; Brooks Hedstrom, *Monastic Landscape;* Orlandi and Suciu, 'The End of the Library', 891–918; Suciu, 'Sitting in the Cell', 141–171; Suciu, 'Revisiting', 301–325.

of requests from ascetics who sought the guidance of experienced elders: 'give me a word!' or 'how can I be saved?'[19] The recipients memorised the answers and repeated them throughout the day—as they also did with scriptural passages[20]—reflecting on their significance in prayerful recollection. It is for the same purposes that, with the time passing, these sayings were collected and disseminated, becoming part of a sapiential tradition that later came to be written down. As we read in the prologue of the alphabetic collection:

> This book is an account of the virtuous asceticism and admirable way of life and also of the words of the holy and blessed fathers. They are meant to inspire and instruct those who want to imitate their heavenly lives, so that they may make progress on the way that leads to the kingdom of heaven.[21]

Given the gradual accumulation of stories and sayings, unknown monastic editors undertook to catalogue the material. Three collections resulted: the alphabetic one, organising the material by the names of the elders whose stories were selected; the systematic one, thematically structured; and the anonymous one, amassing a wide range of *apophthegmata* ('sayings'), whose authors could not be identified and/or that did not meet the criteria of systematization.[22] More than several anecdotes and aphorisms overlap in the three collections, undoubtedly due to their importance.

While the origin of these three collections in the same oral tradition is unquestionable, the impetus for recording the wisdom of the elders must have come from Evagrius' works. In most of his works, he followed the literary genre of *kephalaia* ('chapters'), conveying the message by way of more or less succinct formulations. Evagrius himself pointed out that his 'chapters' were easy to memorise, repeat, and ponder, guiding

---

19 Ammonas 1; Euprepius 7; Hierax 1; Macarius the Great 23, 25, 27, 41; Matoes 11, 12; Poemen 69, 111; Pambo 14; Pistus 1; Sisoes 35; Serapion 2; Or 7.
20 Wortley, 'How the Desert Fathers 'Meditated'', 315–328.
21 *The Alphabetic Collection*, xxxv. The same text prefaces the systematic collection. See *The Book of the Elders*, 3.
22 Harmless, *Desert Christians*, 167–180; Wipszycka, *The Second Gift*, 179–188; Wortley, 'Introduction', 1–7.

the daily monastic practice of spiritual contemplation.[23] His 'chapters' shared this purpose with the monastic collections of sayings.

Before turning to the matters under consideration, a final word is in order regarding the universe of the alphabetic collection, which is of immediate interest here. It contains stories and sayings related to more than a hundred and thirty elders.[24] Of these, only three are women, but this by no means indicates the real number of female ascetics in Egypt's deserts, particularly hermits.[25] Most *apophthegmata* refer to practical matters pertaining to asceticism—namely, retreats, almsgiving, fasting, prayer, obedience, or issues such as balancing prayer, work, and rest. Other stories refer to pilgrimage, foreign and local visitors, selling merchandise, and tensions between various ascetics. Still other passages address scriptural reading and meditation, spiritual discernment, the guarding of one's mind from subconscious upsurges and demonic attacks, as well as charismatic, visionary, and ecstatic experiences.[26]

In short, similar to the other two collections, the alphabetic one vividly depicts a complex world of everyday life, were personal experiments—of which many were failures—and shared aspirations combined into a vibrant way of life: philosophical, profoundly Christian, and realistically human. On this note, I must now turn to the Egyptian elders' sense of discipleship.

Enter the Elders

Earlier on I mentioned that, for the pioneers of Egyptian monasticism, life was not only a matter of ageing; it was an ongoing opportunity for discipleship, for learning and for personal betterment. Monastic eldership did not always amount to being old, but ageing definitely was a matter of growing wiser. Understanding Christ's call to conversion (see Matt. 4:17) as referring to the Christian journey from beginning to end, the early Egyptian ascetics saw discipleship as a

---

23 Evagrius, *Letter to Anatolios*, 8–9.
24 Chryssavgis, *In the Heart of the Desert*, 19–30; Harmless, *Desert Christians*, 193–210.
25 Chryssavgis, *In the Heart of the Desert*, 89–91; Wipszycka, *The Second Gift*, 401–438.
26 Chryssavgis, *In the Heart of the Desert*, 37–109; Harmless, *Desert Christians*, 227–250.

matter of measured spiritual advancement and gradual transformation. Discipleship entailed progressing beyond Christian conversion. Full ecclesial membership was merely the beginning of a lifelong transformative journey. More specifically, while building on the shared foundations of faith commitment and baptismal regeneration, monastic discipleship opened further avenues for personal healing and advancement. It required progression from novitiate to taking the vows to attaining perfection in the form of eldership.[27] In so doing, monasticism took its cue from the philosophical curricula of the Classical world, which outlined progression from ethical formation through contemplative achievements to holiness. What facilitated the monastic iteration of these curricula were Clement and Origen's relevant elaborations.[28]

The three monastic stages roughly correspond to the biological phases of youth, maturity, and old age. Novitiate, as youth, entailed assiduous learning under competent guidance, which led to a correct upbringing; the monastic vows, corresponding to maturity, marked the age of commitment to and consistency on the path; eldership, corresponding to old age, marked one's becoming the monastic *kalogeros* or *kalogria*, wise and compassionate.[29] It went the same, indeed, for both men and women. Sarah (early Fifth Century), a *kalogria*, a beautiful elder acutely aware of the ephemerality of life,[30] progressed to the extent that her heart was pure, equally open to all people.[31] She was

---

[27] What inspired this understanding was Christ's own post-baptismal life. The topic is briefly discussed by a monastic writer from Sinai, but from a later timeframe, the Sixth Century, namely, Hesychius the Priest. See his *On Watchfulness and Holiness*, 12, in *The Philokalia*, 1:164. Another author from the Fifth Century, contemporary with many heroes of the *Sayings*, shared the view that embracing the ascetic life was part and parcel of progressing after baptism. See Diadochus of Photiki, *On Spiritual Knowledge and Discrimination*, 78–79, 89, in *The Philokalia*, 1: 288.

[28] With reference to the philosophical curricula prescribing advancement in three stages, see Hadot, 'Les divisions', 201–223. These curricula became standard ways of mapping the spiritual journey in the early Christian and monastic literature. Bucur, 'Hierarchy', 2–45; Bucur, *Angelomorphic Pneumatology*, 18–24; Costache, 'Christian Gnosis', 260–261, 264–267; Costache, 'Being', 57, 59; Costache, 'Adam's Holiness', 345–350; Louth, *Origins*, 56–60.

[29] See Bucur, 'Hierarchy', 10–16, 38–43. For the transformative dimension of what he called the 'school' of early Egyptian monasticism, see Chryssavgis, *In the Heart of the Desert*, 75–77.

[30] Sarah 6.

[31] Sarah 5. This seems to be the same with what Evagrius calls showing the greatest gentleness to all people. See Evagrius the Solitary, *Texts on Discrimination*, in *The Philokalia*, 1:46.

an *amma*,³² a spiritual mother. Her life illustrated the Pauline principle that in Christ there is neither male nor female (Gal. 3:28). In her words, 'according to nature I am a woman, but not according to my thoughts'.³³ This remarkable saying captures the essence of eldership as amounting to possession of wisdom divine.

A hallmark of this transformative process, the very engine of progress in the spiritual life, was the humble approach. As we read in the prologue of the same alphabetic collection, 'they hid themselves away, and by their supreme humility in keeping most of their good works hidden, they made progress on the way that leads to God'.³⁴ Working discretely upon themselves,³⁵ the more they advanced, the more they realised the need to undergo spiritual healing. In this they replicated the experience of the Therapeutae, the seekers of personal healing through ascesis. What matters is that this realisation determined them to revisit the fundamentals of monastic discipleship, again and again, seeking healing in order to become true disciples. In so doing, they avoided pride—the enemy of all progress. Discretion and humility, therefore, secured their advancement.

This was precisely John the Dwarf's (d. after 407) philosophical exercise. After being a most obedient novice to his elder, he became a widely respected guide to others, without ever considering himself close to perfection. One day, he 'was sitting in church [. . .] and he gave a sigh, unaware that there was someone behind him. When he noticed it he lay prostrate before him, saying, 'Forgive me, abba, for I have not yet made a beginning".³⁶ In the same vein, his disciple, Arsenius (d. 450), one of the most taciturn elders of the Egyptian desert, managed to convince himself he was an inexperienced novice. Therefore, in times of temptation, he prayed, 'God, do not leave me. I have done nothing good in your sight, but according to your goodness, let me now make a beginning of good'.³⁷ But perhaps the most striking account of this

---

32 Sarah 1.
33 Sarah 4. See also Sarah 9.
34 *The Alphabetic Collection*, xxxv.
35 Syncletica 21–22.
36 John the Dwarf 23.
37 Arsenius 3.

sort is that regarding the end of Sisoes (d. 429), an ascetic who, sharing in Adam's paradisal glory,[38] proved the Lord's promise (Matt. 13:43) true by resembling him transfigured (Matt. 17:2). Surrounded by a number of awestruck elders and disciples, as resplendent as the sun, he confessed, 'Truly, I do not think I have even made a beginning yet'.[39] Humility kept them on their toes (as we say in common parlance) so that they continued to work on themselves until the very end, thus attaining perfection. Old age could not excuse relaxation of their routine; they were vibrant and youthful until the very end, singing their love for wisdom.

Wisdom and glorification earned through humility and patience were not the only signs of elders' perfection. Teaching others according to personal experience, not according to theories and hearsay, was equally remarkable.[40] But more relevant here is their compassion towards sick and elderly people,[41] a direct outcome of inner transformation.[42] Macarius the Great (d. 390) went far beyond the proverbial extra mile out of love for the neighbour:

> One day he came to the cell of an anchorite who happened to be ill, and he asked him if he would take something to eat, though his cell was stripped bare. When the other replied, 'Some sherbet,' that courageous man did not hesitate, but went as far as Alexandria to fetch some for the sick man.[43]

Walking from Sketis to Alexandria for the sake of his ill confrère, a trip longer than 90 kilometres, revealed the character of Macarius' heart— to play around the Coptic name of his dwelling place, Šihēt ('Measure of the Hearts'). His abnegation implicitly confirmed Antony's wisdom, that 'our life and our death is with our neighbour'.[44] But this extreme solicitude was not reserved for other monastics. Going to town to sell

---

38 Pambo 12. See Costache, 'Adam's Holiness', 338–339.
39 Sisoes 14. Similarly, Pambo 8.
40 Syncletica 12. Neilos the Ascetic also was a vehement critic of inexperienced pretenders. See *Ascetic Discourse*, 215. See also Burton-Christie, *The Word in the Desert*, 144–146.
41 Crislip, 'Illness and Ascetic Merit', 154–162; Crislip, *From Monastery to Hospital*, 68–98.
42 Chryssavgis, *In the Heart of the Desert*, 81.
43 Macarius 8, *The Book of the Elders*, 3.8; 4.74; 4.78; 7.53; 11.47; *The Anonymous Collection*, 4; 30.
44 Antony 9.

the work of his hands, Agathon (d. early Fifth Century) encountered a sick traveler whom all the passersby ignored; emulating the Good Samaritan, the monk rented a room and remained with the foreigner until he was well again.[45] Another elder would always welcome the sick in his home, taking care of them until they were healed.[46] The commandment of love or the 'school of love', as Douglas Burton-Christie remarked, took precedence for them regardless of the costs involved—this was wisdom they impressed on their disciples too.[47]

The same 'school of love' determined, we have seen above, even staunch hermits to allow prospective disciples and visitors to reach them. In many cases, hospitality entailed breaking monastic rules, such as fasting and prayer, or taking the necessary measures to protect the old age, the weaknesses, and the sensitivities of others.[48] Love and respect led them to abandon the daily routine to visit dying elders. The case of the visitors gathered around Sisoes' deathbed, mentioned above, falls in this category, and so do others.[49]

In short, committed to a lifelong process of conversion, humbly and discretely, the beautiful elders considered themselves disciples, learners, or beginners. Awareness of their own imperfections led to sustained efforts towards improvement. In turn, through prolonged ascetic exercises they acquired wisdom, necessary to guide others, and experienced God's glory to unparalleled degrees. Ageing crowned their lifetime journey. But their spiritual achievements did not make them less sensitive to the neighbour, whose needs, sickness, and old age they prioritised above all else. As a result, truly beautiful—that is, kind and compassionate—they never died alone, being surrounded by other seekers of wisdom, or monastic philosophers.

---

45 Agathon 27; see also Agathon 30.
46 Isidore the Priest 1; *The Book of the Elders*, 16.6.
47 *The Book of the Elders*, 17.22; 17.29; Burton-Christie, *The Word in the Desert*, 261–266, 282–291. See also Moberg, 'Illness', 585–591; Crislip, *From Monastery to Hospital*, 76–81. Sometimes, however, the elders would go to visit the sick without relaxing their own routine. Sisoes 32.
48 Arsenius 24; Cassian 1; Eucharistus 1; Eulogius 1; Lot 1; Macarius 4; Moses 13; Sisoes 15, 20, 30. *The Book of the Elders*, 4.72; 4.85; 8.4; 10.76; 10.105; 10.147; 13; 14.29; 20.2; *The Anonymous Collection*, 596. See also Burton-Christie, *The Word in the Desert*, 249–255, 263–264, 288.
49 See also Pambo 8; Romanus 1.

Enter the Disciples

Since the elders considered themselves—out of humility—disciples and beginners, the novices had to adopt the same cast of mind, which they learned from their guides both intuitively, through witnessing their lives, and explicitly, by heeding their teaching. Following the Lord's clarification (John 14:15), their obedience to the elders was an act of love. Of course, to love the elders (namely, obeying them) was not always easy. Not all of their advices were readily graspable, especially when they concealed tests.

Here is one example. A young monk paid a visit to Serapion (former disciple of Antony and then bishop of Thmuis), enquiring about humility. Contrary to the custom demanding the senior lead the prayer, the elder asked the visitor to pray and then attempted to wash his feet. The young man refused to pray instead of the elder and protested against having his feet washed by him. Noticing disobedience, Serapion further tested the visitor's forbearance, this time eliciting a violent reaction on his part. It was only then that the elder disclosed the wisdom of his pedagogy: 'If you want to be humble, learn to bear generously what others unfairly inflict upon you and do not harbour empty words in your heart'.[50] As a rule, and again in the Lord's footsteps (see Mark 4:10–20), after they offered a difficult lesson, the elders proceeded to explain their meaning. This was a widespread approach. Joseph from Panephysis (end of the Fourth Century) disclosed the nature of their pedagogical approach: 'At the beginning the fathers do not speak to the brothers as they ought to do, but rather in an ambiguous manner, and if they see that they do what is right, then they no longer speak like that, but tell them the truth when they know they are obedient in all things'.[51] Pedagogy changed according to the disciples' progress.

At times, given the humble obedience and the patience of the novices, the tests were not needed or were not deployed for long. Isaiah

---

50 Serapion 4. See also Theodore of Ferme 2.
51 Joseph of Panephysis 5. Evagrius adopted a different pedagogy, teaching the novices in simple, straightforward ways, and increasing the difficulty of the tests according to the disciples' progress. See *The Gnostic* 44.9–13.

from Sketis (Fifth Century) praised the beginners who heeded the advices of their elders, saying, 'just as young shoots are easily trained back and bent, so it is with beginners who live in submission'.[52] Obedience to the elders denoted monastic aptitude, being considered a great gain. As Rufus (late Fourth Century) had it, 'he who remains sitting at the feet of his spiritual father receives a greater reward than he who lives alone in the desert'.[53] The most moving example of rewarding obedience is undoubtedly that of John the Dwarf:

> It was said of Abba John the Dwarf that he withdrew and lived in the desert at Sketis with an old man of Thebes. His abba, taking a piece of dry wood, planted it and said to him, 'Water it every day with a bottle of water, until it bears fruit'. Now the water was so far away that he had to leave in the evening and return the following morning. At the end of three years the wood came to life and bore fruit. Then the old man took some of the fruit and carried it to the church saying to the brethren, 'Take and eat the fruit of obedience'.[54]

This example denotes the power of humility, obedience, and patience, whose combination changes both the person who acquires these virtues and the environment. This is not the place to pursue the topic of asceticism and its environmental dimension. Suffice it to point out that the monastic literature of the time established this nexus based on a great many illustrations.[55]

Equally important in the spiritual relationship of disciples and elders were the former's honesty and disclosure to the latter. According to Antony, 'if he is able to, a monk ought to tell his elders confidently how many steps he takes and how many drops of water he drinks in his cell'.[56] This view was common.[57] Examples of this kind may sound

---

52 Isa. 2.
53 Rufus 2. See also Syncletica 16–17.
54 John the Dwarf 1.
55 See Costache, 'John Moschus', 21–34.
56 Antony 38.
57 See for example Evagrius' *The Monk* 94. See also Cassian the Roman, *Regarding the Holy Fathers of Sketes,* in *The Philokalia,* 1: 236, 239–240, 243.

strange to modern readers, accustomed as they are to defend privacy and individuality. But one's personal freedom and rights were not threatened by these monastic standards and expectations. These standards considered one's capacity for transformation through free submission to experienced guides. This conviction shows that the algorithm of youth indeed includes wisdom.

In short, humility, obedience, and honesty indicated the disciples' love towards their elders. But love took further shapes. Corresponding to the elders' own example, it entailed concrete service to people, including the elders themselves.[58] Thus, the disciples who initially had to cope with strange impositions—whose purposes were to test their obedience—ended by becoming dedicated carers for their ageing spiritual guides. Their love indeed took many forms. Some became advisers to their own guides,[59] others won their sick elders' full trust with storing and distributing the gifts received from donors,[60] while others earned their elders' respect and gratitude for lifelong service.[61] For example, Aios (Fourth Century) mentions with great admiration the solicitude of certain disciples: 'There was a certain old man in the Thebaid, Abba Antianus, who did many good works while he was young, but when he grew old he became sick and blind. Since he was ill, the brethren took great care of him, even putting his food in his mouth'.[62] Antianus' own compassion and almsgiving paid off, eliciting a proportionate response on the part of the immediate witnesses of his way of life—that is, his disciples. This is not an isolated case, although sometimes the disciples' solicitude was not met with kindness. Isaac of Kellia (the Fifth Century) tells the story of a novice who out of love tempted his elder to eat when he was sick.

> Abba Isaac had a serious illness which lasted for a long time. The brother made him a little broth out of flour into which he put some fruit. The old man did not want to taste it so the

---

58 Maximus the Confessor referred to love manifested in 'looking after people in their physical needs'. See his Four *Hundred Texts on Love* 1.26, in *The Philokalia*, 2: 55.
59 Antony 31.
60 Ammoes 3.
61 *The Book of the Elders*, 16.5.
62 Aios 1.

brother tempted him saying, 'Take a little, Father, because you are ill'. But the old man said to him, 'Truly, brother, I should like this illness to last for thirty years'.[63]

At a first glance, the elder's response appears to be intemperate and irrational—a sign of youthful haste and carelessness. He not only refused the kindness of the disciple: as a youth whose wisdom is to love, he welcomed suffering. We have seen above, however, that many Egyptian monastics considered illness an opportunity for testing their own spiritual fortitude, thus a spiritual exercise.[64] What matters here is the solicitude of the disciple who went, beyond obedience, to take care of his elder from whom he learned the ways of asceticism and compassion.[65]

The relationship between disciples and elders was complex. The training routine imposed on many novices was not always easy to understand and follow, but humility and obedience helped the young ascetics to overcome difficulties. This tough training was at times, however, motivated by elders' love, whose purpose was the transformation of the disciples. These, in turn, learned from the elders both explicitly, by submitting to the training routine, and implicitly, by paying attention to how the elders lived. In time, the relationship evolved. The elders put more and more trust in their disciples, while the disciples increasingly loved their elders. Their love took the form of patient service when the elders were sick or grew older. And while the elders advanced by humbly cultivating discipleship, the disciples progressed by learning at the 'school of love', becoming forbearing and compassionate through honouring their elders as they did the angels.[66]

Conclusions

Early Egyptian monasticism represented a radical form of Christian discipleship, having humility as its main engine. Humility propelled

---

63 Isaac 10.
64 Crislip, *From Monastery to Hospital*, 92–99; Moberg, 'Illness', 574–575, 591–599.
65 For more on this, see Costache, 'Asceticism'.
66 Evagrius, *The Monk* 100.5-6.

both elders and novices. In one case, it helped them realise their imperfections, giving them occasion for ongoing improvement. In the other case, it helped them to withstand the training obediently and to mature spiritually. Their humility marked their profound commitment to philosophy understood as a way of life leading to healing and perfection. For the disciples, philosophy entailed appreciation for wisdom and for the elders who embodied it. Progress was impossible without eldership, without wise and experienced guidance. As Andrew Louth observed about monastic experience, it was 'not so much a tradition of the fathers [and mothers], as a fatherly [and motherly] tradition, in which fathers [and mothers] help their children to enter into the fruits of their experience'.[67]

Indeed, the central figure of early monastic philosophy was the elder, *abba* or *amma*, *kalogeros* or *kalogria*. The elder was the embodiment of experience, wisdom, and love, the result of humble discipleship and of a lifelong process of growing spiritually. He or she represented the heroic proof that spiritual healing and maturity are possible—that life is not about travelling towards death, or an ongoing experience of dying, but an opportunity to progress, to better oneself, to add life to one's days. The elder, indeed, was a genuine hero, a warrior of light, but one whose battle was with his or her old self. At the end of this spiritual battle, the elder was victorious, utterly tamed, gentle and noble. His or her play and song were serenity and silence. His or her love were wisdom and altruism. The elder was, therefore, the perfect guide, for he or she—being experienced in spiritual matters—attained mature wisdom, manifested in his or her selflessness and compassion. Ultimately, the elder was the wisdom the disciples were expected to absorb and emulate. No wonder, therefore, the elder was surrounded by the disciples' love and care.

What we learn from the world of the *Sayings*, from the stories of the early Egyptian monastics, is that life is not a matter of decline, at least not in what concerns its inner dimensions. Understood as ongoing discipleship, as a trajectory of learning and healing, life maintains its vibrant dynamism from beginning to end. The child's play and the

---

67 Louth, 'The Theology of the *Philokalia*', 359.

youth's song are integral to the quietness of elderly wisdom. As such, life thrives if one pursues wisdom; the undying beauty we seek is within, the beauty of a pure heart, and not in the illusion of ageless youth. A change of paradigm, therefore, is in order. Childishly, out of the fear of death, we refuse the reality of ageing and keep away from the elderly. We must relearn what life is. We must turn towards wisdom; it will make us beautiful, gentle, loving elders. The result would undoubtedly be a more compassionate society.

Acknowledgements

This chapter was written during my adjunct senior lectureship with the School of Philosophy and Theology, the University of Notre Dame Australia, Sydney (2017–2019), being based on research undertaken both there and at St Cyril's Coptic Orthodox Theological College.

Bibliography

Athanasius: The Life of Antony and the Letter to Marcellinus (The Classics of Western Spirituality; Mahwah, NJ: Paulist Press, 1980; tr. from Greek).

Blaga, L.   *Poemele luminii* [The poems of light] (Bucharest: Cartea Românească, 1919).

Brakke, D.   *Athanasius and the Politics of Asceticism* (Oxford Early Christian Studies; Oxford: Clarendon Press, 1995).

Brooks Hedstrom, D. L.   'The Archaeology of Early Monastic Communities', in William R. Caraher et al. (eds.), *The Oxford Handbook of Early Christian Archaeology* (Oxford University Press, 2019), 147-165.

Brooks Hedstrom, D. L.   *The Monastic Landscape of Late Antique Egypt: An Archaeological Reconstruction* (Cambridge University Press, 2017).

Bucur, B. G.	'Hierarchy, Eldership, Isangelia: Clement of Alexandria and the Ascetic Tradition', in Doru Costache et al. (eds.), *Alexandrian Legacy: A Critical Appraisal* (Newcastle upon Tyne: Cambridge Scholars Publishing, 2015), 2-45.
Bucur, B. G.	*Angelomorphic Pneumatology: Clement of Alexandria and Other Early Christian Witnesses* (Supplements to Vigiliae Christianae 95; Leiden and Boston: Brill, 2009).
Bunge, G.	*Despondency: The Spiritual Teaching of Evagrius Ponticus on Acedia* (Crestwood, NY: St Vladimir's Seminary Press, 2011; tr. from German).
Burton-Christie, D.	'Athanasius (c .295–373) *The Life of Antony*', in Arthur Holder (ed.), *Christian Spirituality: The Classics* (London and New York: Routledge, 2010), 13-24.
Burton-Christie, D.	*The Word in the Desert: Scripture and the Quest for Holiness in Early Christian Monasticism* (New York and Oxford: Oxford University Press, 1993).
Cain, A.	*The Greek Historia Monachorum in Aegypto: Monastic Hagiography in the Late Fourth Century* (Oxford Early Christian Studies; Oxford University Press, 2016).
Casiday, A.	*Reconstructing the Theology of Evagrius Ponticus: Beyond Heresy* (Cambridge University Press, 2013).
Casiday, A. M. C.	*Tradition and Theology in St John Cassian* (Oxford Early Christian Studies; Oxford University Press, 2007).
Casiday, A. M.	*Evagrius Ponticus* (The Early Church Fathers; London and New York: Routledge, 2006).
Chadwick, O.	*John Cassian: A Study in Primitive Monasticism* (Cambridge University Press, 1950).
Chryssavgis, J.	*In the Heart of the Desert: The Spirituality of the Desert Fathers and Mothers* ('Treasures of the World's Religions; Bloomington, In: World Wisdom, 2003).
Cioran, E.	*Pe culmile disperării* [On the heights of despair] (Bucharest: Humanitas, 1990; first edn. 1934).
Costache, D.	'Asceticism, Well-Being, and Compassion in Maximus the Confessor', in Peter G. Bolt and James R. Harrison (eds.). *Justice, Mercy, and Well-Being: Interdisciplinary Perspectives* (Eugene: Pickwick, 2020): 134-47.

Costache, D.	'Christian Gnosis: From Clement the Alexandrian to John Damascene', in Garry W. Trompf et al (eds.), *The Gnostic World* (Routledge Worlds; London and New York: Routledge, 2019), 259-70.
Costache, D.	'Being, Well-being, Being for Ever: Creation's Existential Trajectory in Patristic Tradition', in Doru Costache et al (eds.), *Well-being, Personal Wholeness and the Social Fabric*, (Newcastle upon Tyne: Cambridge Scholars Publishing, 2017), 55-87.
Costache D.,	'John Moschus on Asceticism and the Environment', *Colloquium* 48:1 (2016), 21-34.
Costache, D.	'Adam's Holiness in the Alexandrine and Athonite Traditions', in Doru Costache et al (eds.), *Alexandrian Legacy: A Critical Appraisal* (Newcastle upon Tyne: Cambridge Scholars Publishing, 2015), 322-68.
Crislip, A. T.	*From Monastery to Hospital: Christian Monasticism and the Transformation of Health Care in Late Antiquity* (Ann Arbor: The University of Michigan Press, 2005).
Crislip, A.	'Illness and Ascetic Merit: The Moral Signification of Health and Sickness in Early Egyptian Monasticism', in Warren Kappeler (ed.), *Essays in Honour of Frederik Wisse: Scholar, Churchman, Mentor* (A special issue of *ARC* 33; 2005), 151-82.
Dunn, M.	*The Emergence of Monasticism: From the Desert Fathers to the Early Middle Ages* (Maldon, MA and Oxford: Blackwell Publishing, 2000).

Évagre le Pontique: Le Gnostique ou À celui qui est devenu digne de la science (Sources chrétiennes 356; Paris: Cerf, 1989; tr. from Armenian, Greek, and Syriac).

Évagre le Pontique: Traité pratique ou Le moine (Sources chrétiennes 171; Paris: Cerf, 1971; tr. from Greek).

Finn, R.	*Asceticism in the Graeco-Roman World* (Key Themes in Ancient History; Cambridge University Press, 2009).
Frank, G.	*The Memory of the Eyes: Pilgrims to Living Saints in Christian Late Antiquity* (Berkeley: University of California Press, 2000).

Grant, R. M.	'Theological Education at Alexandria', in Birger A. Pearson and James E. Goehring (eds.), *The Roots of Egyptian Christianity* (Studies in Antiquity & Christianity; Philadelphia: Fortress Press, 1986), 178-89.
Hadot, P.	*Philosophy as a Way of Life: Spiritual Exercises from Socrates to Foucault* (Wiley-Blackwell, 1995; tr. from French).
Hadot, P.	'Forms of Life and Forms of Discourse in Ancient Philosophy' *Critical Enquiry* 16:3 (1990), 483-505.
Hadot, P.	'Les divisions des parties de la philosophie dans l' Antiquité', *Museum Helveticum* 36:4 (1979), 201-23.
Harmless, J. W.	'Monasticism', in Susan Ashbrook Harvey and David G. Hunter (eds.), *The Oxford Handbook of Early Christian Studies* (Oxford University Press, 2008), 493-517.
Harmless, W.	*Desert Christians: An Introduction to the Literature of Early Monasticism* (New York: Oxford University Press, 2004).
Herbel, O.	*Sarapion of Thmuis: Against the Manichaeans and Pastoral Letters* (Early Christian Studies 14; Strathfield, NSW and Banyo, QLD: St Pauls and Centre for Early Christian Studies, 2011).
Katos, D. S.	*Palladius of Helenopolis: The Origenist Advocate* (The Oxford Early Christian Studies; Oxford University Press, 2011).
Krawiec, R.	*Shenoute and the Women of the White Monastery: Egyptian Monasticism in Late Antiquity* (Oxford University Press, 2002).
Louth, A.	*The Origins of the Christian Mystical Tradition: From Plato to Denys* (New York: Oxford University Press, 2007; second edn.).
Louth, L.	'The Theology of the *Philokalia*', in John Behr et al (eds.), *Abba: The Tradition of Orthodoxy in the West* (Crestwood, NY: St Vladimir's Seminary Press, 2003), 351-61.
Louth, A.	'The Literature of the Monastic Movement', in Frances Young et al (eds.), *The Cambridge History of Early Christian Literature* (Cambridge University Press, 2004), 373-81.
Mayers, G.	*Listen to the Desert: Secrets of Spiritual Maturity from the Desert Fathers and Mothers* (Liguori, MO: Liguori/Triumph, 1996).

Meinardus, O. F. A. *Monks and Monasteries of the Egyptian Deserts* (The American University of Cairo Press, 1999; revised edn.).

Moberg, S. 'The Use of Illness in the *Apophthegmata Patrum*', *Journal of Early Christian Studies* 26:4 (2018), 571-600.

Neil, B., D. Costache, and K. Wagner. *Dreams, Virtue and Divine Knowledge in Early Christian Egypt* (Cambridge University Press, 2019).

O'Keefe, J. J. 'Origen (c.185–c.253), Commentary on the Song of Songs', in Arthur Holder (ed.), *Christian Spirituality: The Classics* (London and New York: Routledge, 2010), 1-12.

Orlandi, T. and A. Suciu. 'The End of the Library of the Monastery of Atripe', in Paola Buzi et al (eds.), *Coptic Society, Literature and Religion from Late Antiquity to Modern Times* (Orientalia Lovaniensia Analecta 247; Louvain: Peeters, 2016), 891-918.

Papaconstantinou, A. 'Egyptians and 'Hellenists': Linguistic Diversity in the Early Pachomian Monasteries', in Gaëlle Tallet and Christiane Zivie-Coche (eds.), *Le myrte et la rose: Mélanges offerts à Françoise Dunand par ses élèves, collègues et amis* (Montpellier: Université Paul Valéry, 2014), 15-21.

Philo, vol. 9 (Loeb Classical Library 363 (Cambridge, MA and London: Harvard University Press and William Heineman, 1985; tr. from Greek).

Ramelli, I. L. E. *Evagrius's Kephalaia gnostika: A New Translation of the Unreformed Text from the Syriac* (Writings from the Greco-Roman World 38; Atlanta: SBL Press, 2015).

Rubenson, S. *The Letters of St. Antony: Origenist Theology, Monastic Tradition, and the Making of a Saint* (Studies in Antiquity and Christianity; Minneapolis, MN: Fortress Press, 1995).

Sheridan, M. 'Mapping the Intellectual Genome of Early Christian Monasticism', in Eduardo López-Tello García and Benedetta Selene Zorzi (eds.), *Church, Society and Monasticism* (Roma: EOS Verlag Pontificio Ateneo Sant'Anselmo, 2009), 323-40.

Sinkewicz, R. E. *Evagrius of Pontus: The Greek Ascetic Corpus* (The Oxford Early Christian Studies; Oxford University Press, 2003).

Stewart, C.	'Rethinking the History of Monasticism East and West: A Modest *tour d' horizon*', in Santha Bhattacharji et al (eds.), *Prayer and Thought in Monastic Tradition: Essays in Honour of Benedicta Ward SLG* (London and New York: Bloomsbury T&T Clark, 2014), 3-16.
Stewart, C.	*Cassian the Monk* (Oxford Studies in Historical Theology; Oxford University Press, 1998).
Suciu, A.	'Sitting in the Cell: The Literary Development of an Ascetic Praxis in Paul of Tamma's Writings. With an Edition of Some Hitherto Unknown Fragments of *De Cella*', *Journal of Theological Studies* 68 (2017), 141-71.
Suciu, A.	'Revisiting the Literary *Dossier* of Stephen of Thebes: With Preliminary Editions of the Greek Redactions of the *Ascetic Commandments*', *Adamantius* 21 (2015), 301-25.

The Book of the Elders: Sayings of the Desert Fathers; The Systematic Collection (Cistercian Studies 240; Collegeville, MN: Liturgical Press, 2012; tr. from Greek).

The Philokalia, four vols. (London: Faber & Faber, 1994; tr. from Greek).

The Philokalia: Writings of Holy Mystic Fathers in which is Explained how the Mind is Purified, Illumined, and Perfected through Practical and Contemplative Ethical Philosophy (Belmont, MA: Institute for Byzantine and Modern Greek Studies, 2008; tr. from Greek).

The Sayings of the Desert Fathers: The Alphabetic Collection (Kalamazoo and Oxford: Cistercian Publications and A. R. Mowbray, 1975; tr. from Greek).

Vecoli, F.	'La conversion: Le tournant monastique du IVe siècle', *Théologiques* 21:2 (2014), 17-41.
Veilleux, A.	*Pachomian Koinonia*, three vols. (Cistercian Studies 45, 46, 47; Kalamazoo, MI: Cistercian Publications, 1980, 1981, 1982).
Ware, K.	'The Way of the Ascetics: Negative or Affirmative?' in Vincent L. Wimbush and Richard Valantasis (eds.), *Asceticism* (Oxford University Press, 1998), 3-15.

Wipszycka, E.	*The Second Gift of the Nile: Monks and Monasteries in Late Antique Egypt* (The Journal of Juristic Papyrology Supplement 33; Warsaw, 2018; tr. from Polish).
Wortley, J.	'Introduction' to *The Anonymous Sayings of the Desert Fathers* (Cambridge University Press, 2013; tr. from Greek), 1-7.
Wortley, J.	'How the Desert Fathers "Meditated"', *Greek, Roman, and Byzantine Studies* 46 (2006), 315-28.

CHAPTER 12

Old Age

Matthew Del Nevo

Abstract

In this chapter, I present some thoughts about old age that have principally arisen from reading and re-reading Simone de Beauvoir's book *Old Age* (*La Vieillesse*, 1970), perhaps the greatest study of old age of the last one hundred years. This chapter presents some general considerations regarding the subject of old age and broaches once more the subject of a 'late style'—that is, we are to live to a ripe old age; not only artists, but each one of us, need somehow to develop our own late style or manner. But in this we need to take our cue from artists and, therefore, learn from them. Thus, *Old Age* took me back to Rilke, and it is here I begin.

Introduction

The German lyric poet Rainer Maria Rilke wrote in *The Notebook of Malte Laurids Brigge*, a poetic novel he wrote in Paris in 1910, the peculiar observation that *every new birth is also the birth of a new death*. During our life we are pregnant with that death; we carry it inside us until it is ready to be born at what we call the end of our life. We must take care of our death, as a mother takes care of the new life and death that she carries. We do not die at the end of our life as we would normally imagine. Our death is born with us. It grows with us until at the end it becomes us. We are born pregnant with death. What we call our death is the birth of it that we have been carrying all our lives and that has been growing with us, and has gradually over the course of a life time come to be all that we are at that point i.e. dead. This is natural death Rilke is talking about, not when death is sprung upon us. Then it is a tragic death. Tragic because it is death that has happened to us. Tragic because our own death has not had the opportunity to grow and slowly to ripen and mature within us and to come to fruition at that point in our life others refer to afterward as our death. For death, Malte thinks, has been perverted by religion and civilisation, it has been called a curse, and it is dreaded and hated. It is for these reasons we so often cannot die with natural dignity; we have to be dragged kicking and screaming into death, or we disappear into death drugged and demented because we have lost all sense of death. Death is the grim reaper.

Before, however, as Malte in Rilke's story reflects, things were not this way. Before, 'we carried our death within us, as a fruit bears its kernel. Children had a little death within them, older people a large one. Women had theirs in their womb, men theirs in their breast. One had it, and that gave one a singular dignity, a quiet pride'.[1] But this is long ago.

Most people now assume it is normal to be born in a hospital and to die in one. We live in an age that has medicalised death, as it has birth. As Rilke puts it, 'the whole thing is mechanical'.[2] Furthermore, 'the desire to have a death of one's own is growing more rare. In a little while it will be as rare as a life of one's own'.[3] This 'little while' that Rilke speaks of is now—it is now in our age of mass consumerism. Now, 'we die as best we can', Rilke goes on: 'we die the death that belongs to the disease from which we suffer'.[4] People die in this age of specialised functions 'from one of the deaths assigned to the institution' or wing or ward to which they are sent. Ernest Becker in the 1970s spoke of the denial of death, which is partly Rilke's point, and today we might

---

1   Rilke, *The Notebook of Malte Laurid Brigge*, 9–10.
2   Rilke, *The Notebook of Malte Laurid Brigge*, 8.
3   Rilke, *The Notebook of Malte Laurid Brigge*, 8
4   Rilke, *The Notebook of Malte Laurid Brigge*, 9.

talk instead of the consumption of death. People consume the services put at their disposal for dying and do so willingly and gratefully.

Rilke was not just being poetic. He died in 1926 in Switzerland, in a tower in the countryside that he rented. He died of leukaemia, but he did not allow any diagnosis of his illness to be named or heard in his presence, because it was *his* death that he was dying from, that he had always been carrying; he did not see himself as dying of an illness—not *merely* from that anyway. He accepted no medical intervention; and, intuitively, all along in his work, he talked of the blood, he wrote with his blood, as if he knew all along. And, importantly, he composed the epitaph for his grave. He believed his death was triggered by pricking his finger on a rose in the garden:

> Rose, oh reiner Widerspruch, Lust/ Neimandes Schlaf zu sein unter soviel/ Lindern
>
> ('Rose, oh pure contradiction, joy/of being, no-one's sleep under so many/ lids').

This view of Rilke is one that decides to take death properly, and to take life likewise. Accordingly, to underline this point, when Tolstoy wrote *The Death of Ivan Ilych* (1886), it conveyed the same message. Ivan Ilych had been a pillar of society, a high-court judge, but he had not really lived—at least, not in Rilke's sense of a life that courts death all the way, that remembers death. Not until he is terminally ill does it dawn on Ivan Ilych that nothing he had worked and lived for could save him. Ivan's death was an agony and Tolstoy describes, in lucid detail, the screaming that would not stop, the false words of the visitors to the bedside, and the horrified family members putting on a brave face. Luckily for Ivan his old servant, Gerasim, a peasant, had a sense of death akin to that which Rilke's Malte remembers, so in and through his agony. And although it is too late, Ivan Ilych catches a glimpse of the meaning of life, and it was *not* a successful public career, nor even family.

The psychologist Carl Jung captures a sense of what I am attempting to illustrate through use of a volume of his *Collected Works* entitled, 'The Structure and Dynamics of the Psyche'. He has a paper on 'Stages of Life' and another on 'The Soul and Death'. Let me reiterate some important points here:

> From the middle of life onward, only he remains vitally alive who is ready to *die with life*. For in the secret hour of life's midday the parabola is reversed, death is born. The second half of life does not signify ascent, unfolding, increase, exuberance, but death, since the end is its goal.[5]

This parabola he talks about is the psychological curve of life:

> With the attainment of maturity and at the zenith of biological existence, life's drive towards a goal in no wise halts. With the same intensity and irresistibility with which it strove upward before the middle age, life now descends; for the goal no longer lies on the summit, but in the valley where the ascent began. The curve of life is like the parabola of a projectile which, disturbed from its initial state of rest, rises and then returns to a state of repose.[6]

But while our biological existence has the intelligence to know what it is doing, mentally, many people—even whole cultures—may lack such intelligence. And, indeed, Jung believes this to be the case. The psychological curve of life and the biological curve may be out of accord with each other. We may be hanging on to our younger years or hugging our middle years, attempting to allay what we consider the onset of old age—perhaps by renaming it with a euphemism like 'sixty years young' or 'getting on a bit' or 'late middle age'.

The second point I would make from Jung's paper is that dying has its onset long before actual death: 'this often shows itself in peculiar changes of personality which may precede death by quite a long time'.[7] The body begins before consciousness and very often ceases well after consciousness has left it. It is hard to see the beginnings and endings of these processes Jung observes from his clinical practice in analysis. The

---

5 Jung, *Structure and Dynamics of the Psyche*, 407.
6 Jung, *Structure and Dynamics of the Psyche*, 406.
7 Jung, *Structure and Dynamics of the Psyche*, 411.

psyche is interested in how one dies; the psyche seems uninterested in the actual passing of the individual. By 'how one dies' Jung is referring to the psyche being interested in 'whether the attitude of consciousness is adjusted to dying or not'.[8] Frequently, Jung finds with his patients, many of whom were women, a maladjustment of consciousness, a non-attunement with the psychic or unconscious side of themselves. Why is this? Jung says something in answer to this question that jars with our entire rational, functional hyper-administered and managed civilisation. When he visited tribal peoples in East Africa, Jung stated anyone he met who may have been over 60 was really old, such it seemed they may have always been old 'so fully had they assimilated their age'.[9] This contrasts to European civilisation, where 'we are forever only more or less than we actually are'. We are deeply out of sorts with ourselves in our civilisation due to our overly rational culture. Our biology and mentality are on different wavelengths 'and no longer know how to get along on nature's timing'.[10] Rational civilisation, Jung goes on to argue, has isolated itself psychologically—has alienated itself, Marxists of that period would have said — and 'stands opposed to its own basic human nature'.[11] Adding, 'therefore, rational opinions [about death and dying] come unexpectedly close to neurotic symptoms'.[12] Religion, at least, and religious truths about dying and death, possess a symbolic valence in tune with the psyche from which they originate—unlike the rational opinions, statistically-generated opinions we have today.

As a result of reading Simone de Beauvoir's *Old Age*, I went back to these points about old age and death—Rilke's thoughts regarding death as something that is born within us and something that needs to be nurtured, and Jung's explanation of the psychological curve of life. *Old Age* is a lesser known sequel to *The Second Sex* (*Le Deuxième Sexe*, 1949), which is the most famous and influential feminist text ever written. *Old Age* is a massive text and equally as radical in its own

---

8 Jung, *Structure and Dynamics of the Psyche*, 411.
9 Jung, *Structure and Dynamics of the Psyche*, 407.
10 Jung, *Structure and Dynamics of the Psyche*, 408.
11 Jung, *Structure and Dynamics of the Psyche*, 410.
12 Jung, *Structure and Dynamics of the Psyche*, 410.

way as her feminist work. The introduction to the work begins with a story of the Buddha when he was still Prince Siddhartha, and how he had been cosseted by his father but got out one day and saw 'a tottering, wrinkled, toothless, white-haired man, bowed, mumbling and trembling as he propped himself along on his stick'. The Prince was shocked because the whole world as he knew it was drunk with the vanity and illusions of youth: 'what is the use of pleasures and delights, since I myself am the future dwelling place of old age?'.

And de Beauvoir writes:

> Buddha recognised his own fate in the person of a very aged man because, being born to save humanity, he chose to take upon himself the entirety of the human state. In this he differed from the rest of mankind, for they evade those aspects of it that distress them. And above all they evade old age. The American's have struck the word death out of their vocabulary—they speak only of 'the dear departed'.[13]

Ironically, even de Beauvoir's own book *Old Age* was euphemistically retitled *The Coming of Age* for publication in the United States, where the words 'old age' were too rebarbative for the public's ears. This is part of the American 'war on death', as we might jokingly refer to it. But it is all very Christian. 'Death, where is thy sting?' Paul, the apostle crows, and he did not live to see old age, neither did Peter, neither did Jesus, who died only in his thirties. The Americans are very Christian in their denial of death. The resurrection is the strongest possible condemnation of dying and death. Our Christian and secular culture is the first on earth to ever turn such a blind eye to old age and death and have so much religious self-justification for doing so. De Beauvoir, brought up in a strict Catholic family and convent school, knows this. She knows Nietzsche says this, and this is the subtext of the start of her book—and I do not believe she mentions Buddha anywhere else in her voluminous writings; so to my mind they are telling words.

---

13 de Beauvoir, *Old Age*, 7.

Her work is divided into two parts. Part one deals with biological and ethnological data, followed by an examination of old age in historical societies and in modern society. Even with the dense text of the Penguin edition (it is a 650-page book) the whole of the second half is taken up with examples from real life of how people coped with and assumed old age. It bears out Freud's dictum of, 'there is no such thing as normal'. Freud, of course, is referring here to sexuality. De Beauvoir produces a lot of anecdotal evidence about the sexual life or lack of it in old men, which is fascinating reading for men of a certain age.

Her pages on pain in old age are unremitting. In 1964, she wrote a short work entitled *A Very Easy Death* (*Une Mort très douce*) about the death of her mother. The title is bitter. It was anything but an easy death, but de Beauvoir at her mother's bedside is a relentless observer and, as a reader, I instinctively kept trying to avert my eyes. That is the kind of book it is. But de Beauvoir is also deeply sympathetic and so draws the reader into the closest intimacy with her mother's death on a par with her own.

The French writer Colette, de Beauvoir's near contemporary, receives a small mention in *Old Age* (a couple of lines), but Colette, at 75, crippled with arthritis and internationally famous, wrote a book about her own old age entitled *The Blue Lantern* (*Le Fanal bleu*, 1949). Basically, she was confined to her room and she kept a blue light burning there. In her heyday, Colette wrote the most beautiful books I have ever read about her childhood and mother. In this last book, she talks in terms of the contraction of her fashionable life to this room and bed. But many of her memories are with her in her solitude. When she died in 1954, the Catholic Church refused a religious funeral because of her divorces (no matter that her first husband was abusive), although her best-selling novels from the turn of the century (all still in print in English today), which centred around lesbian relationships in convent school and her account of her early life in a dance troupe, probably did not help her case. She therefore had an honorary state funeral, the first French woman of letters to do so, and was buried in Père-Lachaise cemetery. In *The Blue Lantern*, Colette does not speak of death; it is all about life. She works to the end.

In fact, one of the points that emerges from de Beauvoir's study is the point that what keeps people going in the face of death is work. This is both historically true and true of modern examples that de Beauvoir describes in *Old Age*. Even of herself, in her diary for Sunday 17th April, 1959, she writes: 'I'm getting old. My desire to rush about all over the world has become decidedly blunted, the desire to work has increased. I begin to feel the sense of urgency Sartre has inside him all the time'.[14] Modern life, she points out in *Old Age*, is different from how life used to be; there is not the continuity of father and son, mother and daughter that there was. The modern world will destroy tomorrow what was built yesterday. She writes, 'The son will not re-live the father's life and the father knows it'; adding, 'modern society, far from providing the aged man with an appeal against his biological fate, tosses him into an outdated past, and it does so while he is still living'.[15] Colette would have experienced this 'datedness' within her public persona, which in her case was close to her personal persona. de Beauvoir quotes the nineteenth-century literary critic Saint-Beuve, explaining that 'we harden in some places and rot in others: we never ripen'. Well, not any more. This is what Rilke's Malte was bemoaning as well. 'Old age', de Beauvoir adds, 'is not the *summa* of our life. As time gives us the world with the same motion it takes it from us'.[16] She quotes the 80-year-old Mauriac: 'What am I to say about ideas? Fifty years of reading: and what remains of it?'[17]

Dying is not a medical condition, nor is death. Ageing is not a matter merely of well-being, or a care balance, but of dying, of our descent, and the work of death. Maurice Blanchot borrows from Rilke's idea that we are pregnant with our death, that our death is uniquely our own, like our life—specifically, 'oh Lord, grant to each his own death, the dying that truly evolves from this life/In which they once had love, meaning and need'.[18] Instead, Blanchot, explains Rilke's thought of death gives rise to the prayer:

14 de Beauvoir, *The Force of Circumstance*, 444.
15 de Beauvoir, *Old Age*, 423.
16 de Beauvoir, *Old Age*, 424.
17 de Beauvoir, *Old Age*, 424.
18 Rilke, *Book of Hours*, 90.

> Grant me the death which is not mine, the death of no one, the dying which truly evolves from death, where I am not called upon to die, where death is not an event—an event that would be proper to me, which would happen to me alone—but the unreality and absence where nothing happens, where neither love nor meaning nor distress accompanies me, but the pure abandon of all that.[19]

This is the authentic logic of death, and so dying has to alter life in such a way that it accords with this logic, where my death may be an event for those I leave behind but it is not an event for me. Rilke said that his poetry, his art was 'the road toward myself'. Blanchot adds, 'this road must lead to the point where, within myself, I belong to the outside. It leads me where I am no longer, where if I speak it is not I who speak, where I cannot speak'.[20] We find this seemingly illogical logic that Blanchot explicates here also in Rilke's late Orphic poems. Orpheus—the pure call of music, or poetry—is the god that identifies with the force that dismembers him. This, Blanchot says, is the 'pure contradiction' of Rilke's epitaph: 'The rose becomes for Rilke the symbol of poetic action [of the Orphic rite] and of death, when death is no one's sleep'.[21]

Although death is always our contemporary, as Blanchot puts it, as we enter the parabola of descent, we need a late style, different from the style of youth and middle age. After his 'Duino Elegies' and 'Sonnets to Orpheus' (his great poetic outpouring of 1923), Rilke only had a few years left to live. He was not yet ill; however, something in him knew his days were numbered, and he changed from writing in his native German to writing in French in an almost haiku-like brevity, with a gentle luminous simplicity that perhaps German (as a heavier sounding language) would not allow him. In this manner, he wrote and published over 400 poems in French.

On the parabola of descent, it is time to develop a late style. Perhaps de Beauvoir's book *Old Age* is her tribute to her own ageing, and *The*

---

19 Blanchot, *Space of Literature*, 149.
20 Blanchot, *Space of Literature*, 156.
21 Blanchot, *Space of Literature*, 157.

Second Sex, the work of her life's prime. In using this phrase 'late style', I am of conscious of Edward Said's thoughts in *On Late Style*, as he generated considerable interest in it. His own initial article on the subject pertained to the late style in Beethoven, Lampedusa's very late novel *The Leopard* (1958), and the Greek poet of Alexandria, Cavafy.[22] Perhaps here late style contrasts with youthful rebellion. In any case, a late style pertains not just to the art, but to the life, so I would like to conclude this chapter by presenting some examples of late style in life and some differences with regard to it.

Rilke ceased his homeless wandering life at the end and lived in his tower at Muzot. A late style may mean withdrawal (e.g., Colette to the bedroom with the blue lamp burning). Blanchot, born in 1907, became a recluse after 1968 and died in 2003 at a very old age. But a late style may not mean withdrawal. For Bill Gates (and many other rich Americans) late style may mean becoming a philanthropist.

If Rilke is correct, while we still have time we need to make more of an artwork of our lives; we need to be more conscious that in old age the art of living and the art of dying *are the same art*. Artists do this in their art. I think of Marguerite Duras, from her early novels to the late-style texts such as *The Malady of Death* (*La Maladie de la mort*) and *Emily L*. I think of Samuel Beckett from his early trilogy of novels through to the middle period of How it Is and Company, to the late style minimalism of *Nohow On* (1989), with Waiting for Godot being the turning point (1953). With James Joyce it was the other way around, from the early Flaubertian short stories (*Dubliners*, 1914) and *Epiphanies* through to *Ulysses* (1922) and on to the linguistic confusion of *Finnegan's Wake* (1939). T. S. Eliot led the spirituality of his century through his own soul, from *The Lovesong of J. Alfred Prufrock* (1915) through to *The Waste Land* (1922) and on to the accomplishment of *The Four Quartets* (1943), with their wisdom, harmony and serenity of a late style.

In music, Wagner, after his last opera, *Parsifal*, had plans for an opera about Buddha (among other things) because he was still full of passion and plans. At 70 he was in love with a 24-year-old (Carrie Pringle), but

---

22 Said, 'Thoughts on Late Style', 3–7.

he died in Venice unexpectedly of a heart attack, which it is said came on after an argument with Cosima, his wife, over the girl. Verdi, in his 80s, produced the feisty jocular opera, *Falstaff*. Verdi reached old age and his work matured, but one cannot say he had a late style. He held steady all his life. Richard Strass (1864–1949) reached his 80s, but the last 20 years of his life were sorely affected by the rise of Hitler and the Nazis in Germany, much the same as Prokofiev was adversely affected in his creativity by Stalin's rule in Russia. Strauss fell into deep depression during his denazification process after the war. He was eventually cleared. His 'Four Last Songs', as they were latterly called by Ernst Roth, scored for a soprano voice and symphony orchestra, are perhaps the quintessence of late style. Olivier Messiaen (1908–1992) was like Joyce. He began in 1945 with 'Trois Petites Liturgies de la Présence Divine', a vocal and instrumental piece, and his last work was the massive five-hour opera, 'Saint Francois D'Assise'. The opera premiered on the 28th of November, 1983, in Paris and, as in his first works, critics were divided. Benjamin Brittan (1913–1976) at 59 experienced some heart problems but did not then realise his days were numbered. Ill health and repeated attempts to cure his heart problems through surgical means catapulted him into premature old age and fast-tracked him to an early death before the age of 65. For a late style, age came too quickly.[23]

I am aware of the reaction to late style.[24] I am not saying all artists have one, the same as not all of the remainder of us have one. Freud wanted to die and could not.[25] He found no solace in work, but kept working. In 1924, he was ready to go, he wrote to Lou Andreas-Salomé, his closest confidante. Abraham, Freud's great hope for the future of psychoanalysis, died the following year. He survived. He had the roof of his mouth taken out due to cancer and replaced with a painful contraption he had to keep in there. Between 1923 and 1939 he had 33 operations on his jaw and mouth. The Nazis closed in on Vienna. In 1933, his books were publicly burnt in Berlin. In 1938, he

---

23 This paragraph summarises parts of the wonderful book by Linda and Michael Hutchinson, *Four Last Songs: Aging and Creativity in Verdi, Strauss, Messiaen, and Brittan*.
24 See for example, *Late Style and its Discontents: Essays in Art, Literature and Music*, edited by Gordon McMullan and Sam Smiles.
25 See de Beauvoir, *Old Age*, 575–583

escaped to London thanks to Ernst Jones, leaving his sisters and his wider family to perish in the Holocaust. He escaped by the skin of his teeth in 1938. He refrained from suicide for love for his wife and daughter, Anna, who went with him. Even in excruciating pain, the whole time he was calm. His dog was afraid of him because part of his face was decomposing while he was still alive. Freud had the stench of death on him. In the end, Freud asked his private doctor, who administered his morphine, to push him over the brink. Freud had no late style he was uncompromising. Neither did Jacques Lacan, who Freud never knew, and who, with other great names like Melanie Klein, kept his flame alive. Lacan, like the Freud he loved, endured to the end in the same headstrong manner with which he began.[26] Carl Jung had a late manner. From his early work on typology and psychology in a white coat, he went through what he called his 'night sea journey', an archetypal inner journey with his lover Toni Woolf, who he trained as an analyst. He became Jung and built the tower at the lake at Bollingen along with the stonesmiths, choosing all the stones from the quarry himself and famously carving many. Father and grandfather of a growing clan, by the end he was like a biblical patriarch. Deeply meditative, he became a sage, full of health and humour and levity in old age. He wrote and illustrated *The Red Book*, a monument to his inner *imago*. His work gave rise to the Eranos conferences in Switzerland, to Joseph Campbell's work and James Hillman's archetypal psychology in America. The night before he died, he took his most prized red wine from the cellar at Bollingen and opened it and said goodbye as he looked out on the sun sinking over the lake. He knew. He died that night in his sleep. I do wonder if he washed his wine glass, or whether it still stood there in the morning on his bedside table. Nietzsche knew about late style, but he did not have one because his life broke into two. This occurs as well, sometimes. Therefore, a late style is not always the case, but nor is a happy life. And yet, we can work on it, and if philosophy and psychoanalysis are correct, we need to.

---

26 See Millot, *Life with Lacan*.

Bibliography

de Beauvoir, S.   *The Force of Circumstance* [1963]. Translated by Richard Howard. Harmondsworth: Penguin Books, 1978.

————,   *Old Age*. Translated by Patrick O'Brien. Harmondsworth: Penguin, 1972.

Blanchot, M.   *The Space of Literature*. Translated by Ann Smock. Lincoln, Nebraska; University of Nebraska, 1982.

Hutcheon, L., and Hutcheon M.   *Four Last Songs: Aging and Creativity in Verdi, Strauss, Messiaen, and Brittan* (Chicago: University of Chicago Press, 2016).

Jung, C. G.   *Structure and Dynamics of the Psyche* (London: Routledge, 1960).

Millot, C.   *Life with Lacan* (London: Polity Press, 2018).

McMullan, G., and Smiles, S.   *Late Style and its Discontents: Essays in Art, Literature and Music* (Oxford; Oxford University Press, 2016).

Rilke, R. M.   *The Notebook of Malte Laurid Brigge* [1910]. Translated by John Linton. London: Hogarth Press, 1959.

————,   *The Book of Hours* [1905]. Translated by Stevie Krayer. Saltzburg: Universitat Salzburg, 1995.

Said, E.   'Thoughts on Late Style' *London Review of Books*, Vol. 26 No. 15 (5 August 2004).

Epilogue

We thank all the contributors to this volume for their insights into one of the great questions of humanity, *How do we age well?* They have grappled with this question from theological, practical, and clinical perspectives.

The challenges of ageing cut profoundly to the heart of who we are as a Christian community. Our theological understanding of the nature of God demands more than mere kindness towards the elderly. Respect, care, and dignity are practical hands-on concerns. As C.S. Lewis noted in *The Problem of Pain*, 'kindness without love leads to indifference, even contempt', and we are surely called to something higher than kind tolerance towards our seniors.[1] As Saunders writes, the 'gentle neglect of people with dementia is not a worthy strategy for the church—and yet this is often the case in practice'.[2]

The great challenge for Christian communities is to explore how our theology can best inform our practice, so we are the hands of God acting with compassion and grace towards the disadvantaged we are serving. From a Christian perspective, providers of care need to emphasise the whole person. Our personhood is connected to our soul, not our physique. As such, every person is immeasurably valuable and the focus for Christian care should always emphasise human flourishing as a reflection of the nature of God at work in the world today.

Editors:
Stephen Smith
Edwina Blair
Catherine Kleemann

---

1   C.S. Lewis, *The Problem of Pain* (New York: Macmillan, 1944), 28.
2   J. Saunders, *Dementia: Pastoral Theology and Pastoral Care* (Cambridge: Grove Books, 2002), 21.

www.ingramcontent.com/pod-product-compliance
Lightning Source LLC
Chambersburg PA
CBHW071726080526
44588CB00013B/1907